A HISTORY

OF THE

EPISCOPAL CHURCH

A HISTORY OF THE EPISCOPAL CHURCH

Revised Edition

ROBERT W. PRICHARD

MOREHOUSE PUBLISHING

Cover Illustration:
Robert Hunt, Samuel Seabury, William White,
and Harriet Cannon,
Trinity Memorial Church, Warren, Pennsylvania
(courtesy of Willet Stained Glass Studio)

© 1999 by Robert W. Prichard
First Edition Published 1991.

Morehouse Publishing
P.O. Box 1321
Harrisburg, PA 17105

Library of Congress Cataloging-in-Publication Data
Prichard, Robert, W., 1949–
    A history of the Episcopal Church : revised / Robert W. Prichard.
        p.   cm.
    Includes bibliographical references and index.
    ISBN 0–8192–1828–6 (pbk.)
      1. Episcopal Church—History.   2. Anglican Communion—United States—History.
      3. United States—History. I. Title.
BX5880.P75   1999
283' .73—dc21   99–22978
                                                         CIP

Printed in the United States of America

to Ed and Nancy Prichard,
my loving parents

Contents

Illustrations

Tables

Preface 1999

The greater part of a decade has passed since the publication of the first edition of *A History of the Episcopal Church.* That first edition ended with an optimistic vision of a renewed Episcopal Church that was on the brink of a period of growth and new life. The passage of time has taught me, as it has taught generations of authors before me, that historians do a better job of describing the past than of predicting the future. The second edition, written at the end of the 1990s rather than their beginning, contains a more sober assessment of the last decade of the twentieth century.

I have rewritten the final portion of chapter 10 and have reconfigured and retitled chapter 11. I have included information, such as the adoption of electronic means of communication and the need to evangelize the members of the X generation, which I certainly had not foreseen when I last wrote. I have also added an extended section on the ongoing debate over sexuality. The earlier portions of the book remain unchanged except for minor corrections.

Those who read the final chapter of the book will find that I have not given up entirely on my earlier anticipation of a period of growth and new life in the Episcopal Church, I have only postponed the expected date of its arrival. My persistent optimism may call to mind the closing paragraph of E. Clowes Chorley's *Men and Movements in the American Episcopal Church* (1946). Chorley, writing at the end of a decade and a half of economic depression and international war, dreamed of an era in which the various elements of the Episcopal Church would give up their feuding and cooperate with one another. "The vision," he wrote, "may seem to tarry, but the world is very young and its most surprising songs are yet to be sung."

Robert W. Prichard
Alexandria, Virginia
July 1999

Preface
to the First Edition

A quarter century has now passed since the publication of the last general history of the Protestant Episcopal Church.[1] The mere passage of time—twenty-five years of rapid change that have brought the ordination of women to the presbyterate and episcopate, the Charismatic movement, a rise in Hispanic membership, the publication of a hymnal and a prayer book, and the first meaningful level of racial integration—is a sufficient cause for a new look at the subject. Yet, there are other reasons as well for a new study. A flowering of new scholarship has called attention to the roles of women, minorities, and the laity in the church that had often been overlooked in previous accounts. The continuing ecumenical dialogue in which the Episcopal Church has been involved in this century underlined the importance of relating the story of the Episcopal Church to that of other American denominations. Historians with an interest in social context have provided clues to the social context in which Episcopalians lived.[2] In addition, a series of recent period studies have provided new insights into ways of approaching the general story of the Episcopal Church.[3]

These and many other questions have influenced the way in which I have shaped the narrative that follows. It differs therefore from the histories of the Episcopal Church that have preceded it in a number of ways. I would, however, like to draw attention to five particular elements. First, I have attempted to broaden the base of the story to be more inclusive of laypersons, females, blacks, Hispanics, Asian Americans, and the deaf. In large measure, I am relying on the excellent scholarship of others in this area.[4] Second, I have come to believe that an understanding of the apostolic succession-baptismal covenant argument (the belief that ordination by bishops is a necessary part of the relationship into which God draws the redeemed at baptism) provides a key to understanding many Anglican attitudes from 1700 to the end of the nineteenth century. I have used the concept in my explanation of the success of the Society for the Propagation of the Gospel in New England, of the shock caused during the Awakening by George Whitefield (who rejected the argument as invalid), and of the crisis produced by a growing Roman Catholic Church (which also had apostolic succession) in the nineteenth century.[5] I believe the concept is also useful in understanding the relationship of the Episcopal Church to other denominations.

Third, my reading of the correspondence between Anglican clergy and England during the Great Awakening that is contained in the *Fulham Papers* has led me to suggest a new model for the understanding of the Great Awakening. Previous historians have wrestled with the mixed response that George Whitefield received from his coreligionists in the colonies. I have used a chronological device—differentiating a negative response up to 1759 and an increasingly positive one after that date—to make sense of this data. I believe that this approach allows both for a clearer description of the relationship between Episcopalians and Methodists and for the incorporation of more information about lay piety.

Fourth, the passage of time has allowed me, I think, to take a new look at the 1920s. Those historians who wrote in the thirties and forties played down the divisions in the church at that time.[6] I have, in contrast, called attention to the effects of the modernist-fundamentalist debate in the church and have noted the lack of agreement on such basic issues as rights of female and black Episcopalians. Fifth, I have, in addition, continued the narrative to 1990.

I thank all of those who have helped me with this work, particularly, Marcia, Daniel, and Joseph, my patient wife and sons; Guy F. Lytle, Samuel Garrett, Bruce Mullin, Roland Foster, and Charles Henery, fellow historians who have given me advice and counsel at various points; the members of the

Women's History Project, who have taught me to look at historical evidence in new ways; and a decade of students at the Virginia Theological Seminary, who have taken my class in the history of the Episcopal Church.

Robert W. Prichard
Alexandria, Virginia
January 1991

Notes

1. In the decade following the American Revolution, American Anglicans chose the name "The Protestant Episcopal Church in the United States of America." This remains the official name of the denomination. The General Convention did, however, authorize the shorter title *Episcopal Church* as an alternative in 1967. In 1976, the Convention amended the declaration of conformity required of clergy (article viii of the constitution) to employ this shorter title.

Raymond W. Albright's *A History of the Protestant Episcopal Church* (New York: Macmillan, 1964) was the most recent history of the denomination.

2. See, for example, Kit and Frederica Konolige, *The Power of Their Glory, America's Ruling Class: The Episcopalians* (U.S.A.: Wyden Books, 1978); E. Brooks Holifield, *The Gentlemen Theologians: American Theology in Southern Culture, 1795–1860* (Durham: Duke University Press, 1978); David L. Simpson, Jr., "A Data Base for Measuring the Participation Levels of Episcopalians in Elected Office and Including a List of Lay Delegates to the General Convention of the Church from 1789 to 1895," (M.T.S. thesis, Protestant Episcopal Theological Seminary in Virginia, 1987); and W.J. Rorabaugh, *The Alcoholic Republic* (Oxford: Oxford University Press, 1979).

3. See, for example, John Frederick Woolverton, *Colonial Anglicanism in North America* (Detroit: Wayne State Press, 1984); R. Bruce Mullin, *Episcopal Vision/ American Reality: High Church Theology and Social Thought in Evangelical America* (New Haven: Yale University Press, 1986); and David Sumner, *The Episcopal Church's History, 1945–1985*

(Harrisburg, PA: Morehouse, 1987).

4. See, for example, Mary Donovan, *A Different Call: Women's Ministries in the Episcopal Church, 1850–1920* (Harrisburg, PA: Morehouse, 1986), Joan Gundersen, *"Before the World Confessed":All Saints Parish, Northfield, and the Community* (Northfield, Minn.: Northfield Historical Society, 1987), and Joanna Bowen Gillespie, "'The Clear Leadings of Providence:' Pious Memoirs and the Problems of Self-Realization for Women in the Early Nineteenth Century," *Journal of the Early Republic* 5 (Summer 1985) on the roles of women; Carleton Hayden, "Black Ministry of the Episcopal Church: An Historical Overview," in *Black Clergy in the Episcopal Church: Recruitment, Training and Deployment,* ed. Franklin Turner and Adair Lummis (New York: Seabury Professional Services for the Episcopal Office of Black Ministries, n.d.), J. Kenneth Morris, *Elizabeth Evelyn Wright, 1872–1906, Founder of Voorhees College* (Sewanee: University of the South, 1983), and Odell Greenleaf Harris, *It Can be Done: The Autobiography of a Black Priest of the Protestant Episcopal Church Who Started under the Bottom and Moved up to the Top,* ed. Robert W. Prichard (Alexandria, Va.: Protestant Episcopal Theological Seminary in Virginia, 1985) on the roles of black Episcopalians; Owanah Anderson, *Jamestown Commitment* (Cincinnati: Forward Movement, 1988) on Native Americans; and Otto Berg, *A Missionary Chronicle* (Hollywood, Md.: St. Mary's Press, 1984) on the role of the deaf.

5. For a more detailed discussion of the covenant argument, see Robert W. Prichard, "Theological Consensus in the Episcopal Church, 1801–1873," (Ph.D. diss., Emory University, 1983), 103–140.

6. William Wilson Manross, *A History of the American Episcopal Church,* (New York: Morehouse-Gorham, 1935); and E. Clowes Chorley, *Men and Movements in the American Episcopal Church* (New York: Charles Scribner's Sons, 1951).

1
Founding the Church in an Age of Fragmentation (1585–1688)

Early Colonization in America

Following a series of exploratory visits (Florida, 1565; California, 1579; Newfoundland, 1583; etc.), the English made their first attempt at American colonization at Roanoke Island (1585–87). They named the colony Virginia after Elizabeth the Virgin Queen (1558–1603), though the island is in what is now the state of North Carolina. The Roanoke effort was unsuc-

Fig. 1 St. Luke's Church, Smithfield, Virginia, ca. 1632

cessful, but twenty-two years later an English mercantile company (the London Company) did plant a permanent colony further north, which it named Jamestown after James I (James VI of Scotland), who had followed Elizabeth to the English throne.

During James's reign (1603–25), this Virginia colony was the primary focus of English colonial efforts. It was not, however, the only English settlement. Navigation was still an inexact science in the seventeenth century, and not all the ships headed for the new colony reached their intended destination. In 1612, the wreck of a ship bound for Virginia led to the establishment of an English colony in Bermuda, a collection of islands 580 miles to the east of the coast of North Carolina. In 1620, the Pilgrims, also bound for Virginia, landed at Plymouth, considerably to the north. In 1624, a group of English colonists reached Barbados.

English Christianity and the Reformation

The colonists who came from England to America brought with them the religious faith of their native land. Like that of much of northern Europe, the faith of the English people in the early seventeenth century was a Protestant Christianity that had been profoundly shaped during the sixteenth-century Reformation. Colonists often disagreed about details, but the broad outlines of English Protestantism were clear enough.[1]

That English Protestantism was very different from the late medieval catholicism that had been the faith of England at the start of the sixteenth century. English Christians at that time subscribed to a penitential theology according to which individuals made themselves acceptable to God with good works, pilgrimages, indulgences, and memorial celebrations of the Mass. Beginning in 1519, however, a group of theologians at Cambridge University began to question this theology. Had not the church gone astray, they asked, by limiting the love of God to those who could first perform good works? Did not the New Testament speak of a love that God gave to those who were still sinners (Rom. 5:8)? Were not good works a result rather than a cause of the love of God's forgiveness?

At first only mild voices of protest, these early English Protestants, whose number included Thomas Bilney (1495?–1531), Robert Barnes (1495–1540), John Frith (ca. 1503–33), William Tyndale (1495–1536), Miles Coverdale (1488–1568), Hugh Latimer (ca. 1490–1555), and Richard Cox (ca. 1500–81), made themselves increasingly heard. Bilney told of the sense of forgiveness he had found while reading 1 Tim. 1:15 ("Jesus Christ came into the world to save sinners"). Barnes warned that the pomp and ceremony of the church could obscure the simple meaning of the gospel. Frith rejected the popular depiction of the eucharist as a resacrifice of the natural body of Christ that produced merit for those who paid the priest for the celebration. Tyndale and Coverdale worked on a translation of the Bible into English.

The monarch at the time, Elizabeth I's father King (1509–47) Henry VIII, could not ignore the activities of the Cambridge Protestants. In the 1520s and again in the 1540s, he persecuted them, but in the years in between he turned to them for assistance. Henry chose two men with sympathy for the Cambridge Protestants—Cambridge graduate Thomas Cranmer (1489 –1556) and merchant Thomas Cromwell (1485?–1540) —as his Archbishop of Canterbury and his secretary to the royal Council. He chose one of the Cambridge Protestants (Hugh Latimer) as a bishop and another (Richard Cox) as the tutor of his son Edward VI. He approved the publication of an English Bible translated by two other members of the group (Tyndale and Coverdale).

Henry never entirely trusted the Cambridge Protestants. They, for their part, reserved judgment about the king, accepting him as a possible instrument of reform without forgetting the dangers that political leaders could present for the church. In periods of cooperation, they were able to take the first rudimentary steps toward the reformation of the English church. They issued a Bible and a form of public prayer (the Great Litany) in English, began to dissolve the monastic orders that, as the custodians of the primary relics and pilgrimage sites, were the strongest supporters of the medieval penitential system, and raised questions about the medieval doctrine of purgatory. The alliance proved only a temporary one, with Henry turning more conservative in the 1540s. Yet the decade of cooperation gave the English Reformation a character that distinguished it from that on the continent. In Germany, Martin Luther moved within three years from mild criticism to total rejection of the episcopal hierarchy of the church. In England, in contrast, the circle of Protestants at Cambridge existed more or less openly for ten years (1520–1530). While some ran afoul of the authorities or felt the need to flee to the continent, others were able to move into positions of authority. That they were able to do so gave the English Christians a sense that many continental Christians could not share—that reform and the church's episcopal hierarchy need not be incompatible.

The reigns of Henry's children—Edward VI (1547– 53), Mary I (1553–58), and Elizabeth I—strengthened this perception for the English people. During the short reign of Edward, the Cambridge men quickened the rate of reform; they prepared two editions of the *Book of Common Prayer* (1549 and 1552), published a series of sermons for use in English churches (the *Homilies*), introduced legislation to allow for clerical marriage, and drafted a reformed statement of faith (Edward's Forty-two Articles, which would form the basis for the later Thirty-nine Articles of Religion). During Mary's Roman Catholic reaction, the Cambridge men lost their church positions but discovered a leadership of another kind—that of martyrdom. (Together Henry and Mary burned twenty-five Cambridge men for heresy.) When Elizabeth came to the throne, she chose bishops for the church who had studied with the Cambridge reformers and who shared a conviction about the compatibility of tradition and reform. It was this reformed Christianity that colonists brought with them to Roanoke and Jamestown.

The Religious Character of the Virginia Colony under Elizabeth and James

During the years that Elizabeth I and James I occupied the throne, the primary focus of English colonial efforts was Virginia. The records of that effort bear out the central role that religion played in their lives. The Virginia martial law provisions of 1610, for example, specified that members of the colony should gather to give thanks and to seek God's assistance at daily Morning and Evening Prayer, Sunday morning worship, and Sunday afternoon instruction in the catechism. Clergy were to preside at daily worship and preach each Sunday and Wednesday.[2]

The colonists believed that their day-to-day struggle to found a settlement was religiously significant for two important reasons. First, they could preach the gospel to an Indian population that had not yet heard the good news of Jesus Christ. Thus, Governor John White's account of the Roanoke colony, which English clergyman and geographer Richard Hakluyt (1552?–1616) included in *Principal Navigations* (1589), recorded with pride the baptism of Manteo (the first Native American baptized by an Anglican).[3] Jamestown colonist John Rolfe (1585– 1622) explained that his marriage to the Indian maiden Pocahontas (1595?–1617) was "for the converting to the true knowledge of God and Jesus Christ an unbelieving creature."[4] The first Virginia legislature (1619) declared its commitment to the "conversion of the Savages."[5]

Fig. 2 Pocahontas by an unidentified engraver after Simon van de Passe

A second motive for colonization was closely related. By spreading the gospel, colonists helped to unfold God's plan for the world, thereby hastening the coming of the kingdom. In a

November 1622 sermon to the members of the Virginia Company (the new name adopted by the London Company in 1609), poet and Anglican clergyman John Donne (1573–1631) used the Acts 1:8 promise that the Holy Spirit would assist the disciples to preach "to the end of the earth" to make the point. He noted that the members of his congregation had an advantage over the first-century Christians, who knew nothing about such places as the West Indies and, therefore, could not reach the ends of the earth. Colonists of the Virginia Company could, in contrast, create a "bridge . . . to that world that shall never grow old, the Kingdom of heaven." By adding the names of new colonists, the members of the Company could "add names . . . to the Booke of Life."[6]

Such prospects attracted serious-minded young clergy. Indeed, at a time when university education was still the exception rather than the rule among ordained Anglicans, most of those who volunteered for service in Virginia were university graduates. Alumni of Magdalen College, Oxford, and King's, Emmanuel, and St. Johns, Cambridge, were well repre-

sented in the rolls of colonial clergy.[7] Robert Hunt (d. 1608), the first Vicar of Jamestown, had, for example, earned his M.A. from Magdalen College.

The managers of the Virginia Company screened such volunteers and sent out the most qualified to fill newly established parishes or vacancies created by the high mortality rate in the colony.

Fig. 3 Robert Hunt

(Forty-four of the sixty-seven clergy who served before 1660 died within five years of arrival.)[8] When the members of the company appointed clergy for their colonies, they were following the English custom of patronage. In England, the individual or institution that built a church building and provided the support for its clergy had the right (the advowson) to present a

6

candidate for rector or vicar to the bishop for his consent. Since the Virginia Company created parishes in each of its settlements, set aside glebe lands to provide income, and directed that glebe houses and churches be built, it also claimed the right to nominate candidates to the Archbishop of Canterbury.

Colonization under Charles I and during the Commonwealth

For so long as James I occupied the throne, the majority of English colonists came to Virginia. With his death, however, the situation began to change rapidly. The number and the religious variety of the colonies increased. The uniform religious character of the Jacobean colonies, broken only by the small and relatively late Plymouth settlement, gave way to a broad religious spectrum.

While most English Christians during Charles's reign agreed that a Reformed insistence on justification by faith was compatible with a national church, they disagreed strongly on what a properly Reformed national church should look like. In particular, they could not agree on the externals of worship or on the role of the laity in church government.

One party in Caroline England, which the English at mid-century would call *episcopal* because of its support of the episcopacy, believed that the process of reform had already gone far enough.[9] If anything, members of this party argued, Anglicans had already abandoned too much of the medieval tradition. The English *Book of Common Prayer* and such attempts at Christian education as the *Homilies* had corrected major theological abuses. The reforming legislation of the sixteenth century had ended the excessive concentration of power in the hands of the clergy and had given the laity a sufficient voice in church government through the Parliament. Members of a second church party, whom the English called *puritans*, disagreed. They hoped further to purify Anglican worship by eliminating catholic elements such as liturgical vestments, which they feared might obscure the changes that had taken place in theology. They also believed that the laity and the lower clergy needed a stronger voice in the church.

Unlike Elizabeth I and James I, who had avoided identification with any single faction within the church, Charles I sided squarely with the episcopal party. He appointed priests with episcopal party sympathies as his bishops and supported a campaign by William Laud (1573–1645), his choice for Archbishop of Canterbury, to reintroduce more catholic ritual in England. Puritans objected, and Charles and Laud used arrest and corporal punishment to force compliance.

In 1637, Charles and Laud intensified the religious campaign in two important ways. First, Charles invited a papal legate to join the royal court in order to minister to his queen (Roman Catholic Henrietta Maria of France), thereby signaling to the nation his intention to modify the anti-Roman Catholic stance of his two predecessors. Second, he required the use of an edition of the *Book of Common Prayer* in Scotland, of which he (like all British monarchs after 1603) was also monarch.

The religious policy of the king and prelate solidified puritan opposition. Most puritans came to favor parliamentary authority over that of the king and to favor forms of church government in which primary authority was exercised by either regional gatherings of clergy and laity (presbyterianism) or congregational meetings (congregationalism) to government by bishops.

The colonists in Virginia were not particularly concerned with many of the issues that were hotly debated in Charles's England. Colonial life was still too rough and tumble, for example, for ecclesiastical vestments to be a real option.[10] Similarly, the role of bishops was more of a theoretical than a practical question, since no English bishop visited the colonies during the whole of the colonial period. Yet even so, the English debate during the years of Charles's reign had a profound effect on the religious character of the colonies. It provided so great a distraction from the effort at colonization that settlers were able to remake religious institutions to fit their circumstances. It also changed the character of emigration.

In 1624, Charles prevailed upon his father, the then failing James I, to revoke the charter of the Virginia Company. Charles explained the action by referring to the high mortality rates and dissatisfaction among colonists in Virginia, but his major motive was political. He wanted a source of income that would be free of the control of a Parliament that was becoming increasingly critical of his policies.

Charles's actions in the remainder of the decade made this motivation clear. He did not suggest major reforms in the management of the Virginia colony and generally paid less attention to it than had the officers of the Virginia Company. He allowed, for example, the Virginia Company's clergy placement system to lapse without providing for any alternative procedure. When he did summon the colonial legislature in 1629, it was only to demand tax concessions. The colonial legislators rejected the tax proposal but took advantage of the session to adopt a plan for the designation of clergy. The members of the lower house of the legislature (the House of Burgesses) claimed the right to present clergy to the colonial governor for induction into parish positions. In the 1630s and 1640s, the burgesses would also provide legal regulations governing colonial vestries.[11]

The vestries were evolving institutions in England at the time. From the thirteenth to the sixteenth century, English Christians used the name *vestry* to refer to the regular meetings in which parishioners gathered to provide for the maintenance of church property. The situation changed, however, in 1598 when the English Parliament passed a law making vestries responsible for the care of the poor, a function carried out by monastic institutions before the Reformation. English Christians quickly learned that congregational meetings were not the most efficient means to meet such obligations. They began to elect *select vestries* composed of leading men in the parish who provided for the poor between sessions of the congregational meeting. During the seventeenth century, the

English vestries took on additional duties that are carried out today by county governments. They cared for roads and replaced the decaying manorial court system in certain judicial matters.[12]

English puritans saw the evolving vestry as a vehicle by which laypersons might acquire greater authority. Members of colonial vestries in Virginia shared that perception. Indeed, the indifference of the king and their distance from London made it possible for them to gain a concession that English vestries would be unable to secure: during the 1630s, Virginia vestries began to select their own rectors. By 1643, the legislature abandoned its claim to designate clergy and incorporated vestry appointment in its religious statutes.[13] The Virginia precedent would not be followed by Anglicans in all of the remaining colonies, however. When, for example, the English government established the Anglican Church in Maryland at the end of the century, it gave to the governor the authority to assign clergy. After the American Revolution, however, the Virginia practice became the general rule in the American church.[14]

Virginia vestries attempted to revise English vestry-clergy relations in another way. English clergy, once inducted into their parishes, could only be dismissed by their bishops and then only for grave offenses. In a similar way, Anglican clergy in the Virginia colony, once inducted into their parishes by the governor, had life tenure; their vestries could not dismiss them. Colonial Anglicans tried to get around this situation by neglecting to present their new rectors to the governor, offering their clergy a series of one-year contracts instead. In most cases, these contracts were renewed each year, producing a stable relationship between vestry and clergy. Where disputes did arise, however, nonpresentation provided the vestry with an effective weapon.[15] Again, not all the colonies would follow the Virginia practice of nonpresentation during the colonial era. But after the American Revolution, the Episcopal Church in the United States adopted a canon (1804) that bore some resemblance to the *de facto* Virginia arrangement; it made it possible for vestries in dispute with their clergy to appeal to their bishops for a termination of the rector's tenure in circumstances that would never have been allowed under English canon law.

The second way in which Charles's religious policy affected colonial religion was through emigration. In 1630, whole communities of members of the Church of England who favored congregational polity took advantage of a generous royal charter and moved to New England. Almost from its inception, this settlement was larger in population than Virginia. Indeed, the colonists soon moved beyond the Massachusetts Bay territory into what would later become the separate colonies of New Hampshire and Connecticut. Going beyond the innovations of the settlers in Virginia, they limited church membership to those who could give accounts of their conversion and abandoned use of the *Book of Common Prayer.* With king and bishops safely distant in London, they were in little danger of being contradicted. On the contrary, John Winthrop (1588–1649) and other members of the new colony hoped that their innovations would provide a model that would be followed back home.

The religious policy of the growing New England colony distanced it not only from the church in England but also from the Virginia colony to the south. The two colonies, separated geographically by the Dutch colony of New Netherlands, attracted colonists from different parts of England. Two-thirds of the New England colonists came from the eastern counties of England's East Anglia.[16] The clergy in Virginia, whose geographical patterns usually matched those of the parishioners whom they served, came predominantly from the north and west of England.[17] Differences that already existed in England were only amplified in America.

Massachusetts Bay was not the only new colony chartered by Charles. Interested in the fortunes of Roman Catholics at the royal court, he also gave his Roman Catholic secretary of state, George Calvert (1580?–1632), permission to create a colony (Maryland, charted in 1632). The first colonists sailed two years later. The majority of the wealthier emigrants would be Roman Catholics, but from the start they only constituted a minority of the settlers. Many of the lower-income colonists remained sympathetic with the episcopal party in the Church of England.

In the following decade, Charles was no longer in a position to authorize new colonization. He was locked in a losing power struggle with the puritans that required all his attention. In 1640, Scottish presbyterians, unhappy with the Scottish *Book of Common Prayer*, invaded England. Charles summoned two sessions of Parliament to raise money for an English army, but a presbyterian majority in the House of Commons allied itself with the Scots against the king. The presbyterians joined with the army of Oliver Cromwell (1599–1658), composed primarily of puritan independents (congregationalists), to win the resultant Civil War. The victors executed both Archbishop Laud (1645) and Charles I (1649). With the king and archbishop removed, the Parliament reshaped the Church of England, abolishing the prayer book, the episcopate, and the Thirty-nine Articles of Religion. An assembly of puritan divines, summoned by the Parliament to meet at Westminster Abbey, drew up a new confession of faith and a directory of worship.

The victory of the presbyterian party was, however, only partial. Backed by Oliver Cromwell, independent puritans were able to resist Parliament's efforts to bring all of English puritanism under the new presbyterian form of church government. In 1653, Cromwell asserted his authority over the Parliament more openly; he dissolved the legislative body and ruled alone as England's Lord Protector. He continued to rule until his death in 1658.

English colonists in the New World acted in a predictable manner. New Englanders, from the same East Anglian towns that were centers of presbyterian and congregational opposition to the crown, supported the Parliament. The colonists in Virginia, Maryland, and Bermuda, from areas of England in which loyalist sentiments were strong, favored the royal family. A third group of colonists, dissenters who objected not only to the episcopal but also to the presbyterian and congregational forms of discipline and doctrine, took advantage of the confusion in England to form a colony in Rhode Island (first charter in 1644) and to establish a dissenting foothold in the Bahamas (arrival of dissenters from Bermuda in 1648).

The Colonies after the Restoration

Charles I's son, King (1660-85) Charles II, returned to England from exile on the continent in 1660, invited by a Parliament that was dissatisfied with Richard Cromwell's attempt to succeed his father. With Charles II's restoration, the episcopal party recaptured the Parliament and ended the Church of England's experiment with presbyterian government. Anxious to prevent any repetition of the Civil War, the episcopal party in Parliament not only reestablished the episcopacy, the prayer book *(Book of Common Prayer* 1662), and the traditional Thirty-nine Articles of Religion but also enacted legislation to guarantee continued dominance in the Church of England. The Parliament required, for example, that all clergy in the Church of England who were ordained during the presbyterian years be reordained by bishops or forfeit their positions. It also strengthened the language in the prayer book's preface about the requirement that clergy read Morning and Evening Prayer daily.

Many presbyterians, congregationalists, and independents—particularly among the clergy—refused to accept the Parliament's terms. Approximately 300,000 laypersons and one-fifth of the clergy withdrew from the Church of England and formed separate dissenting denominations.[18] The Parliament tolerated the new groups but adopted the Clarendon Code to limit their privileges. The code's Five Mile Act, for example, forbade dissenting ministers from living within five miles of any town or parish in which they had served.

The strategy led to a rapid decline in the number of dissenters in England; there were only 50,000 left in 1750.[19] It provided, however, an increased motivation for dissenting emigration to the colonies, where the provisions of the Clarendon Code were not systematically enforced. The puritans in

Massachusetts, for example, retained rights and privileges under their royal charter, despite the fact they organized as a denomination (the Congregational Church) outside of the Church of England. Charles II, moreover, granted a new royal charter to congregationalists in the Connecticut Valley (1662). The Church of England, a majority church at home, was soon outnumbered more than three to one by dissenters in the colonies. Only in Virginia, Bermuda, and a few British possessions in the Caribbean (Jamaica, Barbados, Antigua, etc.) did colonists remain within the church, and even they were slow to enforce Parliament's new religious legislation. As late as 1686, a Virginia vestry, for example, elected a rector who had not complied with the requirement for episcopal ordination.[20]

The Restoration did not, however, finally settle the religious debate in England. The Parliament was strongly episcopal in sentiment, but both Charles II and his brother King (1685-88) James II were deeply attracted to Roman Catholicism. Charles II made a deathbed profession to Rome, and James followed an open Roman Catholic policy. When James II introduced Roman Catholic worship at the universities, put Roman Catholics at the head of the army, and arrested seven Anglican bishops, the Parliament ejected him from the throne.

Charles and James pursued their religious goals in a way that contributed to the growth of Presbyterian, Congregational, and other dissenting groups in the colonies. Believing that granting toleration to dissenting Protestants in the colonies was the first step toward toleration of Roman Catholics, Charles renewed the charter of Baptists in Rhode Island (1663) and granted a charter to Quaker William Penn for Pennsylvania (1681). In addition, he made no provisions for the establishment of the Church of England in the charters for the Carolinas (1663) or the territory in New Jersey and New York (1664) that the English had taken from the Dutch. In the year before he was removed from the throne, James attempted to follow his brother's colonial policy with a Declaration of Indulgence, which would have removed legal penalties against dissenting Protestants and Roman Catholics in England itself.

During Charles II's reign, Presbyterians emigrated in increasing numbers to New York and New Jersey, where neither the Congregational nor Anglican Church was established and where the Dutch Calvinists, who predated the English, represented a theological tradition similar to their own. By the next century, English, Scottish, and Irish Presbyterians would prove as numerous in the British colonies on the American mainland as the Anglicans.

By the time that James II abandoned the English throne in 1688, the American colonies were well on their way to becoming the most denominationally diverse territory on earth. Anglicans, Congregationalists, Roman Catholics, Presbyterians, Baptists, and Quakers all had their spheres of influence. The colonists had lost forever the religious simplicity of the first colonies in Virginia and Bermuda.

The Divided Church and the Failure of Moral Vision

The religious disagreements that colonists brought with them from England contributed to the zeal and the excitement of the competing religious enclaves. The same disagreements, however, resulted in both an intolerant attitude toward others and a lack of moral vision.

In one sense the colonists were simply mimicking the actions of the British toward them. When the English authorities paid attention to the religious life of this diverse group of colonists, it was most often for negative reasons. In 1638, Archbishop Laud proposed sending a colonial bishop, not to Virginia or Bermuda, where episcopal sympathies were strong, but to New England, where such a bishop might be used to replace congregational polity.[21] Oliver Cromwell would likewise send a delegation with military authority, not to friendly territory, but to royalist Virginia in order to convince the colonists there to abandon the *Book of Common Prayer* with its petitions for the king and royal family.[22]

The colonists' record was hardly better than that of their motherland. In 1643, Virginia's legislature banned all who

15

were not members of the episcopal party from the colony. Groups of Maryland Protestants led armed insurrections against the Roman Catholic gentry (1655–58 and 1689). Massachusetts authorities executed four Quakers for heresy (1659–61) and nineteen residents of Salem for witchcraft (1692). The various groups of colonists had won for themselves the control of their own religious lives, but they were unwilling to grant the same privilege to minorities within their midst.

The English disagreements about religion also diverted energy that could have been directed to shaping the moral character of the colonies. The preoccupation with congregational orthodoxy in New England, the lack of a resident episcopate in Virginia, the minority position of the Roman Catholic gentry in Maryland, and the general fragmentation of the colonies into small religious groupings made any united church response on moral issues impossible. In particular, the colonists were not in a strong position to respond to the decaying relationships with the Indians and the advancement of slavery.

Dutch traders brought the first slaves to America in 1619. The institution of slavery did not have the same strong negative connotations to the seventeenth-century English that it has today. Peasants were bound to the land in parts of Europe into the nineteenth century; Arab slave traders were active in Africa; and the Spanish had already pioneered the use of slaves in the Americas in their colonies. The number of slaves was relatively small; there were only 16,000 in 1690. But the decisions made in the seventeenth century laid the groundwork for the much larger institution of the following two centuries.[23]

There was little legal precedent for the establishment of racial slavery. It would not be until 1662 in the confusing early years of the Restoration of Charles II that the Virginia House of Burgesses put slavery on a firmer legal footing, setting aside the English precedent that the status of a child depended on that of the father. For black slaves, the status of the child would thereafter depend on that of the mother. This action would be followed in other colonies. That clergyman Morgan Godwyn's *Negro's and Indians Advocate* (1680) protested the treatment of colonial slaves and that the Virginia legislature found it necessary in 1705 to enact a fine of ten thousand pounds of tobacco for any clergyman who married a black to a white suggest some opposition from clergy to the establishment of slavery. But with the colonists divided into competing religious groups and with only limited support from England, little could be done.[24]

The situation was similar in regard to the evangelization and treatment of the Indians. In the years from 1625 to 1688 in which James I's son and grandsons occupied the English throne, some colonists did follow the example of such early colonists as Thomas Harriot, who had preached to the Indians at Roanoke, and Alexander Whitaker, who had prepared Pocahontas for baptism.[25] Such colonists met with an almost insurmountable problem, however. They had the greatest success among small coastal tribes that saw the English settlers as potential allies against tribes in the interior. Yet it was precisely the coastal tribes that were being displaced by incoming colonists. Those engaged in serious work among the Indians were isolated from the general population and lacked the political clout to change settlement patterns. When the inevitable hostilities with the Indians developed, such as Virginia's Great Massacre (1622), colonial authorities adopted the use of military force to move the Native Americans further west.

The divided colonial churches could not speak with a united voice on behalf of Native or black Americans.

NOTES

1. Since the nineteenth century, many Episcopalians have avoided use of the adjective *protestant* to describe their church, choosing instead language that enables them to establish a middle ground between Roman Catholicism and Protestantism. It was, however, common for Anglicans of the sixteenth and seventeenth century to refer to or identify themselves as Protestants.

2. George MacLaren Brydon, *Virginia's Mother Church and the Political Conditions Under Which It Grew,* 2 vols.(Richmond: Virginia Historical Society, 1947), 1:411-13.

3. Louis B. Wright, ed., *The Elizabethan's America* (London: Edward Arnold, 1965), 136.

4. Ibid., 234.

5. Owanah Anderson, *Jamestown Commitment: The Episcopal Church and the American Indian* (Cincinnati: Forward Movement Publications, 1988), 18.

6. John Donne, *The Sermons of John Donne,* ed. George R. Potter and Evelyn M. Simpson, 10 vols. (Berkeley and Los Angeles: University of California Press, 1959), 4:280–81.

7. John Frederick Woolverton, *Colonial Anglicanism in North America* (Detroit: Wayne State Press, 1984), 37.

8. Ibid., 48.

9. *The Oxford English Dictionary* notes the use of "Episcopal Party" in a 1651 work by Richard Baxter (1615–91). Eight years later, Edward Stillingfleet identified the three major English church parties in his *Irenicum* as "congregational men," "presbyterians," and "episcopal men." This history has followed this seventeenth century usage for two reasons: (1) it is a more neutral term than the *Orthodox* label used by Archbishop William Laud or the *Anglican* designation followed by some later historians (Laud distinguished his *orthodoxy* from the *heterodoxy* of the puritans. The use of *Anglican* can mislead readers into believing that pre-Restoration puritans were not members of the Church of England.); (2) *episcopal* would be the word that American Anglicans adopted for their church after the American Revolution.

10. Brydon, *Virginia's Mother Church,* 1:25.

11. Ibid., 1:87–88.

12. Borden W. Painter, "The Anglican Vestry in Colonial America," (Ph.D. diss., Yale University, 1965), 12.

13. Ibid., 56.

14. The English still follow the patronage system. In much of the remainder of the Anglican world, the bishop meets with a committee that includes parish representation in order to choose a rector. In the United States, however, there is one remainder of the patronage system. In many dioceses, the bishop retains the right to appoint the vicars of missions.

15. Painter, "Anglican Vestry," 61–71.

16. Robert McCrum et al., *The Story of English* (New York: Elisabeth Sifton Books, Viking, 1986), 116.

17. Woolverton, *Colonial Anglicanism,* 27.

18. Robert Currie, Alan Gilbert, and Lee Horsley, *Churches and Churchgoers: Patterns of Church Growth in the British Isles since 1700* (Oxford: Clarendon Press, 1977), 27; Gordon Donaldson, *James V–James VIII,* vol. 3 of *The Edinburgh History of Scotland,* Gordon Donaldson, gen. ed. (Hong Kong: Wilture Enterprises, 1965), 366.

19. Currie, *Churches and Churchgoers,* 27.

20. Woolverton, *Colonial Anglicanism,* 53.

21. Arthur Lyon Cross, *The Anglican Episcopate and the American Colonies* (New York: Longmans, Green, and Co., 1902), 21.

22. Brydon, *Virginia's Mother Church,* 1:122. Brydon noted that the Virginia colonists reached a compromise with Cromwell's commissioners. The commissioners allowed the colonists to continue to use the *Book of Common Prayer* for one year, provided that they omitted the royal prayers. Brydon assumed that the colonists used the prayer book even after the expiration of the year.

23. David Burner et al., *An American Portrait: A History of the United States,* 2d ed. (New York: Charles Scribner's Sons, 1985), 59.

24. James Hugo Johnston, *Race Relations in Virginia and Miscegenation in the South 1776–1860* (Amherst: University of Massachusetts Press, 1970), 173.

25. Anderson, *Jamestown Commitment,* 16–18.

2
The Age of Reason and the American Colonies (1688–1740)

In 1688, the Parliament invited James II's Protestant son-in-law and daughter from Holland to assume jointly the British throne as King (1688–1702) William III and Queen (1688–94) Mary II. Mary's younger sister Anne supported their accession and succeeded them as monarch (1702–14). Collectively, the reign of the three marked an important turning point in the religious life of England and her colonies. Well aware of the turmoil that preceded them, the monarchs sought to quiet the tempers of English subjects by adopting a series of practical compromises (retention of the 1662 *Book of Common Prayer* and the Thirty-nine Articles; adoption of an Act of Toleration for Protestant dissenters; and granting of broader authority to Parliament). In Scotland (a separate kingdom with a shared monarch until united with England in 1707), they abandoned their predecessors' attempt to conform the church to that in England; the Church of Scotland would thereafter be Presbyterian. These measures were successful in maintaining the peace; the Glorious Revolution was the last revolution of the English people.

The peace in England was due, not only to specific legislation, but also to a number of people who advanced new ways of thinking about English religion and society. The impact of this shift would be felt by English colonists in the New World. While it is impossible to point to all those involved in bringing the "Moderate Enlightenment" to England following the Glorious Revolution, it is possible to single out two important groups: the Royal Society and the latitudinarian bishops.[1]

The Royal Society

In 1649, a group of scholars at Oxford University began to meet informally in order to gain what one member called "the satisfaction of breathing a freer air, and of conversing in quiet with one another, without being ingag'd in the passions, and the madness of that dismal age."[2] In the midst of civil war and dogmatic debates, members of the group sought only the opportunity to discuss issues of common interest. At the Restoration, Charles II gave the group a charter (1662) and a name (the Royal Society). During the remainder of the seventeenth century, the society's membership would include both prominent church figures and the leading intellectual lights of England: chemist Robert Boyle (1627–91), astronomer Edmund Halley (1656– 1742), philosopher John Locke (1632–1704), mathematician Isaac Newton (1642–1727), Bishop of Rochester Thomas Sprat (1635–1713), Bishop of Salisbury Seth Ward (1617–89), Bishop of Chester John Wilkins (1614–1712), and architect Christopher Wren (1632–1723).[3]

Members of the society shared a bold vision—that a marriage of reason and faith provided a truly pious alternative to the violence that English Christians had experienced early in the century. They believed, moreover, that this vision would not only bring peace to the church but would also bring progress and prosperity to their nation. The same minds that solved religious controversies with patient application of reason could also solve scientific and mathematical problems, providing a basis for the continuing expansion of English industry, navigation, and trade. In the early eighteenth century, society president (1703–27) Isaac Newton presided over a transition in the society's focus; church leaders played a declining role, and members focused more narrowly on scientific investigation. By that time, however, a broad spectrum of English Christians had accepted the vision of the society's first generation as normative.

John Locke's *Reasonableness of Christianity* (1695) was a

classic statement of the faith of the society's first generation. In his work, Locke attempted to escape from the intense theological argumentation, which had divided English Christians for most of his century, by characterizing the message of the New Testament with a few simple and logical propositions. Others, who were not themselves members of the society, supplemented Locke's exposition. In *The Analogy of Religion* (1736), Bishop Joseph Butler (1692–1752) explained that this reasonable Christianity was consonant with the laws of nature. Catherine Cockburn (1679– 1749), a playwright who turned to theological writing, echoed similar themes. Christian belief—and most particularly the Anglican understanding of it—was a reasonable faith, whose propagation went hand in hand with domestic peace, scientific advancement, and the success of the British Empire. This vision deeply influenced English and colonial Christians of all denominations.

The Latitudinarian Bishops

When William III and Mary II came to the throne, all of the Scottish bishops and seven English bishops, including Archbishop of Canterbury William Sancroft, refused to swear allegiance to the new king and queen. These nonjuring bishops (i.e., bishops who refused to swear allegiance) would provide the apostolic succession for a dissenting church that would continue as a separate institution into the nineteenth century. It would be particularly strong in Scotland, where William and Mary agreed to a Church of Scotland with presbyterian polity. Nonjuring bishops from Scotland would consecrate American Samuel Seabury to the episcopate in 1784.

The new monarchs and the Parliament removed the seven English bishops from office and replaced them with popular London clergy who had supported the Glorious Revolution. Among the new appointees were Gilbert Burnet (1643–1715), who became Bishop of Salisbury; John Tillotson (1630–94), who became Archbishop of Canterbury; Simon Patrick (1627–1701), who became Bishop of Ely; and Edward

Stillingfleet (1635–99), who became the Bishop of Worcester. Three of the four men had studied at Cambridge, and the fourth (Burnet) admitted that he was deeply influenced by a group of teachers there, popularly known as the Cambridge Platonists. Ralph Cudworth (1617–88) was the most influential of these teachers. Drawing on the work of third-century Neoplatonic Egyptian philosopher Plotinus, they characterized religious faith as a mystery that could never be entirely reduced to logical propositions.

The bishops who studied with the Platonists saw no conflict between this more mystical approach to theology and scientific investigation of the sort advocated by the members of the Royal Society. Burnet, a historian and an amateur chemist, joined the Royal Society in 1664. Patrick was the probable author of *A Brief Account of the New Sect of Latitude Men* (1662), which explained that the Platonists encouraged science by freeing it from the metaphysical categories of Aristotelian thought.

The bishops' approach dovetailed nicely with the Royal Society's vision of a reasonable faith in a second way.[4] If one stressed practical morality and philanthropy rather than the difficult points of doctrine, it was far easier to show the reasonableness of the Christian faith. Shaped by this conviction, the new bishops argued for a wider toleration in the English church. They questioned, for example, the need for the heated debate over predestination that divided English Protestants of their day into competing Calvinist and Arminian camps.[5] Gilbert Burnet wrote an *Exposition of the Thirty-nine Articles* (1699) in which he suggested that either position was in keeping with the English Thirty-nine Articles. This advocacy for toleration soon earned the bishops the title *latitudinarian,* a label that had also been used of their Cambridge teachers.

Like the members of the Royal Society, the latitudinarian bishops recognized the importance of the English colonies in America. They were a rich resource whose scientific management would bring prosperity to England. They were also diverse and divided religious communities to which a moderate enlightened Anglicanism could offer a unifying vision.

Henry Compton (1632–1713), the Bishop of London who, like the latitudinarians, was a Cambridge graduate, was also an important figure in regard to the colonies in America. Before appointment to the see of London in 1675, Compton had served as Charles II's chaplain of the Chapel Royal. In that capacity he had been responsible for the religious education of both Mary and Anne. He was an active supporter of the Glorious Revolution, and after it he was a trusted adviser who was able to encourage royal patronage for religious and benevolent projects in the colonies.

New Legislation

In the last two decades of the seventeenth century, English monarchs gradually expanded the authority they exercised over the American colonies. In 1684, Charles II cancelled the proprietary charters of Massachusetts and Bermuda, making the territories royal colonies. As Duke of York, James Stuart was himself the proprietor of New York (1664), but after following his brother to the throne as James II (1685), he added New York to the number of royal colonies. In 1691, William III and Mary II designated Maryland as a royal colony as well.

With a larger number of the colonies directly under royal control it became possible for sympathetic monarchs to follow policies favorable to the Anglican Church. William and Mary, and Anne, chose just such a course of action. They instructed their royal governors to lobby the colonial legislatures for the establishment of the Church of England (an action that required subsequent approval by the English Privy Council). The policy was successful in Maryland (establishment in 1702) and South Carolina (1706), and partially successful in New York. (In 1693 the royal governor of New York persuaded the state assembly to adopt an act providing for "Protestant" clergy in New York City and in Richmond, West Chester, and Queen's counties; the governor interpreted "Protestant" to mean "Anglican," but a non-Anglican majority in the assembly made the system largely unworkable.) It was unsuccessful in

25

New Jersey. Queen Anne's successors would, however, later expand establishment to Nova Scotia (1758), Georgia (1758), and North Carolina (definitive legislation in 1765).[6]

The colonial governments in these territories had the responsibility of founding and providing support for Anglican parishes. They fulfilled this responsibility most consistently in Maryland, a former Roman Catholic colony in which a large percentage of the populace had always been Anglican, and in South Carolina. The colonial religious establishment was less successful in North Carolina and Georgia, both because of the late date of enactment and because of the presence of those who had chosen to settle there precisely because of dissatisfaction with the religious situation in Virginia and South Carolina. The late date of establishment would prove less detrimental in Nova Scotia, because the church's favored status would not end with the American Revolution.

While Anglicans in England were not in complete agreement about the wisdom of the church-state alliance that the English government expanded in America after 1688, many of them shared a common conception that was quite different from the dream for world evangelism of the first generation of colonists. Bishop of Gloucester William Warburton (1698–1779) would later explain this new understanding of the relationship of religion and nationhood in his *Alliance between Church and State* (1736). For him, the church was the soul of the state; it taught a natural religion to individuals who, as a result, became better citizens.[7] Residents of the colonies with established Anglican churches came to share a similar opinion; for them, the Anglican Church and civic responsibility became increasingly intertwined.[8] This integrated view would, however, create problems when the American Revolution severed the ties between church and state.

Anglicans would not be able to expand their establishment to include all of the American colonies. With the exception of the partial establishment in New York, no colony between Maryland and Nova Scotia would have an established Anglican Church; Congregationalists, Presbyterians, and other non-Anglicans were too firmly entrenched. The monarchs were, however, able to take steps to encourage and support individual Anglican congregations in those areas. Queen Anne, at the urging of the latitudinarian bishops, designated certain annates and tithes, which had been diverted to the state by Henry VIII, as a fund for the support of low-income clergy. From this fund—the so-called Queen Anne's Bounty—she also authorized gifts to clergy willing to travel to the colonies as missionaries. In addition, the queen made gifts to individual congregations.

During this period, Anglicans founded their first parishes in Massachusetts (King's Chapel, Boston, 1688), Pennsylvania (Christ Church, Philadelphia, 1694), New York (Trinity, New York City, 1697), Rhode Island (Trinity, Newport, 1698), New Jersey (St. Mary's, Burlington, 1703), and Connecticut (Christ Church, Stratford, 1707).

The Commissary System

In England, bishops appointed representatives, called commissaries, to perform functions in distant portions of their dioceses. In 1689, Henry Compton, the Bishop of London (1685–1715) decided that he would use this system in the American colonies. Though the colonies were not formally a part of his diocese, governmental offices and commercial houses in his diocese controlled the commerce and government of the colonies. Finding no other provision for the supervision of colonial religion, Compton adapted the commissary system to provide some leadership for the Anglican Church in the colonies.

In 1689, Compton appointed James Blair (1656– 1743) as his first commissary. Blair was already in Virginia. A Scot who had come to England with the support of latitudinarian Gilbert Burnet, Blair had escaped the uncomfortable reign of James II by volunteering for the mission field. He had quickly established roots in the colony, gaining an entry into the local gentry by marrying Sarah Harrison. Miss Harrison anticipated later liturgical revision in the *Book of Common Prayer* by refusing pointedly on three askings in the marriage service to say that she would obey her husband.[9]

As commissary in Virginia, Blair began to establish some order in the church. He set up a convocation system, sought to enforce morality laws, called annual conferences, proposed —but did not receive—ecclesiastical courts, and attempted to standardize the value of the tobacco in which clergy were

Fig. 4
Commissary James Blair

paid. In 1693, Blair founded the College of William and Mary, the first Anglican institution of higher learning in the American colonies. The Virginia House of Burgesses agreed to the idea, and English contributors, whose number included Gilbert Burnet, John Tillotson and Robert Boyle, provided needed financial resources. Blair planned for his school to educate both Indians and colonists. The college proved more successful with the latter group than the former, however. A large portion of Virginia-born Anglican clergy who served in the colony before the Revolution would be graduates of William and Mary.

Blair's success convinced Bishop Compton of the usefulness of the commissary system. Compton and his successors not only appointed commissaries for Maryland and the Carolinas, which like Virginia had Anglican establishment, but also for colonies in which Anglicans were a distinct minority. The commissary system reached its apogee during the episcopate of Edmund Gibson (Bishop of London, 1724–49). By the 1740s, commissaries were supervising Anglican clergy in nine of the colonies.[10]

The commissary system had certain inherent weaknesses, however. So long as the colonial clergy were in relative agreement, the commissaries were effective spokesmen. In a number of circumstances, they were able to lobby effectively for the removal of colonial governors with whose policies they disagreed. They lacked, however, the canonical authority of a bishop and were able to discipline errant clergy with only the greatest of difficulty.[11]

Within a few years of the introduction of the first commissaries, therefore, some colonial Anglicans were already calling for resident bishops. In 1706, for example, fourteen New York, New Jersey, and Pennsylvania clergy sent one of their number to England to plead for a colonial episcopate.[12] By 1713, such advocates had caught the attention of Queen Anne. She instructed her chief minister to prepare legislation that would have authorized consecration of bishops for the colonies. Unfortunately, she died before any action could be taken.[13]

With Anne's death in 1714, any real possibility for a colonial episcopate was lost. Anne's successor, George I, had a limited knowledge of either the English language or the English church. He delegated his right to appoint bishops to his prime minister and left other issues of religious policy to the Parliament. In 1718 and 1719, a new Whig majority in Parliament replaced the Tory government that had defended the authority of the church during Anne's reign. Rather than seeking to expand the sphere of influence for the episcopate, the Whigs sought to contract it. Parliament, for example, forbade the convocation of bishops to meet as a separate body, preferring to have Anglican prelates carry on their deliberations in the more public forum provided by the House of Lords, in which lay nobles and bishops met jointly.

Some individual Anglicans continued, however, the campaign for a bishop after 1714. In 1718, for example, a number of clergy from Pennsylvania, New Jersey, and Maryland signed a petition to the English bishops and archbishops requesting the appointment of a prelate.[14] Six years later, a call by New England clergy for a bishop brought philosopher and later bishop George Berkeley (1685–1753) to Rhode Island as part of an unsuccessful effort to create a second Anglican college and, the New England clergy hoped, a resident episco-

Table 1. A Partial List of Colonial Commissaries

Virginia

James Blair	1689–1743	(Pres. W & M, 1693–1743)
William Dawson	1743–52	(Pres. W & M, 1743–52)
Thomas Dawson	1752–61	(Pres. W & M, 1755–61)
William Robinson	1761–68	(Visitor W & M, 1759–68)
James Horrocks	1771–71	(Pres. W & M, 1764–71)
John Camm	1772–77	(Pres. W & M, 1771–77)

With the exception of William Robinson, all Virginia commissaries served as presidents of the College of William and Mary (W & M).

Maryland

Thomas Bray	1695–1704	
Christopher Wilkinson		
	1716–29	(Eastern shore only)
Jacob Henderson	1716–30	(Western shore only)
	1730–34	(All of Maryland)

North and South Carolina

Gideon Johnson	1707–11
William T. Bull	1716–23
Alexander Garden	1725–49

The rector of St. Philip's, Charleston, often served as the commissary to the Carolinas.

New York

William Vesey	
(1674–1746)	1715–46

Mr. Vesey served as rector of Trinity Church, New York City.

Pennsylvania (and Delaware)

Archibald Cummings	–1741
Robert Jenney	1742–62

The commissary in Pennsylvania also served as the rector of Christ Church, Philadelphia.

Massachusetts

Roger Price	1730–62

Mr. Price was the rector of King's Chapel, Boston.

The Bishop of London did not appoint commissaries for New Hampshire, Georgia, Connecticut, or Rhode Island. The commissary system fell into disuse in every colony except Virginia during the episcopate of Thomas Sherlock (1748–61). Sherlock hoped that his refusal to appoint commissaries would pressure the English government to send a colonial bishop.

Sources: *The Fulham Papers in the Lambeth Palace Library*, ed. William Wilson Manross (Oxford: Clarendon Press, 1965); *Classified Digest of the Record of the Society for the Propagation of the Gospel in Foreign Parts, 1701-1892*, 4th ed. (London: S.P.G., 1894); Olsen, "Commissaries"; Cross, *The Anglican Episcopate*; Joan Rezner Gundersen, "The Anglican Ministry in Virginia 1723–1776: A Study of a Social Class," (Ph.D. diss., Notre Dame, 1972); Carl Bridenbaugh, *Mitre And Sceptre* (New York: Oxford, 1962); and *The Episcopal Church in North Carolina 1701–1959*, ed. Lawrence Foushee London and Sarah McCulloh Lemmon (Raleigh: Episcopal Diocese of North Carolina), 87. Because of the time needed to communicate the choice of a commissary from England to the colonies, there is often a discrepancy of a year in the dates of service listed by the various sources.

Fig. 5. The Bermuda Group, John Smibert's 1729 portrait of George (right) and Anne (seated with child) Berkeley and other planners of the expedition that eventually reached Rhode Island.

pate.[15] Others on both sides of the Atlantic would sound similar calls throughout the remainder of the colonial period. It would only be after the American Revolution, however, that the Whigs in English Parliament reversed their opposition to resident bishops. So long as the American colonies were part of the British Empire, they feared that an expanded episcopate would only support the authoritarian policies of the Tory party. An episcopate in a separate nation, however, would present no challenge to liberties back at home.

The Missionary Societies

First commissary James Blair served in Virginia as commissary for fifty-seven years. Bishop Compton's appointee in Maryland, Thomas Bray (1656–1730), followed a very different course of action. Though chosen in 1696, Bray did not actually visit the colony itself until 1700. His initial efforts in Maryland were much like those of Blair in Virginia. He summoned a convocation of the clergy, charged them to teach the catechism to their parishioners, and cautioned one of their number about his scandalous conduct. He urged vestries to help in the suppression of evil conduct, and he raised an offering for the assistance of the Church of England in Pennsylvania.[16] The establishment was new in Maryland, and the legislative act for which Bray successfully lobbied did not include any funds for his own salary. After less than three months in the colony, he sailed for England. He would not return to Maryland.

Bray's major contribution, however, was not pastoral; it was organizational and educational. Bray had come to the attention of Bishop Compton because of his intellectual ability. He had been a scholarship student at Oxford whose studies had advanced so quickly that he had graduated before the canonical age for ordination. He had written a popular set of *Catechetical Lectures* that was already in print in 1697. Once appointed by Compton, he immediately recognized the need for educational materials in the colonies. In 1698, he organized the Society for Promoting Christian Knowledge (SPCK), to which Princess Anne contributed forty-four pounds and Bishop Burnet fifty, to purchase books for colonial libraries.[17] In keeping with the Enlightenment marriage of science and religion, the titles included both works in theology and the natural sciences. Bray hoped that these SPCK libraries, which would eventually number almost forty, would be both tools for parish clergy and effective evangelical materials. Dissenters or non-Christians who read the books would learn of the reasonableness of the Anglican cause.

Bray's inability to gain a stipend from the Maryland legislature convinced him that a missionary organization to support colonial clergy was also needed. He began to campaign for such a body. His *A General View of the English Colonies in America with Respect to Religion,* written before his visit to Maryland (1698), had detailed the woeful condition of colonial Anglicanism. In all of New England, there was only one Anglican parish, the newly founded King's Chapel. Long Island had thirteen dissenting churches and no Anglican parishes. East New Jersey had no Anglican church; and Pennsylvania had only one. The Carolinas boasted only one church in Charleston. The situation was better in Bermuda (three ministers in nine parishes), Jamaica (eight ministers in fifteen parishes), Barbados (fourteen ministers in fourteen parishes), Maryland (sixteen ministers in thirty parishes,) and Virginia (thirty ministers in fifty parishes), though Bray had some criticism for the church in those areas as well.[18] Bray's account caught the interest of his fellow Anglicans, and in 1701 he and others secured a charter from William III to form the Society for the Propagation of the Gospel in foreign parts (SPG).

The SPG's first missionary was an ex-Quaker named George Keith (1638–1716). While on his voyage to America, Keith convinced ship's chaplain John Talbot (1645–1727) to join him. In 1702, the two began a grand tour of the colonies, traveling more than eight hundred miles from Maine to the Carolinas. Keith was a Scot who had taught at a Friend's school in Philadelphia before his conversion to Anglicanism. He brought the certainty of a new convert and a willingness to engage in controversy that would mark many of the SPG missionaries who would venture into dissenting strongholds. In Boston, he criticized the graduates of Harvard University for defending the doctrine of predestination and engaged in a pamphlet war with Congregational patriarch Increase Mather (1639–1723).[19]

Keith and Talbot's journey confirmed the information in Bray's *General View*. The Anglican Church was almost unknown in the middle colonies, New England, and the Carolinas. The SPG would send the great preponderance of its missionaries to these areas, though it sent a few to Virginia and Maryland. In the years between 1701 and the American Revolution, the SPG would help support two persons in Virginia, five in Maryland, thirteen in Georgia, thirty-three in North Carolina, forty-four in New Jersey, forty-seven in Pennsylvania, fifty-four in South Carolina, fifty-eight in New York, and eighty-four in New England. Missionaries went both to the English colonists and to blacks, Indians, and immigrants from other European nations. The society's records indicate that the missionaries ministered in six European and fourteen Indian languages.[20] Most, but not all, of the SPG's support went to white male clergy. Exceptions to the rule included society support for Harry and Andrew, black evangelists in midcentury South Carolina.[21]

In addition to their efforts in the colonies that would later become the United States, SPG missionaries also went to other British holdings in the Western Hemisphere: Newfoundland (1703), the West Indies (1712), Nova Scotia (1728), the Bahamas (1733), and Honduras (1733). In the second half of the eighteenth century, the SPG would also begin work in Africa and the Pacific.[22]

The society's instructions to the early missionaries conveyed the reasonable tone of enlightened Anglicanism. "Missionaries to heathens and infidels" were to begin their instruction "with the principles of natural Religion, appealing to their Reason and conscience; and thence proceed to shew them the Necessity of Revelation, and Certainty of that contained in the Holy Scripture, by plain and most obvious Arguments."[23] SPG missionaries were to employ both natural reason and revelation in order to bring others to the Christian faith.

Logical arguments were not, however, the only tools that colonial Anglicans used to portray the alliance of reason and revelation. Even the design of their churches bore witness to the relationship. In the first half of the eighteenth century, most other Protestants met in barnlike rectangular meetinghouses, most of which were entered through a door on their long walls. Colonial Anglicans were, in contrast, attracted to the new designs that James Gibbs (1682–1754) was employing for Anglican churches in England. By replacing free-standing bell towers with steeples that rose from roof tops, Gibbs was able to construct churches with unob-
structed facades. To these he intro-
duced columns reminiscent of classical Roman and Greek designs. The resultant pattern was a marriage of Christianity and classical thought, the architectural incarnation of the hopes of Christians of the Moderate Enlightenment. Anglicans introduced the design in the colonies and other denominations soon imi-
tated it.[24]

Not all the colonists were recep-
tive, however, to Anglican influ-
ence. The SPG recognized this fact, warning missionaries that they would need to defend the dis-
tinctive principles of the Church of England against "the attempts of such Gainsayers as are mixt among them."[25] The major point of controversy, one about which George Keith and Increase Mather were already debating in 1702, was the epis-

Fig. 6. St. Michael's Church, Charleston, South Carolina, 1752–58

copacy. SPG missionaries defended the institution from the criticism of Protestants of denominations that had rejected apostolic succession.

George Keith and others sent to America relied upon a well-laid argument that Thomas Bray had already advanced in his *Catechetical Lectures.* English Protestants of the seventeenth and eighteenth centuries explained the gospel by comparing it to an Old Testament covenant, a contract in which both God and the believer agreed to fulfill certain responsibilities. In the new covenant of the gospel, God promised forgiveness of sin and everlasting life, and the believer promised repentance and faith in Christ. Bray was one of a number of post-Restoration Anglican authors who suggested that baptism by a priest in apostolic succession was the appropriate way to accept this covenant agreement. Episcopacy was, therefore, a necessary element of the covenant. This episcopal version of covenant theology would prove extremely useful to generations of Anglican clergy.

The society's first parishioners in New England and the middle colonies were Anglicans who petitioned the SPG for help in the formation of congregations. Initially, many of these were among the poorer and less-privileged inhabitants. Eighteenth-century Connecticut tax rolls indicated, for example, that two-thirds of the Anglicans in that colony were residents of rural areas and that the percentage of poor was higher than among Congregationalists.[26] In western Massachusetts, a number of Dutch settlers, who felt unwelcome in Congregational churches, were active in the formation of early Anglican parishes.[27] In New York City, many early converts to the Church of England were Dutch-speaking graduates of the SPG charity school who had received instruction both in the English language and the *Book of Common Prayer* from schoolmasters William and Thomas Huddleston.[28]

In 1722, Anglicans made their first inroads into the New England upper class. In September of that year, seven faculty members and recent graduates of Yale College signed a statement for the Yale Board of Trustees indicating "doubt [of] the validity" or persuasion of the "invalidity" of nonepiscopal ordination. The seven, all of whom were Congregational clergy, had met in an informal book club to which they had also invited George Pigot, an SPG missionary in Stratford. Pigot called their doubts on the question of episcopacy "a glorious revolution of the ecclesiastics of this country."[29]

Four of the seven—Yale rector Timothy Cutler (1683 or 1684–1765), tutor Daniel Brown (1698–1723), former tutor Samuel Johnson (1696–1772), and recent graduate James Wetmore (d. 1760)—sailed to England for reordination. Brown died of small pox while in England, but the remaining three were ordained and assigned to American parishes by the SPG: Cutler to Christ (Old North) Church in Boston (1723–64), Wetmore to Rye, New York (1726–60), and Johnson to Stratford, Connecticut, which was left vacant when Pigot moved on to Rhode Island. The contributions of the three men were not limited to the individual parishes they served, however. Native born and well educated, they provided needed leadership for the small Anglican Church in New England and New York. Samuel Johnson, for example, served for nine years (1754–63) as the first president of King's (Columbia) College in New York.

The Congregational Church was the established church in Connecticut, Massachusetts, and New Hampshire. As was the case with the Anglican Church in the South, the Congregational Church in New England was tax supported. As the Anglican Church made steady gains, however, the New England legislatures made some concessions. In 1727, Connecticut exempted all Anglicans living within five miles of Anglican church buildings from paying state church taxes. Massachusetts passed similar legislation in 1735.

Thomas Bray's SPG (now the USPG—United Society for the Propagation of the Gospel—as a result of a 1965 merger with the Universities' Mission to Central Africa) and SPCK continue their activities in the twentieth century. A third missionary society, however, would function only until the American Revolution. Dr. Bray's Associates, as the organiza-

Fig 7. Timothy Cutler   Fig. 8. Samuel Johnson

tion was called, secured a charter in the year of Bray's death (1730). The organization's efforts were directed to the evangelization and education of black Americans. It supported schools for blacks in Philadelphia (1758–75?); New York (1760–74); Williamsburg (1760–74) and Fredericksburg (1765–1770), Virginia; and Newport, Rhode Island (1762–1775?). While male clergy served as superintendents of these schools, most of the actual instruction was given by white school mistresses, such as Anne Wager of Williamsburg. After the American Revolution halted all ongoing projects, the society's managers devoted its assets to charitable projects within England.[30]

When, in 1724, Bishop of London (1723–48) Edmund Gibson sent a questionnaire to Anglican clergy in the American colonies, he found that the condition of the Anglican Church had markedly improved since Thomas Bray's *General View* (1698). Bray had found approximately eighty-five Anglican churches, of which almost all were in Maryland or Virginia. Gibson's survey, in contrast, noted one hundred sixty-one places of worship, ranging from South Carolina to Massachusetts. The survey included replies from Virginia (sixty places of worship), Maryland (forty-five), New York (seventeen), South Carolina (fourteen), Rhode Island (eight),

Pennsylvania (four), New Jersey (seven), Connecticut (three), and Massachusetts (three).[31]

Respondents reported that their churches were full. In Virginia, Maryland, and South Carolina, parishes for which complete data were available, the majority of the population attended worship regularly in the Anglican Church, and approximately 15 percent of the population received communion.[32] The latter figure was three times higher than that of parishes in the English Diocese of Oxford.[33]

The Anglican Church's growth in influence and numbers would not continue uninterrupted throughout the century, however. Two important events—the Great Awakening and the American Revolution— would soon leave lasting marks on the denomination.

NOTES

1. In *Enlightenment in America* (New York: Oxford, 1976), Henry F. May distinguished four overlapping periods in the Enlightenment: the Moderate Enlightenment (1699–1787); the Skeptical Enlightenment (1750–89), the Revolutionary Enlightenment (1776–1800), and the Didactic Enlightenment (1800–15). The present chapter focuses on May's first period, a time in which leading intellectuals believed the fruits of new scientific discovery were compatible with revealed religion. While the three subsequent chapters do not pick up May's labels, they deal with issues closely related to May's remaining periods: Chapter 3 discusses enlightened skepticism as a backdrop to the Great Awakening. Chapter 4 deals with religion in the era of the American Revolution. Chapter 5 uses the term *rational orthodoxy* to refer to May's Didactic Enlightenment.

2. Thomas Sprat, quoted in Margaret Purver and E.J. Bowen, *The Beginnings of the Royal Society* (Oxford: Clarendon Press, 1960) 2.

3. Purver and Bowen, *Beginnings of the Royal Society,* 2.

4. James R. Jacob, *Henry Stubbe: Radical Protestantism and Early Enlightenment* (Cambridge: Cambridge University Press, 1983), 3-4. Jacob credits Stubbe with being "the first to point out the character of this alliance between the latitudinarian churchmen and the Royal Society."

5. The debate was a logical offshoot of the Protestant doctrine of justification by faith alone. Protestants agreed that God forgave sinners because of the righteousness of Jesus Christ, rather than because of any righteousness of the sinner's own. Seventeenth-century Christians went on to ask by what criteria God chose to apply Christ's righteousness to some and not others. Those of the Calvinist party, who took their name from Genevan Reformer John Calvin, argued that no human action could influence God's choice. Arminians, drawing their name from Dutch Reformed theologian Jacobus Arminius, believed, in contrast, that God took human response to the gift of grace into account in making a determination. The Calvinist party predominated in the Congregationalist, Presbyterian, and Reformed churches. Both parties were represented in the Church of England.

6. William Fife Troutman, Jr., "Respecting the Establishment of Religion in Colonial America" (Ph.D. diss., Duke University, 1959), 58–62; S. D. McConnell, *History of the American Episcopal Church from the Planting of the Colonies to the End of the Civil War,* 3d ed. (New York: Thomas Whittaker, 1891), 64–5.

7. Robert Sullivan, "The Transformation of Anglican Political Theology, ca. 1716-1760" (Lecture delivered at the Folger Institute, Washington, D.C., 26 September 1986).

8. Rhys Isaac, *The Transformation of Virginia 1740–1790* (Chapel Hill: University of North Carolina Press for the Institute of Early American History and Culture, 1982), 120–21. Isaac notes that the religion of colonial Virginia reinforced the social order.

9. Park Rouse, Jr., *James Blair of Virginia* (Chapel Hill: University of North Carolina Press, 1971), 24.

10. Alison Gilbert Olsen, "The Commissaries of the Bishop of London in Colonial Politics," in *Anglo-American Political Relations, 1675–1775,* ed. Alison Olsen and Richard M. Brown (New Brunswick: Rutgers University Press, 1970), 110.

11. Ibid., 110–13.

12. Edgar Legare Pennington, *Apostle of New Jersey: John Talbot, 1645–1727* (Philadelphia: Church Historical Society, 1938), 38–39.

13. Arthur Lyon Cross, *The Anglican Episcopate and the American Colonies* (New York: Longmans, Green, and Co., 1902), 101.

14. Pennington, *Apostle,* 62–63.

15. Edwin S. Gaustad, *George Berkeley in America* (New Haven: Yale University Press, 1979), 8–13.

16. H.P. Thompson, *Thomas Bray* (London: SPCK, 1954), 52–53.

17. Thompson, *Bray,* 17, 28.

18. Thomas Bray, *A General View of the English Colonies in America with Respect to Religion,* extracted from the author's work entitled Apostolic Charity, first printed in London in 1698 (reprinted for the Thomas Bray Club, 1916).

19. Pennington, *Talbot,* 16–18.

20. *Classified Digest,* 86.

21. R.E. Hood, "From a Headstart to a Deadstart: The Historical Basis for Black Indifference toward the Episcopal Church, 1800–1860," *Historical Magazine of the Protestant Episcopal Church* 51 (September 1982):272.

22. *Classified Digest,* xvi.

23. Pennington, *Talbot,* 16–17.

24. Donald Drew Egbert and Charles W. Moore, "Religious Expression in American Architecture," in *Religious Perspective in American Culture,* ed. James Ward Smith and A. Leland Jamison, 2 vols. (Princeton: Princeton University Press, 1961), 2:374–77.

25. Pennington, *Apostle,* 16.

26. Bruce E. Steiner, "New England Anglicanism: A Genteel Faith?" *William & Mary Quarterly* (3d series) 28 (January 1970):120–35.

27. Mary E. Grothe, "Anglican Beginnings in Western Massachusetts: Gideon Bostwick, Missionary to the Berkshires" (M.T.S. thesis, Virginia Seminary, 1984).

28. Joyce D. Goodfriend, "The Social Dimensions of Congregational Life in Colonial New York City," *William and Mary Quarterly* (3d series) 46 (April 1989):269–71.

29. Francis L. Hawks and William Stevens Perry, eds., *Documentary History of the Protestant Episcopal Church . . . in Connecticut* (New York: James Pott, 1863), 56–57, 65.

30. Edgar Legare Pennington, *Thomas Bray's Associates and Their Work Among the Negroes* (Worcester, Mass.: American Antiquarian Society, 1939); Joan R. Gundersen, "The Non-institutional Church: The Religious Role of Women in Eighteenth-Century Virginia," *Historical Magazine of the Protestant Episcopal Church* (December 1982):352; John Chamberlin Van Horne, "Pious Designs: The American Correspondence of the Associates of Dr. Bray, 1731–75" (Ph.D. diss., University of Virginia, 1979), 75–86.

31. Patricia U. Bonomi and Peter R. Eisenstadt, "Church Adherence in the Eighteenth-century British American Colonies," *William and Mary Quarterly* (3d series) 39 (April 1982):245–86.

32. Ibid., 261.

33. Robert Currie, Alan Gilbert, and Lee Horsley, *Churches and Churchgoers: Patterns of Church Growth in the British Isles since 1700* (Oxford: Clarendon Press, 1977), 22.

3
The Great Awakening
(1740–76)

In the fall of 1740 and the winter of 1741, a shock wave ran through the English colonies in North America. George Whitefield (1714–70), a young English priest who had come to the colonies for the second time in order to support the Bethesda Orphanage in Savannah, ventured north on a preaching tour. He arrived by ship in New England in mid-September. After forty-five days of itinerant preaching, he went on to the middle colonies, where he would spend two months, almost half of them in the cities of New York and Philadelphia.[1] From there he headed south, passing through Maryland and Virginia and arriving in Savannah in December of 1740. He devoted a month to preaching in the coastal areas of South Carolina and Georgia and returned to England in January 1741. As he traveled, particularly in New England and the middle colonies, he drew huge crowds, at times as many as fifteen thousand. He became the first truly American celebrity, and his death (in the midst of his seventh and final visit to America) was the first to be noted in newspapers throughout the colonies.[2] Though an Anglican, he soon established ties of friendship with revivalistic preachers of other denominations—Congregationalist Jonathan Edwards (1703–58), Presbyterian Gilbert Tennant (1703–64), and Reformed pastor Theodore Frelinghuysen (1691–1748)—knitting together their local revivals into a general and "Great Awakening" in the American colonies.

Whitefield's participation in the Awakening was initially a cause of pride for the Anglican clergy. He was a leading preacher, a magnet for large crowds, who was a member of their denomination. They welcomed him to their pulpits. Yet almost from the moment he began to speak, Anglican clergy had misgivings. They learned that he used extemporaneous prayer, rather than confining himself to the fixed forms of the *Book of Common Prayer.* In conversations with them, moreover, Whitefield explicitly rejected a central element of Anglican covenant theol-

Fig. 9. George Whitefield

ogy—the necessity of apostolic succession for a valid ordained ministry. In colony after colony, therefore, local Anglican clergy began to criticize what they saw as Whitefield's lack of regard for the basic elements of Anglican doctrine and liturgy.

Squabbles with Anglican clergy were, therefore, a continuing element of Whitefield's preaching tour. A meeting between Whitefield and a group of Anglican clergy in Boston that included Timothy Cutler and Commissary Roger Price (1696–1762) resulted in such wide disagreements that Whitefield did not even ask to preach in Anglican congregations in that city.[3] Hearing of Whitefield's New England tour, William Vesey (1674–1746), the commissary in New York, refused to let Whitefield preach at New York City's Trinity Church. In Philadelphia, Anglican clergyman Richard Peters interrupted Whitefield's preaching at Christ Church in order to point out what he believed to be doctrinal errors; soon afterwards Commissary Archibald Cummings (d. 1741) denied Whitefield any further access to Anglican pulpits in the area.[4] In Charleston, Alexander Garden (1685–1756), the bishop's commissary, refused communion to Whitefield and attempted to suspend him from the ministry. Only in Virginia, where Whitefield accepted James Blair's invitation to preach at Bruton Parish in Williamsburg, did Whitefield remain on good terms with the Anglican commissary. Yet even Commissary Blair wrote to the Bishop of London soon afterwards to say that if, as he had since heard by rumor, Whitefield was "under any censure or prohibition to preach," he would abide by it on future occasions.[5]

Whitefield, who always had an eye for the dramatic, discovered a way to use these disagreements to increase interest in his tour. On arriving in a community, he asked to preach at the local Anglican church. If given permission, he would then deliver a sermon in which he attacked Anglican doctrine. Pamphlets by Whitefield published in 1740 gave some indication of the scope of his criticism; in them, he denounced both Bishop Edmund Gibson of London and John Tillotson, the highly respected late seventeenth-century Archbishop of Canterbury. When the local clergy responded to him with criticism or a denial of access to the pulpit, Whitefield would complain of persecution. The news of the church fight would spread, and Whitefield would soon be preaching to curious crowds either outdoors or in the Congregational, Reformed, Presbyterian, and Baptist churches, to which he was increasingly invited.

Sentimentalist Preaching and the New Birth

Whitefield's ability to capitalize on church fights may have won publicity in the short run. Taken by itself, however, it could not account for the sustained interest in and the continuing impact of his preaching. There was another cause for his popularity—something new both in his message and in the way in which he delivered it that met the needs of the people of his day. Those critics who detected in Whitefield a departure from the moderate enlightened faith that was the religious inheritance of early eighteenth-century Christians were correct; they would have also been correct had they suggested that his new message would influence the form of tradition that would be passed on to later generations.

Most colonial Anglican clergy agreed with John Locke's affirmation in *An Essay Concerning Human Understanding*

(1690) that the "Understanding" (i.e., the intellect) was "the most elevated faculty of the soul, . . . employed with greater and more constant delight than any other."[6] They recognized that short-term human actions were often the result of human passions, but they believed that in the long term it was the intellectual conviction of the wisdom of some courses of action and the folly of others that shaped human choices. The content and form of their sermons—intellectual treatises read from manuscripts without eye contact or dramatic flourish—were shaped, therefore, to educate the mind without exciting the passions.

As Whitefield and others came to recognize, however, logical demonstration did not always bring personal conviction or amendment of life. Indeed, skeptical thinkers, such as John Toland (1670–1722), had begun to suggest that rational argument might disprove, rather than confirm the central truths of the Christian faith. Toland and other skeptics forced more orthodox Christians to reexamine their premises. Some of these more orthodox believers concluded that rational discourse by itself was not a sufficient tool for Christian proclamation. The good news had to touch the affections as well as the mind.[7]

Those clergy who sought to follow this route could draw on the sentimentalist theories of the third Earl of Shaftesbury (Anthony Ashley Cooper, 1671–1713) and of Francis Hutcheson (1694–1746), in which human affections played a more central role. Accepting the sentimentalist premise that human action did not always arise from dispassionate logic, such clergy abandoned the reading of sermons and adopted extemporaneous styles of delivery and broad dramatic gestures in the hope of reaching their parishioners on a more emotional level.[8] When they did so, they found that their new emphasis provided one effective antidote to skepticism. Parishioners awaited their sermons with excitement, traveled long distances to hear particularly noted speakers, and began to express a new seriousness about religion.

The change in the form of preaching was accompanied by a corresponding change in content. Moderate enlightened clergy sought a change in intellectual conviction on the part of their auditors. Sentimentalist clergy, in contrast, looked for signs of change in the affections of their parishioners. It was not enough to understand intellectually the basic Reformation doctrine of justification by faith; one had to "feel" that doctrine on a personal level. As sentimentalist clergy explained it, this usually involved despair at the realization that all human efforts ended in damnation, which was followed by a "new birth" in the which the individual turned to a reliance on Jesus Christ.

Whitefield was a particularly successful proponent of both the form and content of this new sentimentalist approach to preaching. His own life, about which he would write in a widely published journal, provided, moreover, a striking, concrete example of the new birth. He was the son of a widow who ran a tavern in Gloucester, England. As a child, he confessed, he had been addicted to "lying, filthy talking, and foolish jesting." He stole from his mother, broke the Sabbath, played cards, read romances, and dropped out of school at fifteen. His mother remarried, however, and Whitefield was able to return to his studies. It was the beginning of a new chapter in his life. He completed grammar school and was admitted to Oxford as a scholarship student.[9]

At the university, Whitefield joined a prayer and study group led by John (1703–91) and Charles (1707–88) Wesley, to which other university students referred as the "the Reforming Club," "the Holy Club," or, for their systematic method of pursuing piety, "the Methodists." Though, as his participation in the group indicated, he was concerned about the Christian faith and life, Whitefield was unable to overcome his own doubts until a dramatic and emotional conversion left him prostrate and weeping.[10] On a doctor's suggestion, he withdrew from school for a time, but he never after doubted his Christian faith.

The events of the following years reinforced Whitefield's conviction that the conversion had been a turning point in his life. The Bishop of Gloucester, Martin Benson, sought him out, gave him a small scholarship for the purchase of books, and

Fig. 10. John Wesley and his Friends at Oxford

offered to ordain him before the canonical age of twenty-three. Once he began preaching, Whitefield found that people responded to his message, whether he spoke in London churches, in the American colonies (which, on the advice of the Wesleys, he first visited in 1737), or in fields (as he began to do in 1739).[11] Before his life ended, he would deliver an approximate total of eighteen thousand sermons in England, Scotland (fourteen visits), Ireland (two visits), and America (seven visits). Supporters said that his voice was so rich that he could bring people to tears with the mere saying of the word *Mesopotamia.* He could be heard by thirty thousand and yet speak intimately to a small prayer group.[12]

While he recognized that not all would have—or needed—conversion experiences as dramatic as his own, he was absolutely convinced that, without some experience of new birth, salvation was impossible. That experience had to involve, moreover, real personal struggle:

> My dear friends, there must be a principle wrought in the heart by the Spirit of the living God. . . . If I were to ask how long it is since you loved God, you would say, As long as you can remem-

ber; you never hated God, you know no time when there was enmity in your heart against God. Then, unless you were sanctified very early, you never loved God in your life. My dear friends, I am more particular in this, because it is a most deceitful delusion, whereby so many people are carried away, that they believe already. . . . It is the peculiar work of the Spirit of God to convince us of our unbelief—that we have got no faith. . . . Now, my dear friends, did God ever show to you that you have no faith? Were you ever made to bewail a hard heart of unbelief? Was it ever the language of your heart, Lord, enable me to call thee my Lord and my God? Did Jesus Christ ever convince you in this manner? Did he ever convince you of your inability to close with Christ, and make you to cry out to God to give you faith? If not, do not speak peace to your heart.[13]

Whitefield's reference to peace was an allusion to Jer. 6:14 ("They have healed the wounds of my people lightly, saying 'Peace, peace,' when there is no peace.").[14] He accused those, who said they had a Christian faith without first despairing the possibility of earning their own salvation, of claiming a peace that they did not have.

Whitefield had even stronger words for those "false doctors" who suggested that the New Testament concept of the new birth did not imply personal conversion:

Suppose any of these doctors were to come to any woman when her travailing pains were upon her, and she were crying out, and labour pains came on faster and faster, and they should stand preaching at the door, and say, Good woman, these are only metaphorical pains, this is only a bold expression of the Easterns, it is only metaphorical; I question whether the woman would not wish the doctor some of these metaphorical pains for talking so, which he would find real ones. . . . I am of an odd temper, and of such a temper, that I heartily wish they may be put under the pangs of the new birth, and know what it is by their own experience, know that there is nothing in nature more real than the new birth.[15]

Whitefield explained that the new birth created "a new understanding, a new will, . . . new affections, a renewed conscience, a renewed memory, [and] a renewed body."[16]

Whitefield had rejected the Anglican argument that a valid ministry required ordination in the apostolic succession. His stress on a new birth that was often marked by dramatic conversion meant that he also departed from the covenant teaching of many of his Anglican coreligionists in another way. In *Catechetical Lectures,* Thomas Bray had equated renewal of the covenant with baptism and the eucharist; Whitefield connected it with personal conversion.

After a not particularly successful missionary stint in Georgia and conversion experiences of their own, John and Charles Wesley followed Whitefield on the preaching circuit in England. Never quite as dramatic in the pulpit as Whitefield, they had other gifts that Whitefield lacked. In particular, they had a gift at organization and were able to create a network of societies that sustained the revival between visits of the great preachers.

John and Charles Wesley had loosely patterned the Holy Club at Oxford, which Whitefield had joined, on the English religious society Anthony Horneck had created in 1687. Horneck's society, based on German pietistic models, had been an exclusively male group devoted to prayer, Bible study, and conversation about practical piety. John and Charles Welsey's father, Anglican clergyman Samuel Wesley (1662–1735), had introduced one such group in his Epworth parish. Samuel, however, dissolved the organization when his wife Susanna (1669/70–1742) insisted on active participation.[17]

Whitefield and the Wesleys worked with existing religious societies and also helped to form new ones. They began, however, to change the Horneck model in significant ways, in part to conform with what they had learned from Moravian pietists. (John Wesley had been deeply impressed by the Moravians he met on the ship to Georgia in 1735, had joined their Fetter Lane Society organized by Peter Böhler in London, and had visited the Moravian community in Germany in 1738.) The newer religious societies segregated those who had not yet experienced the "new birth" from those converted Christians who were seeking holiness of life. They opened membership to women, and introduced the singing of hymns, the lyrics of many of which were written by Charles Wesley.[18]

While Whitefield and the Wesleys both made use of such societies, the Wesleys would develop a structure with which to coordinate and connect them. By 1746, John Welsey had established a hierarchy with "class leaders" presiding over "classes" or "bands" of a dozen or so and "lay preachers" leading societies composed of several such classes. The societies were, in turn, grouped into circuits led by "superintendents." The lay preachers and superintendents (some of whom were Anglican clergy) then met together in "annual conferences."[19] Thus, while Whitefield's visits produced more immediate effect, the long-term influence of the Wesleys would be greater.

The Progress of the Awakening

Whitefield's tour of 1739–40 left a permanent mark on the churches in the American colonies. The call for revival was so strong that it was impossible for American Christians to ignore. They had either to align themselves with it or become outside critics of the movement. Congregationalists who approved of the Awakening formed "New Light" congregations. Presbyterian clergy and congregations created a separate "New Side" synod (1741–58). Other supporters of the Awakening came to see adult baptism as an appropriate sign of the awakening of adult faith. They left Presbyterian and Congregational churches altogether and formed Baptist congregations. A small denomination prior to the Awakening, the Baptist Church would grow rapidly and by the nineteenth century become larger in size than either the Congregational or the Presbyterian Church.

Not all were happy with the preaching of George Whitefield and the increasing religious fervor of the American religious scene, however. Sizeable portions of the Presbyterian and Congregational churches feared that zeal for personal experience compromised traditional Reformed theological formulations. These "Old Light" Congregationalists and "Old Side"

Presbyterians insisted on strict adherence to the Westminster Confession of Faith and continued to support the communal implications of covenant theology.[20]

With the exception of Lewis Jones (ca. 1700–44) and Thomas Thompson (fl. 1740) of South Carolina, most Anglican clergy rejected Whitefield during his 1739 tour. He was not consistent in his use of the *Book of Common Prayer* for public worship, he didn't subscribe to the Anglican version of covenant theology with its emphasis on apostolic succession, and he questioned the salvation of those who could not attest to conversion. Timothy Cutler, one of the Yale converts, summed up the opinion of many when he wrote to the Bishop of London about Whitefield's theology: "He contradicted himself, the Church, and whatever Your Lordship has delivered . . ."[21] Thus, while Congregationalists and Presbyterians were divided by the Awakening, Anglicans were united in their opposition to it.

In New England, Anglican opposition had an unexpected result. While some did leave the Anglican Church to follow the revival, as a whole the church grew rapidly in numbers. Timothy Cutler, writing to the secretary of the SPG on behalf of Anglican laypersons in Simsbury, Connecticut, shortly before Whitefield's third visit to the colonies (1744–47), explained his understanding of the phenomenon in this way: "Enthusiasm has had a long Run . . . so that many are tired of it, and if the Door were open would take Refuge in our Church from Error and Disorder."[22]

In the middle colonies, the Awakening contributed to a rapid growth of the Presbyterian Church, which was already expanding as a result of Scotch-Irish immigration. The number of Presbyterian congregations in New York, New Jersey, and Pennsylvania, which stood at one hundred twenty-five in 1740, doubled in the thirty-five years after Whitefield's first visit. Anglican clergy shared their New England counterparts' negative estimation of Whitefield, but some of the laity, especially in Delaware and along the Pennsylvania-Maryland border, were touched by the Awakening. Delaware clergymen John

Pugh (d. 1745) and William Beckett (d. 1743) complained of losing parishioners in 1740 and 1741 to an awakened religious society. In Pennsylvania, William Currie of Radnor and Alexander Howie of Oxford made similar complaints.[23] Yet, as in New England, Anglican congregations grew as well. In New Jersey, for example, Anglican parishes increased from ten to twenty-one in the years between 1740 and 1765.[24]

One indirect result of this anti-Awakening growth was a rising concern for education. Anglicans, believing that sound education could refute what they saw as the errors of the Awakening, became acutely aware of the lack of Anglican schools in New England and the middle colonies. The diverse religious climate in the middle colonies made the establishment of purely Anglican colleges unlikely and probably unwise. Anglicans were, however, able to provide direction for two new institutions in the region. In New York, a group of interested people, the majority of whom were Anglican, secured a charter in 1753 for the establishment of King's College (renamed Columbia during the Revolution). While some non-Anglicans would participate in the school, the leading influence in the early years was clearly Anglican. Two-thirds of the governors (i.e., trustees) of the school were Anglican laypersons. Trinity Church contributed the land for the school.[25] Anglican clergy predominated among the early faculty members. Samuel Johnson, one of the Yale converts, served as the school's first president and was followed in 1763 by a second Anglican cleric, Myles Cooper (1737–85). Neither man had much sympathy for Whitefield or the Awakening.

In order to become president of King's College, Samuel Johnson had to decline an invitation to head the second institution, the College of Philadelphia. Back in 1740, Benjamin Franklin (1706–90) and other interested persons had secured a charter for an academy and college. The school was not on strong footing until the following decade. William Smith (1727–1803), an Anglican cleric from Aberdeen who accepted the call to become provost after Johnson's refusal, reorganized the school and secured a revised charter in 1755. An educational theorist who had aroused interest with an essay on the ideal university (*The General Idea of the College of Mirania*), Smith attempted to give the school an Anglican character similar to that at King's College. With the support of the trustees, two-thirds of whom were Anglican laypersons, he introduced Morning and Evening Prayer and Anglican catechizing.[26] Like his counterparts at King's College, he was deeply suspicious of the Awakening.

Anglicans made gains in other educational circles as well. Between 1725 and 1748, 2 percent of Harvard graduates and 5 percent of Yale graduates entered the Anglican ministry, figures that undoubtedly reflected the proselytizing of Samuel Johnson in New Haven and of his fellow convert Timothy Cutler in Boston. In 1754, Yale president Thomas Clap attempted to stem the tide of converts by forbidding students from attending worship in a newly constructed Anglican church near the campus. Any success on Clap's part was, however, short-lived. By the 1770s, Anglicans were numerous and confident enough to designate a chaplain for the Anglican students at Yale College.[27]

Virginia and Maryland, where the Anglican Church was numerically the strongest, were largely untouched by either the revivalist excitement of 1739 and 1740 or by the surge of growth resulting from opposition to it. Commissary Cummings of Pennsylvania attributed the lower interest to the established position of the Anglican Church; Whitefield suspected it was due to unfaith. He described Maryland, for example, as an area "yet unwatered with the true Gospel of Christ." The lack of large urban centers in which Whitefield could attract large crowds may, however, have been as much a cause of indifference to the Awakening as anything else. The end result was, however, clear enough. With the exception of the coastal area from Savannah to Charleston, inhabitants of the southern colonies had little interest in Whitefield's 1739 tour.[28]

Whitefield's third (1744–47) and fourth (1751–52) visits to the colonies did little to alter this basic pattern: Anglicans opposed the Awakening, Baptists favored it; and Presbyterians and Congregationalists divided into competing factions.

The Anglican Awakening

In the years between Whitefield's fifth (May 1754–March 1755) and sixth visits (August 1763–June 1765), Anglican attitudes began to change, however. While many Anglicans remained skeptical about Whitefield and his methods, a significant number of Anglicans began to think otherwise.

Often it was younger clergy who led the way in this rethinking of the Awakening. For them, Whitefield would have been a fixture on the theological landscape rather than the new phenomenon that he had been in 1739. Whitefield's specific criticism of the Anglican Church's ministry and theology had, moreover, blunted over time. It was possible for the younger clergy to adopt Whitefield's doctrine of new birth and his advocacy of small-group worship without accepting his earlier criticism of the Anglican liturgy and ministry.

In Philadelphia, it was William McClenachan (Mcclenachan or Macclenaghan, ordained in 1755 and died in 1766 or 1767), a recently ordained Irish clergyman with evangelical leanings, that triggered interest in the Awakening. MacClenachan arrived in Philadelphia in 1759 after a brief term as an SPG missionary in Massachusetts. While assisting Robert Jenney (1687–1762), the aging commissary and rector of Christ Church, MacClenachan preached about conversion and established a religious society. When Jenney attempted to silence him, Macclenaghan and his supporters withdrew and began to meet at the state capitol. They formed the new congregation of St. Paul's and by December 1761 had completed a building, which they claimed to be "the largest in this City or Province."[29] Other Anglicans in the city must have been impressed, for by 1764 Jacob Duché (1737–98), the young assistant at Christ Church, had joined with one of the wardens to form private meetings at Christ Church itself.[30] When Whitefield arrived in Philadelphia in the fall of 1763, even his old adversary Richard Peters, who had succeeded Jenney at Christ Church (linked from 1760 to 1836 with St. Peter's as the United Parish), welcomed him. After consulting Duché and other clergy, he decided that it would be preferable to invite Whitefield to preach than to have "further disunion among the members, who might when displeased go over to" MacClenachan. Whitefield accepted the invitation and preached on four occasions. Peters reflected afterward that his decision to extend the invitation had been a correct one. The evangelist preached, he felt, "with a greater moderation of sentiment" than he believed had been the case on earlier visits.[31]

Many younger clergy in other colonies shared a similar interest in Whitefield. Samuel Peters (1735–1826), who took charge of the Anglican congregation in Hebron, Connecticut, in 1758; Charles Inglis (1734–1816), who served Christ Church in Dover, Delaware, beginning in 1759; and Samuel Magaw (1740–1812), who succeeded him in 1767, all supported the Awakening to varying degrees. A somewhat older Hugh Neill (ca. 1725–81), with parish experience in Dover, Delaware; Oxford, Maryland; and Philadelphia, was a cautious supporter of the Awakening.[32]

Interest in this spreading Anglican Awakening was also evident in Virginia, where Whitefield had finally succeeded in lighting the fire of revival during his fifth visit to the colonies. By the 1760s, Robert McLaurine (ordained 1750, d. 1773), Archibald McRoberts (licensed to serve in Virginia in 1761), Devereux Jarratt (1733–1801), Charles Clay (ordained 1768), and perhaps as many as six other Anglican clergy in the state actively supported the Awakening.[33] Of the group in Virginia, Jarratt was to be the best known. Touched by the stirrings of awakening that began in the Presbyterian Church in Virginia during Whitefield's fifth visit, Jarratt traveled to England for Anglican ordination in 1762. While there he heard both Whitefield and John Welsey preach. Returning to Virginia to serve as the rector of Bath Parish in Dinwiddie County, Jarratt began to call for personal conversion and to establish small religious societies in his parish and in neighboring areas.

Clergy who were ordained in the 1770s exhibited an interest in the Awakening similar to the ordinands of the 1760s. In North Carolina, clergyman Charles Pettigrew (1744–1807) became an active proponent of the revival after his ordination in 1775. Pettigrew was a second-generation advocate of awakening; his own father had been converted by the preaching of Whitefield in Pennsylvania.[34] Uzal Ogden (1744–1822), an SPG catechist (1770–72) and priest in Sussex and other points in New Jersey, and Sydenham Thorne of Delaware, both of whose ordained ministry began in 1774, shared a similar interest.[35] Philadelphia clergyman William Stringer, who claimed ordination by an orthodox bishop but who was reordained in England in 1773, also was a clear supporter of the Awakening.[36]

There was strong lay leadership for the Awakening in the colonial Anglican Church as well. This came from two directions: from those colonists, like the parishioners of St. Paul's, Philadelphia, who were touched by the progress of the Awakening in America, and from those recent immigrants who had been touched by the parallel evangelical revival in the Britain.

Some of those in the latter category had been active in the Methodist movement in England. By the 1760s, some who had experience as class leaders and lay preachers in the hierarchy that John Wesley had created to coordinate British religious societies were immigrating to American. Noticing the lack of any coherent structure to promote the Awakening in the colonial Anglican Church, they began to introduce the British pattern. Irish immigrant Robert Strawbridge founded methodist societies in Maryland and Pennsylvania beginning in the early 1760s. In the mid-1760s, Barbara Heck (1734–1804) convinced her cousin Philip Embury (1728–73), who had been a lay preacher before his immigration, to form a methodist class in New York. Heck and Embury found the Anglican Church in New York unconducive to their effort and began attending a Lutheran congregation.[37] Others in New York apparently felt differently. In 1764, Anglicans supportive of the Awakening were influential enough at Trinity Church, for example, to pressure new rector Samuel Auchmuty (1722–77) to hire an assistant who was "a sound Whitfilian." These lay supporters tried to convince Jacob Duché to leave his position as assistant at Christ Church, Philadelphia, and to come to New York. Duché declined the offer, but recommended Charles Inglis of Dover, who became Auchmuty's assistant in 1765.[38]

By the late 1760s, many others had followed Strawbridge, Heck, and Embury's lead in introducing methodist structures in America. French and Indian War veteran Captain Thomas Webb provided a colorful leadership style for New York methodists. Robert Williams, an Irish lay preacher and itinerant, arrived in Philadelphia in 1769. He traveled widely, appearing, for example, in 1772 or 1773 on Devereux Jarratt's doorstep in Virginia.[39] He and others cooperated with Jarratt, producing a flourishing methodist movement that soon became the largest in the country.

In 1769, John Wesley decided to play a more direct role in the expansion of this growing methodist movement in the American colonies. He began to choose lay preachers to send to America. He would eventually send ten, including Joseph Pilmore (Pilmoor, 1739–1825), Francis Asbury (1745–1816), and Joseph Rankin. Pilmore, one of the first two chosen to go in 1769, settled in Philadelphia. Asbury, who on his arrival in 1771 was only twenty-six, would eventually emerge as the most influential leader of the methodist movement. In the short term, however, it was Rankin, an older and more experienced man who arrived in 1773, who provided leadership. In 1773, he summoned the first of what would become regular annual methodist conferences.[40] Those who attended the first meeting adopted the published minutes of Wesley's English conferences as their rule of order and vowed that they would admit no one to their number who did not agree to do the same.[41]

Wesley's appointees were more supportive of the continued link between the methodist societies and the Church of England than were some of the earlier immigrants who had introduced methodist structures on their own initiative. Wesley's designates encouraged members of the methodist societies to worship in the Anglican Church, invited sympathetic Anglican clergy to sessions of annual conference, and tried to restrain preachers like Robert Strawbridge from celebrating the sacraments without Anglican ordination.[42] This attitude won the cooperation of many of the ordained Anglican supporters of the Awakening.

The expanding methodist system also filled an important vacuum. Whitefield had provided a personality that linked awakened congregations in the colonies but no lasting structure or institution that could endure after his own death in 1770. The methodist system, in contrast, provided a structure that was not dependent on one individual and could, therefore, provide continuity and direction over time. Not all who embraced the Awakening joined the methodist societies, however. Colonial clergy regarded the methodist societies as a lay movement that they should assist, rather than join. Lay supporters of Whitefield might have questions about membership as well, for, though Whitefield and the Wesleys agreed on the importance of new birth and the value of private meetings, they disagreed over the doctrine of predestination. Nonetheless, many did join and by 1775 the societies could boast of 3,148 members.[43]

The Effects of the Awakening

The Great Awakening changed the theological character of the colonial Anglican Church. While Anglican advocates of awakening of the 1760s and 1770s never did abandon apostolic succession or the fixed liturgy in the way that Whitefield had been willing to do in 1739, they did adopt sentimentalist styles of preaching and Whitefield's call for adult conversion. Even critics of the Awakening began to pay greater attention to personal religious experience. The attempt to integrate this new appreciation for affections with the received covenant tradition would, in turn, be a major topic of interest for theologians at the end of the century.

Changes were not only theological, however. Indeed, there were few aspects of church life that were left untouched. The membership, the institutions, and even the architecture and church music of the denomination were affected.

The Membership

One way in which the Great Awakening changed the membership was by subtly raising the status of women. Female literacy was considerably lower than male literacy in the eighteenth century; by some estimates it was one-half that of men.[44] The intellectual religion of the Moderate Enlightenment had, therefore, limited appeal to women. The Awakening, however, with its emphasis on affections and its household prayer meetings, provided new opportunities for female involvement. Martha Laurens Ramsay (1759–1811), the daughter of a prominent South Carolina family that attended St. Philip's Church in Charleston, found, for example, that her awakened faith opened doors to a world with greater possibilities. She corresponded with such pious Englishwomen as Selina, Countess of Huntingdon (1707–91) and began a personal religious journal, which was published by her husband after her death.[45]

Similarly, the Awakening would affect the Anglican Church's ministry to black Americans. Anglicans had begun to expand that ministry about the time of Whitefield's tour of 1739–40, in large measure due to rapid increase in slave population.[46] In 1741, the SPG purchased the slaves Harry and Andrew to serve as evangelists among blacks in South Carolina. In the mid-1740s, the clergy of Christ Church, Philadelphia, saw such an increase in their ministry among blacks that they asked the SPG to appoint a catechist to oversee the work. The SPG responded with the appointment of William Sturgeon (d. 1772) in 1747. Sturgeon, a Yale graduate who had traveled to England for ordination, carried on that work until 1762. In the early 1750s, Hugh Neill baptized 162 black persons in his Delaware congregation. Between 1758 and 1765, Dr. Bray's Associates opened schools for blacks in Virginia, Pennsylvania, Rhode Island, and New York.[47]

The fact that the most effective work among blacks was often carried on in the same Anglican parishes in which the Awakening took hold after 1759 may not be entirely coincidental.[48] Anglican clergy may have tested the simple message of personal reliance on Christ as a tool for evangelism for blacks before using the message with white parishioners. Whatever the facts of the matter, however, one thing was clear: an expansion in ministry to blacks coincided with the Great Awakening.

Thus during the Awakening years, Anglicans laid the groundwork for a expanding role for blacks and women in the years following the American Revolution. The formation of independent black congregations at the close of the eighteenth century and the growing women's movement in the nineteenth century were both built upon that foundation.

The membership of the colonial Anglican Church was affected in another way as well. Prior to the Great Awakening, American denominations were arranged in a roughly geographical pattern; Congregationalists predominated in New England, Anglicans in the South, and Presbyterians in certain areas of the middle colonies. The Awakening shattered this pattern. It brought Presbyterians and Baptists to Virginia and contributed to the growth of the Anglican Church in New England. The religious enclaves of the first half of the century gave way to a more heterogeneous pattern.

Provincial Assemblies and the Call for the Episcopate

The Awakening also sparked a renewed call for a colonial episcopate. Whitefield's confrontations with colonial clergy in 1739 and 1740 demonstrated the weakness of the commissary system. Commissaries could complain about Whitefield's preaching, but they lacked the clear authority over him that a colonial bishop would have been able to exercise. Moreover, as Anglicans had pointed out earlier in the century, a colonial bishop would provide a more satisfactory supply of clergy and would avoid the inevitable loss of life of some who took the dangerous trip to England for ordination. Yale convert Samuel

Johnson was well aware of the danger; his son had died on such a trip.

Johnson's fellow Yale convert Timothy Cutler was a leading advocate of the establishment of a colonial bishop. Another vocal figure was Thomas B. Chandler (1726–90), a New Jersey clergyman whose *An Appeal to the Public, on Behalf of the Church of England in America* (1767) sought to rally popular support for the idea. In England, Bishop Joseph Butler (1692–1752), a critic of John Wesley, took up the call for a colonial episcopate, and Bishop of London (1748–61) Thomas Sherlock stopped appointing commissaries in every colony except Virginia in order to pressure the Parliament to take action.[49]

Non-Anglicans reacted negatively to the Anglican campaign for a colonial episcopate. In the tense political climate of the 1760s, any proposal for a new British institution in the colonies was suspect. For Congregationalists and Presbyterians, an Anglican bishop, one who might exercise the political authority of his episcopal counterparts in the House of Lords, was particularly odious.

In Massachusetts, Congregational clergy Noah Welles (1718–76), Jonathan Mayhew (1720–66) and Charles Chauncy (1705–87) were fierce critics of the Anglican Church. In an anonymous pamphlet titled *The Real Advantage* (1762), Welles claimed to have joined the Anglican Church for purely social reasons. Mayhew's *Observations on the . . . S.P.G.* (1763) both criticized Anglican clergyman East Apthorp (1732 or 1733–1816) and suggested that SPG missionaries violated their own charter by preaching to those who were already active Christians.[50] Chauncy challenged Chandler's *Appeal* with his own *Appeal to the Public* (1769), to which Chandler responded with *The Appeal Farther Defended* (1771). The Welles-Mayhew-Chauncy characterization of the Anglican Church as wealthy was hardly accurate; nationally, the church represented roughly the same economic group as the Congregational Church, and in New England its membership was decidedly less well off. The charge did become, nonetheless, a lasting element in American religious imagery. Later

Episcopalians could, however, appreciate the historical irony involved when Mayhew's grandson, Jonathan Mayhew Wainwright (1792–1854), was elected an Episcopal bishop.

In New York, Presbyterians William Livingston (1723–90) and Francis Alison (1705–79) penned the *American Whig* papers in which they were similarly critical of Anglican plans for a colonial bishop. Their opposition, combined with that from New England, proved strong enough to prevent the introduction of bishops. Cutler, Chandler, and Butler were able to interest Archbishop of Canterbury Thomas Secker (archbishop 1758–68), but they could not convince the English Parliament to send bishops against the vocal opposition of non-Anglicans.

While the Anglican attempt to deal with the Awakening did not lead immediately to the sending of a colonial bishop, it did result in the creation of the colonial institutions that would in time play a vital role in the procuring of episcopal ministry. In May 1760, the clergy of Pennsylvania, Delaware, and New Jersey decided to meet in Philadelphia. William Smith of the College of Philadelphia presided at the gathering. William MacClenachan's religious society and the need for a colonial bishop were the major topics of conversation. Smith thought the convention a good idea and wrote to the Archbishop of Canterbury the following year suggesting that the other colonies form provinces, just as New Jersey, Delaware, and Pennsylvania had done. Smith was not, however, impressed by a suggestion advanced by the convention of 1766. College duties kept him from attending that year, and in his absence a majority of the clergy voted in favor of what he characterized as "a kind of Presbyterian or Synodical self delegated Government by Conventions."[51]

New York clergy also met regularly. They invited Anglican clerics from neighboring colonies to a series of conventions (1765, 1766, and 1767) that were largely preoccupied with the campaign for a colonial episcopate. Samuel Seabury (1729–96), a native of Connecticut who served churches in Long Island and Westchester, was the secretary of two of those sessions. In 1767, the New York clergy joined with those in

Pennsylvania, New Jersey, and Delaware to found the Society for Relief of Widows and Orphans of Clergymen.[52] These three organizations—the two regional conventions and the one united charitable society—would provide the framework and leadership for the reorganization of the Anglican Church following the American Revolution.

Architecture and Church Music

The Awakening also affected the interior design of churches. Many earlier Anglican buildings had had two-foci designs with pulpits and altars on adjacent walls. Those buildings that Anglicans designed after the onset of the Awakening were generally single-foci buildings with large central pulpits that emphasized the importance of the sermon.[53] Indeed, as early nineteenth-century Episcopalians would complain, many of these pulpits were so placed that they hid the holy table from the view of the congregation.[54]

Fig. 11. The interior design of Old Chapel, Clarke County, Virginia (ca. 1790) reflected the increased importance of preaching following the Great Awakening.

Similarly, the musical innovations of the Wesleys made a permanent mark on Anglican worship in America. Prior to the Awakening, many Anglicans resisted the use of hymns of recent composition. Christians should, they believed, sing only biblical material or texts like the *Te Deum* that were hallowed by centuries of use. In the early years after the Awakening, many Anglicans continued to look upon the singing of modern hymns with great suspicion. In Virginia, Awakening supporter Archibald McRoberts was tried for the singing of unauthorized hymns some time around 1779.[55] In Maryland, critics charged William Briscoe, Jr., of Shrewsbury Parish of the same offense in 1808.[56]

Yet even such charges did not prevent the inroads of hymn singing. Following the American Revolution, Episcopal General Conventions authorized hymnals in 1789 (27 texts), 1808 (57 texts), and 1826 (212 texts). Two of the 1808 texts and fourteen of those in the 1826 collection were by Charles Wesley.[57] Anglicans, both supporters and opponents of the Awakening, had begun to sing hymns.

As the 1770s approached, Anglicans in North America had, on the whole, cause for thanksgiving. The Great Awakening had led to disagreements among church members but (with the formation of a separate Methodist Church still a decade off) to none of the formal divisions that marked the Old-New splits of the Congregational and Presbyterian churches. Established Anglicanism was losing some ground in the South to the awakened Presbyterian and Baptist congregations, but the church was growing in the middle colonies and New England. Indeed, the church was participating in a spurt of growth that doubled the number of American congregations in the four decades after 1740. Much of that expansion may have been the result of the swelling immigration to America, but it gave colonial Anglicans a sense of progress and growth.[58] This sense of security would, however, soon be shattered by the events of the American Revolution.

NOTES

1. William Howland Kenney, III, "George Whitefield and Colonial Revivalism: The Social Sources of Charismatic Authority, 1737–1770" (Ph.D. diss., University of Pennsylvania, 1966), 85; Stuart C. Henry, *George Whitefield, Wayfaring Witness* (New York; Abingdon Press, 1957), 200–10.

2. Sydney E. Ahlstrom, *A Religious History of the American People* (New Haven: Yale University Press, 1972), 349–50.

3. William Stevens Perry, ed., *Massachusetts,* vol 3 of *Historical Collections Relating to the American Colonial Church* (Hartford, 1873; reprint, New York: AMS Press, 1969), 346; George Whitefield, *George Whitefield's Journals,* a new edition, ed. Iain Murray (London: Banner of Truth Trust, 1965), 457. It was in this conversation that Whitefield rejected the necessity of apostolic succession for a valid ministry.

4. Whitefield, *Journals*, 356. Kenney, "George Whitefield," 68–70, 89–91.

5. Perry, *Virginia*, vol. 1 of *Historical Collections*, 364.

6. John Locke, *An Essay Concerning Human Understanding,* ed. Alexander Campbell Fraser, 2 vols. (Oxford: Clarendon Press, 1894), 1:5.

7. Eighteenth-century Congregational clergyman Jonathan Edwards defined affections as "the more vigorous and sensible exercises of the inclination and will," which were "the springs which set us to work in all the affairs of life, and stimulate us in all our pursuits, especially in all affairs pursued with vigor" (Jonathan Edwards, *A Treatise on Religious Affections* [Grand Rapids: Baker Book House, 1982], 12 and 17.). While Edwards noted that "all affections have in some respects or degree an effect on the body," he distinguished the affections from such bodily sensations (pp. 57–61). In contemporary English, "deep personal conviction" conveys something of the same meaning that "affection" conveyed to eighteenth-century English speakers.

8. Harry S. Stout, *The New England Soul* (New York: Oxford University Press, 1986), 187.

9. Whitefield, *Journals,* 37–38.

10. Stuart C. Henry, *George Whitefield, Wayfaring Witness,* 24.

11. J.C. Ryle, "George Whitefield and His Ministry," in *Select Sermons of George Whitefield with an account of his life by J.C. Ryle and a summary of his doctrine by R. Elliot* (Edinburgh: Banner of Truth Trust, 1985), 13–17.

12. Ibid., 18 and 27.

13. George Whitefield, *Select Sermons of George Whitefield,* 85.

14. Whitefield used the Jeremiah passage as the basis for his oft delivered sermon titled, "The Method of Grace." See Whitefield, *Select Sermons,* 75–95 or John Grillies, *Memoirs of the Rev. George Whitefield,* rev. and cor. (New Haven: Whitemore and Buckingham, 1934), 473–88.

15. George Whitefield, *Sermons on Important Subjects; by the Rev. George Whitefield, A. M. with a memoir of the author by Samuel Drew and a Dissertation on his Character, Preaching, etc. by the Rev. Joseph Smith* (London: Thomas Tegg, & Son, 1836), 735–36.

16. Ibid.

17. Howard A. Synder, *The Radical Wesley* (Downer's Grove, Ill.: Inter-Varsity Press, 1981), 14–16.

18. Henry D. Rack, *Reasonable Enthusiast: John Wesley and the Rise of Methodism* (Philadelphia: Trinity Press International, 1989), 85, 186.

19. Williston Walker, Richard Norris, David Lotz, and Robert Handy, *A History of the Christian Church,* 4th ed. (New York: Charles Scribner's Sons, 1985), 602–03.

20. Historian Perry Miller first suggested in a 1935 essay that Jonathan Edwards and other New England New Light clergy rejected covenant theology. That claim has been the subject of a continuing debate. For Miller's essay, see "The Marrow of Puritan Divinity," in *Errand into the Wilderness* (Cambridge: Belknap Press of Harvard University Press, 1956). For a discussion of the current state of the debate on covenant theology and the Great Awakening, see David D. Hall, "On Common Ground: The Coherence of American Puritan Studies," *William and Mary Quarterly* (3rd series) 44 (April 1987).
Presbyterian and Congregational advocates of covenant theology did not, of course, accept the Anglican argument that episcopal ordination was a condition of the covenant.

21. Perry, *Historical Collections,* 3:346.

22. *Ibid.,* 3:380.

23. John Frederick Woolverton, *Colonial Anglicanism in North America* (Detroit: Wayne State Press, 1986), 196.

24. Patricia U. Bonomi and Peter R. Eisenstadt, "Church Adherence in the Eighteenth-Century British American Colonies," *William and Mary Quarterly* (3d series) 39 (April 1982):272.

25. David C. Humphrey, *From King's College to Columbia, 1746–1800* (New York: Columbia University Press, 1976), 34–5, and 77.

26. Ibid., 77; Ahlstrom, *A Religious History,* 222–23.

27. Humphrey, *King's College to Columbia,* 24–25, and 48; Edwards Beardsley, *Life and Correspondence of Samuel Johnson, D.D.* (New York: Hurd and Houghton, 1874), 200.

28. Kenney, "George Whitefield," 72, 99–100, 108. In South Carolina and Georgia, Whitefield did attract considerable crowds in 1740. In addition to clergymen Lewis Jones (ca. 1700–1744) of St. Helena Parish in Port Royal, South Carolina, and Thomas Thompson (fl. 1740s) of St. Bartholomew's Parish, who have been previously mentioned, the vestries of two vacant congregations (Christ Church Parish and St. John's, Colleton County) were supportive of Whitefield. See Sidney Charles Bolton, "The Anglican Church of Colonial South Carolina, 1704–1754: A Study in Americanization" (Ph.D. diss., University of Wisconsin, 1973), 315–16.

29. Perry, ed., *Pennsylvania,* vol. 2 of *Historical Collections,* 319–24, 355; Wardens and vestry of Saint Paul's Church to Bishop Osbaldeston, 22 June 1762, Fulham Papers, Lambeth Palace Library, London, England, vol. 7, p. 320; Wardens of St. Paul's to Bishop Terrick, Fulham Papers, vol. 8, pp. 48–51.

30. Perry, *Historical Collections,* 2:360.

31. *Ibid.,* 2:392–93.

32. Woolverton, *Colonial Anglicanism,* 198; Robert C. Monk, "Unity and Diversity among Eighteenth-Century Colonial Methodist and Anglicans," *Historical Magazine of the Protestant Episcopal Church* 38 (March 1969):59–60; Perry, *Historical Collections,* 2:365.

33. Joan Rezner Gundersen, "The Anglican Ministry in Virginia 1723–1776: A Study of a Social Class" (Ph.D. diss., Notre Dame, 1972), 214–18.

34. Sarah McCulloh Lemmon, *Parson Pettigrew of the "Old Church"* (Chapel Hill: University of North Carolina Press, 1970), 4.

35. Monk, "Unity and Diversity," *Historical Magazine,* 60.

36. Richard Peters to Bishop Terrick, 12 Dec. 1766, Fulham Papers 8:29; William Smith to Bishop Terrick, 22 Oct. 1768, Fulham Papers, 8:41; Wardens of St. Paul's to Bishop Terrick, 3 Dec. 1772, Fulham Papers, 8:48–49; Clergy of Philadelphia to Bishop Terrick, Fulham Papers, 8:50–51; William Stringer to Bishop Terrick, 28 Oct. 1773, Fulham Papers, 8:56–57.

37. Rack, *Enthusiast,* 484.

38. Perry, *Historical Collections,* 2:365.

39. Rack, *Enthusiast,* 484–85; Devereaux Jarratt, *The Life of the Reverend Devereux Jarratt* (Baltimore: Warner and Hanna, 1806; reprint, New York: Arno Press and the New York Times, 1969), 107–8.

40. Rack, *Enthusiast,* 456–57.

41. Thomas C. Oden, *Doctrinal Standards in the Weslyan Tradition* (Grand Rapids: Francis Asbury Press of Zondervan Publishing, 1988), 29–30.

42. Rack, *Enthusiast,* 486–87.

43. Ahlstrom, *Religious History,* 327. Whitefield believed that God chose particular people for salvation for reasons that were ultimately unknowable to humans (i.e., what has been called the "Calvinist" position). John Wesley argued that God gave the gift of salvation to people based on the foreknowledge that they would make good use of that gift (i.e., the "Arminian" position).

44. Linda K. Kerber, *Women of the Republic: Intellect and Ideology in Revolutionary America* (Chapel Hill: University of North Carolina Press, 1980), 193.

45. Joanna Bowen Gillespie, "'The Clear Leadings of Providence': Pious Memoirs and the Problems of Self-Realization for Women in the Early Nineteenth Century," *Journal of the Early Republic* 5 (summer 1985):197–221.

46. The rise in slave population was the result of a boom in tobacco prices, which began in the 1730s. Planters invested their increased profits in additional slaves. In Virginia, slave population increased from 60,000 to 140,000 in the twenty-year period from 1740 to 1760. David Burner et al., *An American Portrait: A History*

of the United States, 2d ed. (New York: Charles Scribner's Sons, 1985), 63–64.

47. *Classified Digest of the Records of the Society for the Propagation of the Gospel in Foreign Parts, 1701–1892,* 4th ed. (London: SPG, 1894), 38–39, 852; Edgar Legare Pennington, *Thomas Bray's Associates and Their Work Among the Negroes* (Worcester, Mass.: American Antiquarian Society, 1939).

48. Among the parishes in which expanded ministry to blacks preceded a white interest in the Awakening were Christ Church, Philadelphia (catechetical work among blacks leading to the appointment of Sturgeon; Macclenaghan's awakened preaching of 1759, and Duché's Whitfilian groups of the 1760s); Dover, Delaware (Neale's baptisms of blacks; awakening under rectors Inglis and Magaw); Trinity, New York (Dr. Bray's Associates' school; lay interest in awakening, leading to appointment of Inglis); and St. Philip's, Charleston (black catechists; interest of Martha Laurens Ramsay and others in awakening).

49. *Dictionary of National Biography,* s.v. "Joseph Butler" by Leslie Stephen; Arthur Lyon Cross, *The Anglican Episcopate and the American Colonies* (New York: Longmans, Green, and Co., 1902), 129.

50. Carl Breidenbaugh, *Mitre and Sceptre* (New York: Oxford University Press, 1962), 226.

51. Perry, *Historical Collections,* 2:311–24, 413–15; Cross, *Anglican Episcopate,* 247.

52. Clara O. Loveland, *The Critical Years* (Greenwich, Conn.: Seabury Press, 1965), 7.

53. Donald Drew Egbert and Charles W. Moore, "Religious Expression in American Architecture," in *Religious Perspective in American Culture,* ed. James Ward Smith and A. Leland Jamison, 2 vols. (Princeton: Princeton University Press, 1961), 2:374–77.

54. *Christian Journal* 11 (New York, 1827):135; *The Correspondence of John Henry Hobart,* ed. Arthur Lowndes, 6 vols. (New York: priv. print., 1911–12), 2:511–19.

55. Gundersen, "Anglican Ministry," 290.

56. Katherine Myrick DeProspo, *A History of Shrewsbury Parish Church* (Wye Mills, Md.: Chesapeake College Press, 1988), 100.

57. *The Hymnal 1940 Companion,* 3d rev. ed. (New York: Church Pension Fund, 1951), xx–xxi.

58. Bonomi and Eisenstadt, "Church Adherence," 274.

4

The American Revolution
(1776–1800)

In March 1775, a young man, whose uncle was an Anglican cleric, spoke to a gathering at St. John's Church in Richmond, Virginia. The speaker, Patrick Henry (1736–99), chose Jer. 6:14 as his text. The words from Jeremiah—"They have healed the wounds of my people lightly, saying 'Peace, peace,' when there is no peace"—may have triggered memories of George Whitefield for Henry's listeners, for that awakened evangelist had used them to describe the false religious security of the unconverted. Henry, however, dealt with the text in a way quite unlike Whitefield:

> Gentlemen may cry peace, peace, but there is no peace. The war is actually begun. The next gale that sweeps from the north will bring to our ears the clash of resounding arms. Our brethren are already in the field. Why stand we here idle? What is it that gentlemen wish? Is life so dear, or peace so sweet, as to be purchased at the price of chains and slavery? Forbid it, Almighty God! I know not what course others may take, but as for me, give me liberty or give me death![1]

The danger of which Henry warned his audience (the second Virginia revolutionary convention) was political, rather than religious. He was convinced that it was only a matter of time before the fighting with the British that had already begun in New England would reach Virginia.

Henry was not unique in his recasting of a Great Awakening theme in political terms. Both patriots and loyalists recognized what one historian has called a "spill-over" from religion to politics.[2] The preachers of the Awakening had discerned the hand of God in the spreading revivals of midcentury; now political leaders were making the same claim about the American Revolution. Depending on one's point of view, God would guarantee either the success or failure of the Revolution. The choice, therefore, between the patriotic or loyalist side was a choice between faithfulness and infidelity.

With such a potent combination of religious and political themes, it was inevitable that the American Revolution would have major consequences for the religious life. Those churches that sided with the winning side would undoubtedly prosper; those that made the wrong choice would, at least in the short run, suffer.

The Anglicans, more than any other religious group in the colonies, chose wrong. In the early 1770s, they could point to signs of health: a numerical growth from forty-five to almost four hundred parishes in the years from 1660 to 1770, a geographical expansion in the same period from one colony to thirteen, and a ministry to Indians and slaves (largely the work of missionaries supported by the SPG and Dr. Bray's Associates) that was unequaled.[3] By the war's end, these signs of health had given way to indications of a very different kind. Many clergy and laity had fled, parishioners had abandoned church buildings, and the schools for blacks supported by Dr. Bray's Associates had closed. The denomination as a whole had experienced a decline in membership the results of which would be felt well into the following century. By 1820, the church would fall far behind the Congregationalists and Presbyterians, slipping from second or third in number of parishes to sixth among American denominations. Baptists, Methodists, and Lutherans would soon claim more congregations.[4]

The Devastation of War

Loyalists and Patriots

The rubrics of the 1662 *Book of Common Prayer*, which was in use in the colonies at the time of the Revolution, directed "all Priests and Deacons . . . to say daily the Morning and Evening

Prayer. . ." Those prayer offices and the Sunday liturgy all contained a collect for the English monarch with the petition
"strengthen our most gracious Sovereign Lord, King GEORGE
. . . that he may vanquish and overcome all his enemies."[5] In
addition, at the time of ordination all clergy had made a public
promise before God and the church to obey the king.

For many Anglican clergy their moral obligation was clear.
They must oppose the patriots and the American Revolution.
The clergy in the middle colonies and New England, who
received instruction and, in many cases, salaries directly from
England, were particularly clear about their allegiance. The
vast majority sided with the British. Like the nonjuring clergy
at the time of the Glorious Revolution in England, they
believed that their oaths left them little other choice.

The situation was somewhat different in Maryland, Virginia,
North Carolina, South Carolina, and Georgia, where colonial
legislatures had established the Anglican Church. The legislatures there, following the precedent set in Virginia during the
English Civil War, ordered clergy to omit any reference to the
king from the liturgy. Clergy in such states were then faced
with a choice between two legal authorities that demanded
their obedience. Many followed the authority that was closest
at hand and supported the patriots. Others, however, followed
the example of the loyalist clergy to the north.

A significant percentage of the laity in the southern and
lower middle colonies supported the Revolution. The
Anglican laypersons who represented two-thirds of the signers
of the Declaration of Independence were, for example, primarily from these regions.[6] The situation was different in New
York and New England, where laypersons supported the
British side in significant numbers. Four-fifths of the faculty,
two-thirds of the governors, and a probable majority of students and alumni were loyalists, for example, at King's
College in New York.[7] Some loyalists fought for the British in
the King's American Regiment. Others abandoned the colonies
for Nova Scotia and Ontario; ten thousand may have gone to
Ontario alone.[8] The Native American and black population

also demonstrated a high degree of loyalty to the British. Of the six nations of the Iroquois confederacy, only two (the Oneida and the Tuscaroras) supported the patriots, while four (Mohawk, Onodaga, Cayuga, and Seneca) sided with the British. Similarly, promises of freedom led large numbers of blacks to join the British forces. Approximately 15,000 would depart for Jamaica, Nova Scotia, England, and other British holdings with the evacuation of British troops in 1783. Approximately one thousand of the settlers in Nova Scotia emigrated in 1792 to Sierra Leone, where they would play a critical role in the introduction of Christianity to Africa.[9]

The percentage of the clergy in the area supporting the loyalists cause was even greater. The Reverend Charles Inglis, rector of Trinity Church, New York, was exaggerating only slightly when he wrote to the SPG on October 31, 1776, that "all the Society's Missionaries . . . in New Jersey, New York, Connecticut, and so far as I can learn in other New England Colonies, have proved themselves faithful, loyal subjects in these trying times" and that "all the other Clergy of our Church in the above Colonies, though not in the Society's service, have observed the same line of conduct."[10]

Inglis was part of a circle of clergy that attempted to turn public opinion against the Revolution. In addition to Inglis, the informal group included President Myles Cooper of King's College, Thomas Bradbury Chandler of Elizabethtown, New Jersey, and Samuel Seabury of Westchester, New York. Their literary output included Seabury's *Free Thoughts on the Proceedings of the Continental Congress* (1774), Chandler's *What Think Ye of Congress Now?* (1775),

Fig.12. Charles Inglis

and Inglis's *True Interests of the American Impartially Stated* (1776). Seabury was, in addition, the probable author of the anonymous *Letters of a Westchester Farmer* (1774–75).

As Inglis noted in his letter to the SPG, such conduct did not go unnoticed by the patriots. Indeed, loyalist Anglicans were in

a most disagreeable and dangerous situation, particularly the Clergy, who were viewed with peculiar envy and malignity by the disaffected, . . . an abolition of the Church of England [being] one of the principal springs of the dissenting leaders' conduct. . . . [The Clergy were] everywhere threatened, often reviled . . . sometimes treated with brutal violence. [Some were] pulled out of the reading-desk because they prayed for the King, and that before independency was declared. [Other were fined for not appearing] at militia musters with their arms. [Others] had their houses plundered.[11]

Inglis could speak firsthand of such harrowing experiences. In the month before he wrote, patriots had burned Trinity Church, its rectory, and its school. On a later occasion a company of General Washington's soldiers entered Inglis's church in formal military order. Undaunted, Inglis continued with the liturgy and finally convinced the soldiers to take seats. One of the last of the loyalist Anglican clergy to leave the colonies, he left New York with the crown forces in November 1783.[12]

By one numeration, some fifty-six clergymen, serving in ten states, were persecuted during the war. The largest numbers were from Massachusetts (12), New York (10), Connecticut (8), Maryland (6), and Virginia (6). Four of them died as a result of their treatment, and others were victims of physical violence. Patriots arrested fourteen and drove thirty-five from their parishes.[13]

Some of the stories were particularly poignant. John Stuart (1740–1811), for example, worked with the Mohawk Indians at Fort Hunter, New York, beginning in 1770. As part of his efforts he prepared a translation of the catechism and a history of the Bible into the Mohawk language. When he continued to read the prayers for the king after the outbreak of the Revolution, patriots placed him under house arrest for three years. They fined him, confiscated his land, and converted his church building into a bar. They denied him permission to teach school in order to secure an income. In 1780, he emigrated to Canada as part of a prisoner exchange with the British. Many of his Mohawk parishioners followed him to Quebec, where he reported baptizing 104 Indians in 1784 alone.[14]

A mob attacked Alexander McCrae of Littleton, Virginia, and whipped him because of his allegiance to the crown. Many other loyalist clergy and laity suffered for their convictions. Some left the thirteen colonies for Canada, Bermuda, or England. Others, like McCrae, remained despite their treatment.

The Anglican Church in New England lost the majority of its clergy during the Revolution. By the end of the war there were only four active clergymen in Massachusetts, one in New Hampshire, and none in Rhode Island. Connecticut, however, had a more conservative population than its neighboring states. It retained a majority of its twenty clergy at the end of the war.[15]

A larger percentage of the clergy supported the Revolution in states in which the Anglican Church was established. In Maryland, one-third of the clergy supported the patriots, and in South Carolina three-quarters did.[16] In Virginia, vestries served as one of the most effective communication networks for the patriots. Of the one hundred and five clergy in the state in 1776, eighty-five took the oath of allegiance that had been prescribed by the legislature. Others, moreover, were active combatants. William and Mary College president James Madison (1749–1812), a cousin of the later U.S. president, became the captain of the student militia. One Shenandoah Valley parson served as a colonel in the Continental army and a second served as a general. Three other clergymen from the state served in arms.[17]

In North Carolina, where five of eleven clergy were patriots, Hezekiah Ford served as a chaplain to the fifth regiment of the North Carolina Continental line.[18] The thirteen of eighteen South Carolina clergy who supported the Revolution included Robert Smith (1732–1801), rector of St. Philip's, Charleston, and later Bishop of South Carolina, who enlisted in the army as a militiaman.[19] In Georgia, however, the fate of the church was more like that in New England. Though the legislature established the Anglican Church in 1758, most of the activity in the church was confined to congregations in St. Simon's Island, Savannah, and Augusta. There were only four clergy in the colony, of whom two or perhaps three were loyalists. The fortunes of Christ Church, Savannah, were typical of the difficulties such loyalists faced. In 1775, patriots drove away loyalist rector Hadden Smith, who had only arrived from England the year before. Anglican worship halted at Christ Church until the British occupied Savannah (1779–82), at which point loyalists installed a second cleric as rector. Regular worship halted with the departure of the British, however, and it would not be until 1786 that the parish was able to secure a new rector.[20]

In the middle colonies, the situation was somewhere between that of New England and Virginia. A number of loyalist SPG clergy stopped their public worship, rather than omit prayers for the king. In Pennsylvania, where women were exempt from the penalties imposed for praying for the king, some pro-British SPG missionaries found another way to skirt the patriots' prohibitions: they led worship for congregations composed exclusively of women and children.[21] Other middle colony clergy supported the Revolution, however. William White (1748–1836), for example, connected by marriage to some of the leading patriots, served as chaplain to the Continental Congress. He was the only Anglican cleric in Philadelphia and perhaps in the whole state to give unambiguous support to the Revolution. Two of New Jersey's eleven clergy were patriots, as was one of the nineteen clergy in New York—Samuel Provoost (1742–1815). In Delaware, two of five colonial clergy clearly sided with the patriots.[22] One of them, Aeneas Ross of New Castle, was the brother of Declaration of Independence signer George Ross.[23]

Disestablishment

In states such as Connecticut and Massachusetts, the Anglican Church had never been the established denomination. Anglican Church property belonged to a particular minority religious group. Thus the war did little to affect the legal status of the church. Patriots might attack and burn individual buildings, and an American victory in war meant the loss of financial support from the Society for the Propagation of the Gospel, but on the whole the legal status of church properties was clear. They belonged to the Anglicans who worshiped in them.

In the South and, to a lesser degree, the middle colonies, the situation was very different. The state legislatures in the southern states had set aside public land for the Church of England. The legislatures had, moreover, given vestries, which served as public welfare agencies, authority to tax the populace for religious and social purposes.

In the middle colonies, no single group so clearly dominated. Presbyterians were numerous in New Jersey and New York, and the Quakers in Pennsylvania, but there were Dutch Reformed, Swedish Lutherans, Baptists, Moravians, Roman Catholics, Jews, and Anglicans in the region as well. Of these colonies, only New York had a religious establishment; it was, however, a largely unworkable system that applied only to a few eastern cities and counties. The legislature did not give vestries the power to tax, nor had it extended the system to western areas of the state. Anglicans in the middle colonies could, however, point to two public institutions—the College of Philadelphia and King's College in New York—that were strongly Anglican in character.

With the onset of the Revolution, the colonial legislatures moved quickly to insure the support of colonial religious groups. Southern legislatures acceded to a long-standing request by Baptists and Presbyterians that the salaries of Anglican clergy be suspended. Maryland, Virginia, and North Carolina did so in 1776. Georgia and South Carolina followed in 1777 and 1778. The abolition of salaries not only placated dissenters, it also guaranteed that Anglican clergy would be financially dependent on the voluntary offerings of their congregations, a move that made it difficult for loyalist clergy to openly disagree with patriotic congregations. In addition, the legislatures required new oaths of allegiance and drafted new prayers for use in place of the prayers for the king.

The patriots also took steps to guarantee the loyalty of universities with Anglican ties. In 1779, the Virginia legislature eliminated the chair of (Anglican) theology at the College of William and Mary. In the same year, the Pennsylvania legislature reorganized the College of Philadelphia (University of Pennsylvania) in order to undercut the authority exercised there by loyalist Anglicans. The New York legislature acted somewhat more slowly. In 1784, the year after the final departure of British troops, it recast the charter of King's College in order to create Columbia University, over which Anglicans exercised much less influence.[24]

In one sense, the colonial elites were only repeating a lesson that they had learned from the Glorious Revolution. English Whigs had created popular support for the expulsion of a Roman Catholic king by linking it to a curtailing of the exclusive position of the Church of England and an extension of religious liberties to Protestant dissenters. The same Parliament that forced the flight of James II repealed the more obnoxious portions of the antidissenting Clarendon Code. To support the Glorious Revolution was to support religious toleration.

In 1777, the legislature in New York repealed the largely unworkable scheme for establishment in the eastern portion of that state.[25] In the southern states, however, legislatures retained some vestiges of establishment. In Virginia, for example, the legislature retained the right to establish and adjust parish lines; the vestries continued to serve as state welfare agencies; and the governor and Council continued to license clergy to perform marriages. In Maryland, the governor retained the right to appoint parish clergy.

The retention of these elements of establishment provided little advantage to the church. To the contrary, the remaining legislation was a continuing reminder that the church was under the authority of the state. Anglican clergy were, therefore, among the most vocal advocates of a total repeal of establishment.[26] They wanted to be able to regulate their own affairs, free of outside control. It would not be, however, until 1783 that southern legislatures began to grant them the permission to organize as self-governing religious societies.

Reorganization

It was from the middle colonies that the initial leadership for the reorganization of the Anglican Church came. Anglicans in the region were accustomed to a pluralistic, nonestablished religious setting, a setting of the sort that would increasingly become the rule following the Revolution. Anglicans there could also draw upon their experience with local institutions: the College of Philadelphia, King's College, the provincial synods of the 1760s, and the Society for Relief of Widows and Orphans of Clergymen. Anglicans in other regions would soon lend a hand, but it was those in the middle colonies who led the way.

Activity in the Diocese of Maryland

Dr. William Smith left Philadelphia in the year in which the legislature reorganized the College of Philadelphia (1779). He took up residence in nearby Chestertown, Maryland, where he served as the head of the Kent School. Smith presided over the successful attempt to transform the school into Washington College, for which he gained a charter in 1782.

The church in Maryland was in a precarious position. As in other southern states in which the Anglican Church had been established at the time of the Revolution, the legislature had eliminated the benefits of establishment—the ability to tax for the support of the church—without granting the church any clear legal status.

William Smith saw the need to take action. Beginning in 1780, he convened gatherings of Episcopal clergy and laity to discuss the situation. By 1783 they had already taken a number of concrete actions. First, they chose the name Protestant Episcopal Church to replace the no longer favored Church of England as the name of their denomination. The new name combined the word *protestant,* which differentiated the church from the Roman Catholic Church in Maryland, with *episcopal,* the name for the seventeenth-century English church party that favored retention of the episcopacy. Second, they planned a state convention that would exercise the authority for the

Fig. 13. William Smith of the College of Philadelphia
and Washington College

church. They drafted a charter that the legislature approved in
August 1783, granting them title to church property and a government by a synod of laity and clergy. The legislature also
recognized the independence of the church from any foreign
power and the importance of episcopal ordination.[27] Third, they
identified candidates for the ordained ministry and sent two of
them—Mason Locke Weems (1759–1825), who was a cousin
of Smith's wife, and Edward Gantt, Jr.—to England for ordination to the priesthood. The two would face a long wait in
England, however. English law did not yet permit ordination
without an oath of allegiance to the king, which would have
been unacceptable to the Maryland candidates. Fourth, they
elected William Smith as candidate for bishop.

Smith kept his former student William White, who had
remained in Philadelphia, abreast of his efforts. Word of
Smith's efforts would also spread in another direction. Robert
Smith, rector of St. Philip's, Charleston, spent 1780 to 1783 in
Maryland.[28] A patriot, he had moved north when the British
occupied Charleston. When he returned, he brought news of
Smith's efforts in Maryland. In Virginia, the Reverend David
Griffith (1742–89) of Fairfax Parish (Pohick Church), who had
briefly served as an assistant at the United Parish of
Philadelphia, was kept informed of the events in Maryland.

William White and the Case
of the Episcopal Churches Considered

William White was born in 1748 to a wealthy Philadelphia family, which had made its money in real estate. He was a part of the elite in what was then the largest colonial city. His sister married colonial financier Robert Morris (1734–1806), and he himself married Mary Harrison, the daughter of the city's mayor.[29] In 1770, White went to England for study and ordination. On his return, he was appointed assistant to the rector in his home church, the United Parish of Christ Church and St. Peter's. When the Revolution began, White's rector, Jacob Duché, sided with the patriots and became the chaplain to the Continental Congress, but when the British occupied the city in 1777, Duché reversed his allegiance. When the British left, he went with them. White, on the other hand, waited out the British occupation at his brother-in-law's home in Maryland. With the British departure, he returned. The parish vestry

Fig. 14. William White

elected him rector, and the Congress chose him to replace Duché as chaplain. He continued as chaplain so long as the Continental Congress met in Philadelphia and remained rector of the parish for the rest of his life.

Learning in the 1780s of Smith's work in Maryland, White became convinced that similar actions were needed in other states. On August 8, 1782, he published a pamphlet titled *The Case of the Episcopal Churches in the United States Considered* in which he suggested that other states form conventions like that in Maryland. These "general vestries" would elect presiding clergy, who—at least until the nation gained the episcopate—would exercise some of the functions of bishops.

The presiding clergy and elected representatives of the general vestries would attend annual district and triennial national conventions.[30] In all three levels of organization, presiding clergy, other clergy, and laypersons were to meet together in unicameral bodies.

On May 11, 1784, White and other New York, New Jersey, and Pennsylvania Episcopalians gathered in New Brunswick, New Jersey, for the annual meeting of the Society for the Relief of Widows and Orphans of Clergymen. After discussing White's plan, they decided to campaign for organization on a state level and for election of representatives to a meeting later in the year.[31] The meeting that took place in New York in October attracted a larger number. In addition to the four middle states that participated in the widows and orphan society (New York, New Jersey, Pennsylvania, and Delaware), five other states were represented. Dr. William Smith attended from Maryland and David Griffith from Virginia. Delegations from three New England states (Massachusetts, Rhode Island, and Connecticut) also attended, but soon afterward withdrew from the General Convention effort in order to pursue separate plans for organization.

Those who attended the New York gathering adopted a series of resolutions similar to those that had already been adopted at state meetings in Pennsylvania and Maryland: that there was to be a bishop in each state; that the bishops would be ex officio members of a unicameral general convention in which clergy and laity would vote by orders; and that the first meeting of the convention would be in Philadelphia in 1785.[32]

The General Convention met once in 1785 and twice in 1786. Representatives from the three New England states did not return, but delegates from South Carolina attended, so that seven states were represented at these critical Conventions. The Conventions petitioned the English for consecration of three candidates for the episcopacy and adopted a constitution. They prepared the *Proposed Book* (approved by convention, 1785; published, 1786), a revision of the 1662 English *Book of Common Prayer.* The convention's revision simplified

Anglican worship along lines that were often suggested by eighteenth-century Anglicans. In the place of three creeds (the Apostles', the Nicene, and the Athanasian), the book had only a form of the Apostles' Creed from which the clause about Christ's descent to hell had been removed. The Thirty-nine Articles were reduced in number to twenty. The number of psalms required for recitation was decreased. The book also replaced references to clergy as "priests" and dropped the word *regeneration* from the baptismal liturgy.[33]

Some Americans thought that the revision was too conservative. Charles Miller, the rector of King's Chapel, Boston, wanted, for example, to remove all references to the Trinity. When the conventions did not agree to do so, the congregation issued its own book, distanced itself from other Anglicans, and became the first explicitly unitarian church in America (1786). For most Anglicans, however, including the English archbishops to whom copies had been sent, the revision proved too thorough. The conventions of 1786, therefore, abandoned the book. Some features of it would be included, however, in the later 1789 prayer book.

On June 26, 1786, the British Parliament passed legislation providing for the consecration of three bishops for the American church. The following year William White and Samuel Provoost, the rector of Trinity Church, New York, were consecrated to the episcopate for Pennsylvania and New York. (The Parliament also provided for the consecration of bishops to serve in British colonies. The first of these, Charles Inglis, the Bishop of Nova Scotia, was also consecrated in 1787.)

David Griffith, Bishop-elect of Virginia, was unable to raise the funds for the trip. He resigned his election, and in 1790 a new candidate, James Madison of the College of William and Mary, was consecrated. William Smith had been elected in Maryland in 1783, but because of his reputation for consumption of alcohol, he was unable to gain the endorsement from General Convention required by the new constitution. In 1792, Episcopalians in Maryland elected a second candidate, Thomas

86

Claggett (1783–1816). He would become the first bishop consecrated on American soil.

Not surprisingly, perhaps, the state conventions chose candidates for the episcopate who occupied the positions that had once been held by colonial commissaries. Provoost, as rector of Trinity Church, New York City; White, as rector of the United Parish of Philadelphia; and Madison, as president of the College of William and Mary were all successors of the commissaries. Claggett served in a parish in Prince George's County, Maryland, adjoining that which colonial commissary Jacob Henderson had occupied. Like the colonial commissaries, the four new bishops would continue to serve as parish rectors after accepting their leadership positions. There were no endowments and insufficient income to support a full-time episcopate.

Samuel Seabury and the Anglican Church in New England

Representatives from Connecticut, Massachusetts, and Rhode Island had attended the organizational meetings in 1784, but they did not attend the General Conventions of 1785 or 1786. They objected in principle to the approach taken by the clergy of the middle and southern states. Drawing on Anglican covenant arguments that SPG missionaries had been advancing in New England for three-quarters of a century, they believed that the church's essential nature came from the historic episcopate and not from the voluntary association of clergy and laity. White's proposal was for them little better than the congregational polity.

Troubled by White's *Case,* ten of the fourteen remaining clergy in Connecticut met in Woodbury in March 1783. They elected two New York clergymen as potential candidates for bishop. Both were natives of Connecticut and committed loyalists. The older of the two, Jeremiah Leaming (1717–1804), had served parishes in Newport, Rhode Island, and Norwalk, Connecticut, before taking refuge in loyalist territory in New York during the latter years of the war. The younger, Samuel Seabury, had served as secretary for the New York conventions in the 1760s and had been part of the loyalist circle of clergy in New York that had tried to influence public opinion against the war. Imprisoned for a period in 1775 by Connecticut patriots, he had also served as a chaplain to the King's American Regiment. Leaming declined his election; Seabury accepted. Perhaps hearing of the two Maryland candidates who were waiting in England for ordination to the priesthood, he set sail for England in June 1783 on a departing British ship.

Seabury soon found himself facing the same difficulty as the two Maryland candidates. English law required any ordinand to take an oath of allegiance to the crown, an act that would undermine the credibility of an American candidate. Moreover, Seabury faced additional difficulties. The two Maryland candidates had the approval of a state convention that had been chartered by the Maryland legislature. Seabury, in contrast, had been elected by a secret gathering of clergy in a state in which the Congregational Church was established by law. When Parliament responded to American entreaties with a new law on August 13, 1784, it allowed for the ordination to the priesthood of Weems and Gantt of Maryland but took no action on episcopal consecration. It would not be until June 1786 that the Parliament, assured by long negotiation with the middle and southern states' General Convention, would further amend the law to allow consecration of bishops for America.

Undaunted, Seabury went north to Scotland, where on November 14, 1784, he was consecrated to the episcopate by three nonjuring Scottish bishops. The following day he signed a concordat with the Scottish Episcopal Church recognizing the church's legitimacy and agreeing to advocate the use of its prayer of consecration, which was drawn from the 1549 prayer book, rather than from the 1552 book on which the subsequent English con-

Fig. 15. Samuel Seabury

secration prayers were based. Seabury returned to Connecticut.

In Seabury's absence, representatives from New England had attended the fall 1784 meeting in New York, but upon his return they refused to participate further. They joined instead in a series of clergy convocations, the first of which Seabury called in August 1785. In contrast to the General Conventions, Seabury's gatherings were clerical affairs only; no laity attended. Nor were the gatherings organized around a representative form of government. Seabury convened the gatherings, presided at them, preached to and instructed the clergy, and began to ordain candidates to the priesthood and the diaconate. Imitating the usage of the Archbishop of Canterbury, Seabury signed some of his early letters as the "Bishop of All America."[34]

The participants in the middle and southern states' conventions were attempting to deemphasize some of the distinctive elements of their tradition. Elements that they dropped from the *Proposed Book,* such as the Athanasian Creed, the word *priest,* and the use of *regeneration* to refer to baptism, were unfamiliar to most other American Protestants. In New England, Seabury followed the opposite course. The presence of a bishop enabled New England Anglicans to develop their covenant theology in ways that further distinguished them from the Congregational establishment. Bishops could not only lay their hands on the heads of ordinands but also use the office of confirmation to impart the Holy Spirit to lay men and women. Seabury explained this in his first address to his clergy convocation:

> In confirmation. . . we believe the Holy Spirit to be given for sanctification, i.e. for carrying into effect that regeneration which is conferred in Baptism. By Baptism we are taken out of our natural state of sin and death, into which we are born by our natural birth, and are translated, transplanted, or born again into the Church of Christ. . . and by confirmation . . . we are endued with the Holy Spirit to overcome sin, and to perfect holiness in the fear of God.[35]

Bishop Seabury would repeat the same theme at other points during his episcopate. Several years later, for example, he prepared an edition of a catechism by Bishop Innes of Brechin in Scotland for use in his diocese. A form of the catechism would later be used in New York. Bishop Innes had been clear about the relationship between baptism and confirmation: "In our water-baptism the Holy Ghost purifies us and fits us to be a Temple for himself, and in Confirmation he enters in and takes Possession of this temple."[36] Seabury's strong affirmation of the importance of the episcopacy as the agent through which the Holy Spirit was conveyed provided a badly needed response to the Great Awakening for anti-Awakening New England clergy. Thomas Bray's catechism had linked the covenant to the apostolic succession. Seabury sought to tie the presence of the Holy Spirit to the episcopacy as well.

In 1787, the Connecticut clergy elected Abraham Jarvis (1739–1813) as a bishop coadjutor for Seabury. They wrote to the Scottish nonjurors, but the Scots proved unwilling to consecrate him.

The Organization of the Methodist Episcopal Church

Those Anglicans active in the methodist societies were also deeply concerned about the need for organization. They had, like other Anglicans, been devastated by the war. John Wesley's open opposition to the Revolution created obvious difficulties, but even without it loyalist sentiments would have been strong among those methodist leaders who were recent immigrants from the British Isles. Barbara Heck and other New York methodists began emigrating to Canada as early as 1773. Joseph Pilmore (Pilmoor) left for England in 1774. Captain Thomas Webb, a former British officer, spent time in prison but was allowed to emigrate to England in 1778. By that year, so many methodist leaders had fled that only one of the ten lay preachers sent by Wesley—Francis Asbury—remained in the colonies, and even he abandoned his active preaching in Maryland and retired to Dover, Delaware. In addition, some of the Anglican clergy supportive of the methodist movement, such as Jacob Duché of the United Parish of Christ Church and St. Peter in Philadelphia, William Stringer of St. Paul's, Philadelphia, and Charles Inglis of Trinity Church, New York, left the colonies. After 1775, participation at the annual conferences fell to a dangerously low point. In 1779, methodists in the North and South organized separate conferences and met independently of one another.[37]

The local structure that the methodists had created proved resilient even in this time of crisis, however. Local classes, societies, and circuits continued to function well, particularly in Virginia and North Carolina. By 1780, the membership in the methodist societies had risen to 12,000, and by 1784 to 14,988 of whom nearly 90 percent were south of the Mason-Dixon Line.[38] This swelling of the number of society members created a growing need for ordained people to celebrate the sacraments, a demand that came at the time war was thinning the ranks of Anglican clergy. Individual clergy like Devereux Jarratt, Samuel Magaw, Charles Pettigrew, Uzal Ogden, Sydenham Thorne, and Hugh Neill did what they could, but they had serious problems of their own and were ill equipped to cope with the growing need for clerical assistance.

The members of the methodist societies began to look in other directions for help, therefore. In England, Charles Wesley approached Samuel Seabury about ordaining methodist lay preachers. Seabury agreed to do so, provided that he found the candidates properly qualified.[39]

Some methodist society members advocated, however, a different course of action. In 1779 and 1780, the members of the southern conference suggested that methodists themselves adopt a form of ordination. Francis Asbury and others in the northern conference persuaded the southerners to abandon the idea in the short run, but that was the course of action upon which the methodists would finally agree.

John Wesley began to hint at that course about the time that the Americans and British signed the Treaty of Paris (September 1783) ending the war. He designated Francis Asbury as the "General Assistant for America," sketched a plan for church government, drafted a revision of the *Book of Common Prayer (The Sunday Service of the Methodists in North America, with Other Occasional Services),* and chose a delegation of three English methodists to visit America.[40] One of the three, Dr. Thomas Coke (1747–1814), was the first Anglican priest sent by Wesley to America. Wesley and Coke laid hands on the other two, lay preachers Thomas Vasey (1742?–1826) and Richard Whatcoat (1736–1806), before they left England.

The trio landed in New York in November 1784 and headed south. William White and Samuel Magaw greeted them when they reached Philadelphia.[41] In November, the delegation met Francis Asbury for the first time at a quarterly meeting of methodists in Delaware. The annual conference met the following month at Christmas time in Baltimore.

This "Christmas conference" came at a critical moment in the life of the methodist movement. While they may not yet have known of Seabury's consecration in November, the methodists were certainly aware of the attempts by both New England and by middle and southern state clergy to adopt a form of organization and to secure episcopacy.[42] Were they to wait, American methodists would have had a resident Anglican episcopate to whom they could turn for ordination. Yet, as John Wesley himself observed in a letter to the Americans in September, if Anglican bishops ordained methodist clergy "they would likewise expect to govern them," an eventuality to which American methodists looked with decreasing favor.[43] While they had received support and assistance from some ordained Anglicans, the only Anglican clergyman whom they recognized as having authority over them was John Wesley.

The methodists decided, therefore, to act. Francis Asbury, who had to that point opposed ordination, abandoned his opposition. He recorded the action of the Christmas conference in a few short lines:

We then rode to Baltimore, where we met a few preachers; it was agreed to form ourselves in an Episcopal Church, and to have superintendents, elders, and deacons. When the conference was seated, Dr. Coke, and myself were unanimously elected to the superintendency of the Church, and my ordination followed, after being previously ordained deacon and elder. . . . Twelve elders were elected, and solemnly set apart to serve our societies in the United States. . .[44]

The methodist societies had become the Methodist Episcopal Church. (The name *Methodist Episcopal,* an adaptation of the title *Protestant Episcopal* used by Anglicans in Maryland, was revised in a 1939 Methodist merger. The largest Methodist church dropped the word *Episcopal* from its title at that time, though three smaller black Methodist churches continue to use it.)

Not everyone was pleased by the decision. Devereux Jarratt, the Anglican clergyman who had labored long and hard to support the methodist societies in Virginia, was furious; he felt that he had been betrayed by methodist promises of loyalty to the Anglican Church. John Wesley himself had reservations about the increasing independence with which the Americans acted, particularly with a 1787 decision by the Americans to change the title of superintendent to bishop.[45]

Some had questions about the legitimacy of the ordination of the new church. At least four methodist preachers had reservations strong enough that they chose to affiliate with the Episcopal Church. Joseph Pilmore (recently returned from England with testimonial letters from Charles Wesley) and Samuel Roe (d. 1791) of Burlington, New Jersey, sought out Samuel Seabury soon after the latter's return from England. He ordained them both in 1785. The two soon settled in vacant parishes. Pilmore served successively at the United Parish of Trinity, All Saints' and St. Thomas (near Philadelphia); Christ Church, New York City; and St. Paul's, Philadelphia; Roe, at Christ Church, Dover, Delaware. After his consecration, Bishop White ordained a third candidate, Thomas Vasey, who had arrived from England in the delegation with Coke. A fourth Methodist, Levi Heath (d. 1805 or 1806), had, like Thomas Coke, been ordained in the Church of England. He left the Methodist Episcopal Church in 1787, serving in succession a series of parishes in Maryland, New Jersey, Pennsylvania, and Virginia.[46]

This concern about the validity of Methodist orders motivated some Methodists and Episcopalians to remain in conversation during the decade that followed the Christmas conference. Coke corresponded with White and Seabury in 1791 about the possibility of consecration of bishops for the Methodist Episcopal Church. Bishop James Madison of Virginia discussed the possibility of merger at General Convention in 1792.[47] Nothing came of the conversations, however: the discussion ended when Coke returned to England, and the proposal was rejected by the House of Deputies.

The lack of apostolic succession did not hinder the growth of the Methodist Episcopal Church, however. Indeed, the result was quite the opposite. By choosing to ordain those who lacked the university-level education generally required for Anglican ordination, the Methodists were able to tap a large and vigorous source of leadership at a time when the three denominations that had been largest in the colonial period— Congregationalists, Presbyterians, and Episcopalians—faced chronic shortages of clergy. The new church would lag behind the older denominations in educational standards but would be able to draw upon a sufficient body of clergy to meet the needs of America as the nation moved westward. In the nineteenth century, it would become the nation's largest Protestant church.

The General Conventions of 1789

By 1787, American Episcopalians had, in effect, established three denominations: a middle and southern states' church with English lines of consecration and a representative clerical and lay convention; a New England church directed by a bishop with Scottish consecration and governed through a clergy convocation; and a Methodist Episcopal Church with a form of government drafted by John Wesley. Efforts to reunite with the Methodist Episcopal Church proved unsuccessful; the two remaining groups would, however, find a way to combine.

It was not initially evident that this would be the outcome, however. The two groups were not on good terms. The leaders of the middle and southern states' group had been supporters of the Revolution; those in Connecticut had been loyalists. Seabury had been a British chaplain, had drawn maps for the British troops, and was still receiving a pension from Great Britain.[48] The New England clergy doubted the integrity of the middle and southern states clergy who had surrendered so much episcopal authority to the laity; the middle and southern states wondered whether Seabury's brand of episcopal authority was compatible with their new republic.

In 1786, the two groups were outwardly hostile to one another. Seabury ordained candidates from the middle states, and the General Convention responded with legislation instructing member dioceses not to affirm the validity of Seabury's nonjuring orders. White himself refused to open his pulpit to Joseph Pilmore, the former methodist lay preacher who had gone to Connecticut for ordination.

In 1789, the General Convention assembled in Philadelphia for two sessions (July-August and September). Samuel Provoost, a bitter enemy of Seabury, was unable to attend. White, taking advantage of the absence, used the two sessions to make concessions that appeased Seabury and healed the breach. The first session affirmed the validity of Seabury's orders, created a separate House of Bishops with a partial veto (which the House of Deputies could override with a three-fifths vote), and amended the constitution to make participation of lay deputies optional. These changes met many, but not all, of Seabury's objections.

The General Convention made further concessions at the second session in September. It gave the House of Bishops the right to originate as well as act upon legislation, and a stronger veto (The deputies needed a four-fifths majority to override. In

1808, the General Convention raised this to a full veto.) After the approval of these final changes, Seabury and the clerical deputies from Connecticut and Massachusetts took seats at the Convention. In addition to approving the constitution on which they had agreed, the members of the expanded body adopted the *Book of Common Prayer* (1789). This 1789 prayer book eliminated some of the elements of the 1785–86 *Proposed Book* that had aroused the greatest opposition. It, for example, restored the Nicene Creed and the full text of the Apostles' Creed (with the reference to Christ's descent to hell,

Fig. 16. Seabury and White in a portion of a church window at Trinity Church, Warren, Pennsylvania

which an explanatory note adopted by the deputies equated with descent to "the place of the departed spirits"), included some references to priests that had been eliminated in 1785, and put back the word *regeneration* in the baptismal office. The 1789 book included, however, many of the less controversial changes from the *Proposed Book,* such as the omission of references to the English monarchy. In addition, some changes in the 1789 book had not appeared in the 1785–86 revision: the inclusion of a shortened list of psalms, the designation of the proper preface for Trinity as optional, and the adoption of a slightly edited form of the Scottish prayer of consecration. Seabury was apparently not the most vocal proponent of this final action. A second William Smith of Maryland—a Scottish priest with the same name as Dr. William Smith of Washington College and the College of Philadelphia—played that role.[49]

In 1792, White worked out another compromise. Samuel Parker (1744–1804) of Massachusetts asked the convention of 1789 to authorize White, Provoost, and Seabury to consecrate a bishop for Massachusetts. White declined to do so, saying that he had to receive the permission of the English archbishops for any such action. The convention wrote to England but received no answer, not an unexpected event since any answer would require a judgment on the validity of Scottish nonjuring orders.[50]

With the consecration in England in 1790 of James Madison as Bishop of Virginia, it became possible, however, for White to join in a consecration with three bishops (the traditional number at a consecration) of the English line. In 1792, he convinced Seabury, Provoost, and Madison to join with him in the consecration of Thomas Claggett (1743–1816) as bishop of Maryland. In order to lure Provoost into participating with his enemy Seabury, White arranged for Seabury to be absent from the General Convention while the House of Bishops adopted legislation allowing Provoost to become presiding bishop for one session. Seabury died two years later. He took part in no other consecration. Through Claggett, however, his line of consecration mingled with that from England.[51]

By 1792, the Episcopal Church was finally established as an American denomination. It had a governing body, a prayer book, a national constitution, and a mechanism for the creation of new bishops. The effort, however, had exhausted the energy of many in the church. An aging leadership began to die, and new leaders were not immediately forthcoming. The situation was perhaps most extreme in Georgia, in which only Christ Church, Savannah, remained active. The congregation, which did not send a delegation to General Convention, belatedly agreed to use the 1789 *Book of Common Prayer* in 1793.[52] It would not be until 1823 that Georgia was represented at General Convention. Matters were only slightly better in North Carolina. Episcopalians from St. James's, Wilmington, and a few other congregations managed to assemble a state convention and choose a bishop-elect (revivalist Charles Pettigrew) in 1794. Pettigrew's failure to reach General Convention for consecration, however, dampened the hopes of Episcopalians, who soon stopped gathering for state conventions and halted all communication with the General Convention.[53] No North

Carolina delegation reached the General Convention until 1817.

The church had survived but would have to wait for a new generation of leaders to regain the momentum that it had had in the years prior to the American Revolution.

NOTES

1. *Encyclopedia Americana,* international ed. (Danbury, Conn.: Grolier, 1984), s.v. "Patrick Henry" by Philip G. Davidson.

2. David S. Lovejoy, *Religious Enthusiasm in the New World: Heresy to Revolution* (Cambridge: Harvard University Press, 1985), 223.

3. Edwin S. Gaustad, *A Historical Atlas of Religion in America* (New York: Harper & Row, 1962), 9; and R.E. Hood, "From a Headstart to a Deadstart: The Historical Basis for Black Indifference toward the Episcopal Church, 1800–1860," *Historical Magazine of the Protestant Episcopal Church* (September 1982):272.

4. Gaustad, *Atlas,* 43. Dr. Bray's school in Philadelphia reopened following the war. The remaining schools did not reopen.

5. William McGarvey, *Liturgiae Americanae or The Book of Common Prayer As Used in the United States of America Compared with the Proposed Book of 1786 and with the Prayer Book of the Church of England and an Historical Account and Documents* (Philadelphia: n.p., 1895), 23, 123.

6. Raymond W. Albright, *A History of the Protestant Episcopal Church* (New York: Macmillan, 1964), 113.

7. David C. Humphrey, *From King's College to Columbia, 1746–1800* (New York: Columbia University Press, 1976), 140.

8. Alan L. Hayes, ed., *By Grace Co-Workers: Building the Anglican Diocese of Toronto, 1780–1989* (Toronto: Anglican Book Center, 1989), 23.

9. Owanah Anderson, *Jamestown Commitment: The Episcopal Church and the American Indian* (Cincinnati: Forward Movement Publications, 1988), 32; Lamin Sanneh, "Strangers at Home: American Innocence in Africa" (Sprigg lecture delivered at Virginia Theological Seminary, 15 March 1990).

10. *Classified Digest of the Records of the Society for the Propagation of the Gospel in Foreign Parts, 1701–1892,* 4th ed. (London: SPG, 1894), p. 76.

11. Ibid.

12. Ibid., 77.

13. S.D. McConnell, *History of the American Episcopal Church from the Planting of the Colonies to the End of the Civil War,* 3d. ed. (New York: Thomas Whittaker, 1891), 211. In compiling his list of incidents against clergy, McConnell relied upon Lorenzo Sabine's *Loyalists in the Revolution* (1847). He included entries from all of the states except New Hampshire, Delaware, and Georgia.

14. *Classified Digest,* 74, 140, 154, 155, and 800.

15. James Thayer Addison, *The Episcopal Church in the United States 1789–1931* (New York: Scribner, 1951), 52. In addition to the sources named in this and the following seven notes, I am indebted to the Reverend Samuel M. Garrett, professor emeritus of church history at the Church Divinity School of the Pacific, for his calculation of the number of clergy supporting and opposing the Revolution.

16. Sydney E. Ahlstrom, *A Religious History of the American People* (New Haven: Yale University Press, 1972), 351–52.

17. George MacLaren Brydon, *Virginia's Mother Church and the Political Conditions Under Which It Grew,* 2 vols. (Richmond, Va.: Virginia Historical Society, 1947), 2:415–22.

18. Lawrence Foushee London and Sarah McCulloh Lemmon, eds., *The Episcopal Church in North Carolina, 1701–1959* (Raleigh: Episcopal Diocese of North Carolina, 1987), 65.

19. Albert Sidney Thomas, *Historical Account of the Protestant Episcopal Church in South Carolina 1820–1957* (Columbia: R.L. Bryan Company, 1957), 11.

20. Henry Thompson Malone, *The Episcopal Church in Georgia, 1733–1957* (Atlanta: Protestant Episcopal Diocese of Atlanta, 1950), 39–43.

21. *Classified Digest,* 40.

22. Nelson Waite Rightmyer, *The Anglican Church in Delaware* (Philadelphia: Church Historical Society, 1947), 168.

23. Borden W. Painter, Jr., "The Anglican Vestry in Colonial America," (Ph.D. diss., Yale University, 1965), 217.

24. Humphrey, *From King's College to Columbia,* 271. Humphrey noted that his interpretation of the events in 1784 differed from that of Sidney Sherwood in *The University of New York: History of Higher Education in the State of New York* (Washington: United States Bureau of Education, 1900). Sherwood interpreted the

rechartering of the college in 1784 as an Anglican attempt to "capture" a state university. Humphrey's interpretation is the opposite: "If anything was captured in 1784 it was King's College itself."

25. Hugh Hastings, *Ecclesiastical Records: State of New York,* 7 vols. (Albany: J.B. Lyon Company, 1905), 6:4300.

26. Brydon, *Virginia's Mother Church,* 2:440.

27. Clara O. Loveland, *The Critical Years: The Reconstruction of the Anglican Church in the United States of America: 1780–89* (Greenwich, Conn.: Seabury Press, 1956), 29.

28. Thomas, *South Carolina,* 11.

29. John F. Woolverton, "Philadelphia's William White: Episcopalian Distinctiveness and Accommodation in the Post Revolutionary Period," *Historical Magazine of the Protestant Episcopal Church* 43 (December 1974):279–96.

30. White was not explicit about the geographical areas to be included in his general vestries and district meetings. He probably intended the general vestries to be state meetings and the districts to be similar to the regional groups that Dr. William Smith had suggested for commissaries. Smith's proposal, which was made in 1762, was for six districts. One would encompass New Hampshire, Massachusetts, and Rhode Island; another, Connecticut and New York; a third, Pennsylvania, New Jersey, and presumably Delaware; and a fourth, the Carolinas and perhaps Georgia. Maryland and Virginia were in Smith's plan to constitute separate districts. See Arthur Lyon Cross, *The Anglican Episcopate and the American Colonies* (New York: Longmans, Green, and Co., 1902), 247, for details of Smith's plan.

White's three-level system of government proved too complicated for the fledgling denomination and the middle level was never created. It would not be until the 20th century that the Episcopal Church provided for the creation of provinces.

31. Loveland, *Critical Years,* 67–68.

32. Ibid., 89–90.

33. Marion J. Hatchett, *Commentary on the American Prayer Book* (New York: Seabury Press, 1981), 9–10.

34. Marion Hatchett, *The Making of the First American Book of Common Prayer* (New York: Seabury Press, 1982), 5.

35. Samuel Seabury quoted in Loveland, *Critical Years,* 140.

36. George Innes, *A Catechism or The Principle of the Christian Religion Explained in a Familiar and Easy Manner, Adapted to the Lowest Capacities* (Edinburgh; reprint New Haven: T. & S. Green, 1791), 9.

37. Henry D. Rack, *Reasonable Enthusiast: John Wesley and the Rise of Methodism* (Philadelphia: Trinity Press International, 1989), pp. 484–87; *Dictionary of American Biography* (New York: Charles Scribner's Sons, 1943), s.v. "Joseph Pilmore" by Joseph Cullen Ayer; Thomas C. Oden, *Doctrinal Standards in the Wesleyan Tradition* (Grand Rapids: Francis Asbury Press of Zondervan Publishing, 1988), 31.

38. Rack, *Reasonable Enthusiast,* 487.

39. Francis L. Hawkes and William Stevens Perry, *Documentary History of the Protestant Episcopal Church in the United States of America Containing Numerous Hitherto Unpublished Documents Concerning the Church in Connecticut* (New York: James Pott, 1864), 2:261.

40. Rack, *Reasonable Enthusiast,* 509–10.

41. Rightmyer, *Anglican Church,* 120.

42. As recent arrivals from England, Coke, Whatcoat, and Vasey would have known of Seabury's effort. It had been a topic of conversation at the pre–General Convention meetings of May and October 1784. Samuel Magaw, a close associate of Asbury who had also invited Coke to preach in his church, attended those meetings, as did, of course, William White, with whom Coke also had been in contact. In addition, Asbury visited Mason Locke Weems on November 30 in order to talk with him "on the subject of the Episcopal Mode of Church government." (*The Journal and Letters of Francis Asbury,* ed. Elmer T. Clark, J. Manning Potts, and Jacob S. Payton [London: Epworth Press, 1958], 1:473). Weems, both a relative of Dr. William Smith and a recent English ordinand, would have been well aware of Anglican efforts both in Maryland and the United States at large.

43. John Wesley quoted in Rack, *Reasonable Enthusiast,* 514.

44. *Journal of Francis Asbury,* 474–76.

45. Rack, *Reasonable Enthusiast,* 517.

46. William A. Beardsley, "A Registry of Ordination by Bishop Seabury and Bishop Jarvis of Connecticut," *Historical Magazine of*

the Protestant Episcopal Church 13 (March 1944):67; *The Journal and Letters of Francis Asbury,* ed. Elmer T. Clark, J. Manning Potts, and Jacob S. Payton, 3 vols. (London: Epworth Press, 1958), 1:472n; Rightmyer, *Anglican Church,* 121. Vasey later returned to England, where he was active in the the methodist societies.

47. Robert C. Monk, "Unity and Diversity among Eighteenth Century Colonial Anglicans and Methodists," *Historical Magazine of the Protestant Episcopal Church* 38 (March 1969):63–67.

48. Bruce Steiner, *Samuel Seabury: A Study in the High Church Tradition* (Oberlin: Ohio University Press, 1971), 167.

49. Hatchett, *First American Book of Common Prayer,* 116–30.

50. In the eighteenth century, some members of the Church of England questioned the validity of the nonjuring churches of England and Scotland. By the end of that century, however, most of the members of the nonjuring church in England, of which the last regularly consecrated nonjuring bishop died in 1779, had been reabsorbed into the Church of England. In the century that followed, however, the Church of England would recognize the nonjuring Scottish Church as a legitimate part of the Anglican Communion.

51. Loveland, *Critical Years,* 279–88.

52. Malone, *Episcopal Church in Georgia,* 53.

53. Pettigrew abandoned his first attempt in 1795 because of a yellow fever scare in the port of Norfolk, through which he had to pass. Three years later, his plans were thwarted a second time by the cancellation of the 1798 General Convention. Pettigrew made no further attempt to contact General Convention members. See London and Lemmon, *Episcopal Church in North Carolina,* 84–87.

5
Rational Orthodoxy
(1800–1840)

Episcopalians had reacted to the American Revolution in much the same way that their English ancestors had responded to the Glorious Revolution. Some objected to the Revolution and tried to remain aloof from the new republic, much in the way English and Scottish nonjurors had done in 1688. A majority of the laity and perhaps 50 percent of the clergy had, however, followed the example of the English Whigs. They saw the Revolution as an extension of individual rights and attempted to remake their church in a more democratic pattern.

The democratic dream was not an exclusive property of the Episcopal Church. Americans of all religious traditions saw the Revolution as an extension of personal liberties. Presbyterians and Baptists in the South saw the Revolution as a guarantee of equal rights for their denominations. Methodists and Quakers saw the abolition of slavery as a logical outcome of the Revolution. New England Congregationalists saw the war as a vindication of their right to determine their religious tradition free from the interference of the British government.

By 1800, however, Americans had begun a gradual retreat from some of the ideals of 1776. The equality of blacks and whites, or of men and women, for example, no longer seemed wise goals for many Americans who feared the more radical notions of equality of the French and Haitian revolutions. American fear of a French invasion at the end of the eighteenth century contributed to a more conservative United States in the nineteenth century.

By 1800, American Christians began to look for change

from a different direction. The patriots of 1776 had secured greater personal freedom with the force of arms. The citizens of 1800 looked, in contrast, to education. It was the instrument that would both safeguard existing freedoms and provide the opportunities to take advantage of them. It would, in addition, provide a public morality and an identity to a nation of people who could no longer understand themselves simply as English men and women.

Fig. 17.
The elderly William White

Episcopalians, though struggling to recover from the effects of the Revolution, were active in the attempt to educate and edify the new nation. Led by Bishop William White, the only one of the first four bishops to remain active in the national church after 1800, they worked at colleges and secondary schools, founded theological seminaries, and campaigned for public morality.

Morality and the Church

Many Episcopalians perceived that their nation and their church were in the midst of a moral crisis. The Revolution both caused the flight of many of the more conservative members of American society and the abandonment of a form of government that at least in theory combined religious values and state functions. Stripped of these influences, Americans were guilty of a variety of moral excesses during the period of mild prosperity that followed the war. The per capita consumption of alcohol rose to three times that of modern America.[1] The practice of dueling spread rapidly in the rough and tumble new republic with both a vice president (Aaron Burr) and a future president (Andrew Jackson) killing men in duels. The theater, perceived by many as an exciter of passions and a promoter of vice, became a popular entertainment in the growing cities.

Episcopalians were among the first to respond to this situation. Using church legislation, pamphlets, and works of fiction, they campaigned against major American ills. Canons that had been adopted by the General Convention of 1789 advised clergy to avoid "taverns or other places most liable to be abused to licentiousness." The provision was modeled on such seventeenth-century English works on pastoral care as George Herbert's *Country Parson* ("Neither is it for the servant of Christ to haunt Inns, Taverns, or Alehouses . . .") and Gilbert Burnet's *A Discourse of the Pastoral Care* ("A priest . . . must not only not be drunk, but he must not set a tippling, nor go to taverns or alehouses, except some urgent occasion require it.").[2] The canons also directed the clergy to refuse communion to "any persons within this church offend[ing] their brethren by any wickedness of life."[3] Subsequent legislation was more specific. The General Convention of 1808, for example, forbade clergy to bury any person who had participated in a duel. The action was in keeping with what was already the pastoral practice of many clergy. In 1804, for example, Bishop Benjamin Moore (1748–1816) of New York initially refused communion to the dying Alexander Hamilton on the grounds that the latter had participated in a duel.[4] The Reverend Walter Addison of Maryland was another cleric who was adamant about the evils of dueling. Famous in the Washington, D.C., area for his opposition to the practice, he became an officer of the court so that he could arrest those engaging in that pastime. He even entered Jefferson's White House in the pursuit of suspected duelists.[5]

In 1817, Francis Scott Key (1779–1843), the active Georgetown lawyer best known for his authorship of the National Anthem, suggested to the General Convention that the Episcopal Church go on record as opposing "vain amusements of the world, frequent horse races, theatres, and public balls, playing cards, or . . . any other kind of gaming" as "inconsistent with Christian sobriety, dangerous to the morals of the members of the Church, and particularly unbecoming the character of communicants."[6]

While the resolution was not adopted in its entirety, one quite like it was adopted in the House of Bishops. Bishop White, himself the author of pamphlets critical of the theater, probably drafted the language used:

> The House of Bishops . . . are induced to impress upon the clergy the important duty, with a discreet but earnest zeal, of warning the people of their respective cures, of the danger of an indulgence in those worldly pleasures which may tend to withdraw the affections from spiritual things. And especially on the subject of gaming, of amusements involving cruelty to the brute creation, and of theatrical representations, to which some peculiar circumstances have called their attention,—they do not hesitate to express their unanimous opinion, that these amusements, as well from the licentious tendency, as from the strong temptations to vice which they afford, ought not to be frequented. And the Bishops cannot refrain from expressing their deep regret at the information that in some of our large cities, so little respect is paid to the feelings of members of the Church, that theatrical representations are fixed for the evenings of her most solemn days.[7]

The House of Bishops objected to the production of theatrical performances on Sundays and on Christmas Eve.

Mason Locke Weems, the cousin of Mrs. William Smith who had traveled from Maryland to become one of the first two postrevolutionary ordinands in England, was one of the many who carried on this campaign on a literary level. After spending ten years in the parish ministry in Maryland, Weems became interested in writing. He first planned a volume of Episcopal sermons. Finding some support from fellow clergy but little excitement from potential publishers, he adopted another tack. He wrote and sold tracts on moral topics with such titles as *God's Judgment on Dueling* and *God's Judgment on Adultery.* From these he turned to biography, recording the stories of George Washington, Benjamin Franklin, and Francis Marion. He wove his moral advice into the fabric of the narrative, carefully pointing out to his readers that these leaders had met with success because of the moral choices that they had made in their personal lives. Numerous negative examples were used to suggest the end of those who did not follow so righteous a course. Weems's works were widely read, undoubtedly helping with the moral reformation of the American people.

Other authors included novelists Susanna Haswell Rowson (ca. 1762–1824) and Sally Sayward Wood (1759–1855) and poet Sarah Wentworth Apthorp Morton (1759–1846). Mrs. Rowson was an English-born actress who pioneered the American sentimental novel. Her *Charlotte Temple* (1791) was the first American best-seller. She was a communicant of Trinity Church, Boston, and for a time the president of the Boston Fatherless and Widow's Society. Mrs. Wood, a parishioner of St. Paul's, Portland, Maine, continued the tradition of the sentimental novel with *Amelia; or the Influence of Virtue* (1802). Mrs. Morton, a parishioner of Christ Church in Quincy, Massachusetts, pursued similar themes in such poems as "The Virtues of Society, A Tale Founded on Fact" (1799).[8]

Together these literary and canonical attempts at moral reform seemed to have contributed to a revival of personal piety among many Episcopalians. Such devotions as regular family Morning and Evening Prayers, which had grown rare in the years following the onset of the American Revolution, became common once again.[9]

Education

Equally important for American Episcopalians was the improvement of the American educational system. Perhaps because they were children of a church so intimately connected with education in England, Episcopalians proved willing to embrace a variety of extradenominational educational projects. Clergy often divided their time between parishes and teaching. In Virginia, clergymen James Madison, John Bracken, and William H. Wilmer (1782–1827) served as presidents of the College of William and Mary. After the Revolution, William Smith left Washington College, of which he had been president, and returned to Philadelphia, where he served as provost of the College of Philadelphia. In New York, Bishop Provoost's successor, Benjamin Moore (1748–1816), served as the president of Columbia from 1801 until 1811. Bishop Robert Smith of South Carolina opened an academy that would later become South Carolina College. In Kentucky, Benjamin Boswell Smith (1794–1884) became the state superintendent of schools. Second Bishop of Maryland James Kemp (1764–1827) served as provost of the University of Maryland from 1815 until his death.

Female literacy was only half that of men at the beginning of the Revolution. At the end of the century, a flurry of reformers would seek to advance female literacy. Episcopal clergy and laity were also active in that effort. Mason Locke Weems was one of many who taught at a female academy. Episcopal laywoman and First Lady Martha Washington (1732–1802) helped endow the first free female academy in Virginia. Novelist Susanna Rowson wrote textbooks for these and similar institutions. These institutions proved amazingly successful, for by 1840 female literacy would equal that of men.[10]

The increasingly literate females would staff one of the most effective institutions for promoting literacy in America. In 1780, English publisher Robert Raikes (1735–1811) gathered a group of children who worked in the Gloucester pin factories. He hired a Mrs. Meredith and three other women to instruct them on Sunday in reading and the church catechism. This Sunday school idea proved so successful that within five years Raikes was able to join with others to establish a national society to promote the idea in Britain. William White, who visited a Raikes school while in England in 1787 for consecration, was one of many who helped to transplant the institution to America. In 1790, he and other Philadelphians formed the First Day Society, which ran one of America's first Sunday schools. Some Christians opposed holding school on Sunday as a violation of a restful sabbath, but they soon abandoned these objections. In the first two decades of the nineteenth century, American Protestants formed a series of regional interdenominational Sunday school agencies. Several of these combined to form the American Sunday School Union in 1824.

Prior to the Sunday schools, only New England had a public school system. In the South, free education was provided on a limited basis only to the poor. In the middle states, a variety of private academies offered educational opportunities. The Sunday school would be the first national effort to provide free education for the rapidly expanding number of American children. The public school system would follow the path blazed by the Sunday school teachers.

Black Episcopalians

Many black Americans had believed deeply in the promises of the American Revolution. In the last decade of the eighteenth century, a number of those who had gained their freedom took steps to assert their right to self-determination in matters of religion. When, for example, a white organist in a Maryland Roman Catholic Church used alcohol and a cloth to ostentatiously wipe the organ keys that had been used by a black musician, black parishioners stormed out to form their own congregation. Black Methodists in Philadelphia and New York walked out of congregations in which they were given second-class treatment.

The Philadelphia Methodists, who were led by Absalom Jones (1746–1818) and Richard Allen (1760–1831), left St. George's Methodist Church.[11] The members of the departing group, who had already formed the Free African Society (1787), built a church of their own (1794), and joined the Episcopal Church, taking the name St. Thomas's African Church. Jones served the con-

Fig. 18. Absalom Jones

111

gregation as lay reader and, after ordination by Bishop White, as deacon (1795) and priest (1804). He was the first black American to be ordained by a hierarchical denomination.

St. Thomas African Church was a busy center of activity. The congregation boasted one of the nation's oldest black women's groups (the African Friendly Society of St. Thomas, 1793), a men's group (1795), and a school. By 1815, the congregation was the second largest in the Diocese of Pennsylvania.[12]

Absalom Jones's coworker Richard Allen remained in the the Methodist Church until 1816, when he joined with other black Methodists to form the African Methodist Episcopal (AME) Church.

The New York Methodists, also complaining of discrimination, left the John Street Methodist Church in New York City in 1796. James Varick (1750–1827) and some thirty other black Methodists then formed Zion Church, the first black church in New York City (1801). In 1818, Zion joined with other black Methodist congregations to create the African Methodist Episcopal (Zion) Church. Peter Williams, Jr., the son of one of Varick's cofounders, took a different course, however. After the departure from John Street, he joined Trinity Episcopal Church in New York. He was confirmed around 1798, elected a lay reader in 1812, and ordained to the priesthood in 1826. The church that he founded in 1818, St. Philip's, became a center for black Episcopalians. Williams was one of the founders of the first black American newspaper, *Freedman's Journal* (1827); a promoter of the first National Conference of Negro leaders (1830); and a manager of the American Anti-Slavery Society.[13]

In the years before the Civil War, fourteen other black men followed Williams and Jones into the Episcopal ministry. In most cases they served free black congregations in northern cities.[14] In the South, white clergy generally ministered to blacks as appendages of the white families for whom they worked. White priests baptized and married blacks and often provided some Sunday school instruction. Even where slave owners provided for separate black chapels, however, blacks did not organize vestries and take part in the leadership of the congregation in the way that they were able to do in the North.

In the early nineteenth century, black Americans lost much of the ground that they had gained in the immediate years after the Revolution. Congress banned importation of slaves in 1808, but the resultant shortage of slaves, especially in the Deep South where plantation owners were devoting new lands to the cultivation of cotton, created a booming internal slave trade. Black Christians like Absalom Jones and Peter Williams, Jr., continued the campaign against slavery. Some individual white Episcopalians also remained faithful in that effort. The members of the Jay family of New York were, for example, consistently active. Chief Justice John Jay (1745–1829) signed the act abolishing slavery while governor of New York. His son William (1789–1858) participated in the founding of the New York Anti-Slavery Society in 1833 and in the 1850s published pamphlets against slavery. His grandson John (1817–94) was a leader in the successful effort in the 1840s and 1850s to admit St. Philip's Church on equal footing with white congregations in the New York diocesan convention. As a whole, however, the predominantly white denominations of Christians—with the noticeable exception of the Quakers—dropped their protest against slavery.[15] All of the original thirteen states that limited slavery in their borders did so by 1804; the division between free and slave states in the East would remain unchanged until the Civil War.

One benevolent society concerned with slaves was, however, active in the South after 1804. Presbyterians, Episcopalians, and other interested Christians formed the American Colonization Society in 1816. The society followed the British example in Sierra Leone and the initiative of a black American sea captain named Paul Cuffee (1759–1817), who had campaigned for emigration to Africa during the War of 1812. Layman Francis Scott Key and later bishop of Virginia William Meade (1789–1862) were among early supporters of the society. Free blacks in the North, such as

Absalom Jones and Richard Allen, opposed the efforts of the society, but, whatever the fairness or wisdom of the idea of emigration to Africa, the society was the most effective advocate of some form of abolition in the South in the years before the Civil War. It offered a "solution" to what southern whites saw as the major social cost of abolition—the creation of a large class of poor blacks in America. By offering such a solution, the society made emancipation seem more palatable to whites. It was not a coincidence that the last serious attempt to eliminate slavery in a southern state, an 1832 vote in the Virginia legislature for a plan of gradual abolition that failed by a single vote, came at a time in which the Colonization Society was sending a record number of freed slaves to Liberia.[16]

It was as a result of the Colonization Society's efforts that the first American Episcopal clergyman served as an overseas missionary. Joseph R. Andrus, a New Hampshire priest who had also served as rector of St. Paul's, King George, Virginia, sailed for Africa with three other society members in 1821. Andrus died of fever before the end of the same year. Elizabeth Mars Johnson Thompson (1807–64), a black missionary who devoted most of her adult life to educational work in Liberia, was one of the many Episcopalians who would continue the work in Liberia as the century progressed.[17]

Institutional and Theological Change

Back in 1782, Bishop White's *Case of the Episcopal Churches* had defined the Episcopal Church as that church that professed "the religious principles of the Church of England."[18] The definition accorded with the religious perspective of most Americans in the first half of the nineteenth century. Churches were identified by principles and doctrines; good churches were those that could be most clear about what they believed.

Bishop White and other national leaders recognized that there was still much to be done in order to clarify the principles of the Episcopal Church. True, General Convention had

114

adopted a prayer book and constitution in 1789. But it had yet to adopt the Thirty-nine Articles or to identify a body of doctrine with which new candidates for the ministry should become acquainted. Perhaps more pressing still, the church had yet to shape a concerted response to the divisions of the Great Awakening. How could Episcopalians combine the best insights of both those who supported the Awakening and those who opposed it?

Fig. 19. The books—the Bible, Hooker's *Ecclesiastical Polity,* and Cranmer's Works—upon which Bishop William Meade rested his elbow in this portrait by John Neagle suggested the common Episcopal concern for correct doctrine.

William White and the bishops, priests, and laypersons who appeared at General Convention after 1800 turned their attention to this clarification of doctrine. Many of the bishops and deputies had themselves become active in the church after 1789. They looked to White as a father figure. He led them well, serving with a gentle hand as presiding bishop in the critical years between 1795 and 1836. Toward the end of his life, he would write the only firsthand history of the events that led to the formation of the Episcopal Church.

In 1801, White convinced the General Convention to adopt the Thirty-nine Articles with only minor political alterations. In 1804, he responded to a request from the Convention by preparing the Course of Ecclesiastical Studies, a list of textbooks that every candidate for the ministry was to read before ordination.[19]

In 1804, candidates for the ministry studied privately with either an important parish cleric or a college divinity professor. In 1808, however, a group of Congregationalists, worried by the unitarian leanings of the divinity professor at Harvard, developed another educational pattern. They established Andover Seminary, the first three-year, Protestant, postgraduate theological school. The institution was an immediate success.

Episcopalians, Presbyterians, Baptists, Lutherans, and Reformed Christians soon created their own seminaries based on the Andover model. In the 1820s, Episcopalians opened three: General Seminary in New York (1822), Virginia (the Protestant Episcopal Seminary in Virginia, 1823), and the theological department of Kenyon College in Ohio (Bexley Hall, 1824). Many early faculty members of these institutions had themselves attended Andover. The new seminaries, capable of producing a larger number of candidates for the ministry than the older patterns of study, rapidly replaced reading for orders as the primary path to ordination.

In the same years, a major shift was taking place in the character of the ordained ministry. Parish clergy, who during the colonial era enjoyed at least theoretical life tenure to the parishes into which they had been instituted, lost that privilege in 1804. In that year, General Convention adopted a canon giving bishops (or, in their absences, diocesan convention and standing committees) the right to mediate in disputes between clergy and congregations. The canon gave bishops little new authority over truculent parishes but did grant them the authority to suspend clergy involved in such disputes. The provision was written to resolve the ongoing conflict between Uzal Ogden, who had been a pro-Awakening ordinand of the 1770s, and his parish. The combination of the Convention's new canon and its failure to endorse him as Bishop-elect of New Jersey convinced Ogden to join the Presbyterian Church.[20]

Changes were taking place in the nature of the episcopate as well. The church leaders that were most familiar to colonial Anglicans before the Revolution were the commissaries, who had represented the Bishop of London and presided over convocations of clergy. The first bishops, who often occupied the same parishes as the commissaries that preceded them, modeled themselves after these colonial leaders. Unlike the commissaries, they did ordain new clergy. Little else that they did, however, differentiated their ministries from that of the commissaries. Few—Seabury may have been the major exception—made parish visitations. Few followed through on Bishop Seabury's early advocacy of confirmation. They did not address pastoral letters to their dioceses. They had no diocesan budgets to administer. Like the commissaries, they spent the majority of their time in the parish or teaching positions that provided their livelihood and exercised their authority over the diocese primarily by presiding over the occasional meetings of diocesan conventions. Such commissary bishops were able to meet the single greatest need of the new church, the ordination of new candidates for the ministry. They did not, however, provide vital diocesan leadership.

In 1811, a new assistant bishop was consecrated for the state of New York. John Henry Hobart (1775–1830) was a young assistant at Trinity Church who had prepared for the priesthood with Bishop White. He married Mary Chandler, the daughter of Thomas Bradbury Chandler, the New Jersey priest who had campaigned for a colonial episcopate and against the American Revolution.

Hobart, initially consecrated to assist an ailing Bishop Benjamin Moore, provided a new model for the American bishop. An active speaker, an ardent pamphlet writer, and an able administrator, he was not content simply to preside at annual convention. He saw, for example, the need for episcopal leadership in missions. With the western end of his state swelling with a tide of New England and New York pioneers who were following the Erie Canal to the West, he led the way in establishing new congregations for the settlers. He orga-

Fig. 20. John Henry Hobart

117

nized an offering for missions, addressed the parishioners of his diocese in parish visitations and pastoral letters, and played a personal role in the recruiting and placement of clergy.[21]

Other dioceses received ample evidence of the wisdom of Hobart's approach; New York was soon the country's largest diocese. Episcopalians elsewhere quickly emulated Hobart's active leadership. In 1814, for example, Virginians elected Richard Channing Moore (1762–1841), a New York priest who had seen the vigorous style of Hobart close up, as their second bishop. Two years later, New York priest Adam Empie came to St. James's, Wilmington, North Carolina. He began a revival of the Episcopal Church in the state and a continuing link between the diocese and that of New York.[22]

The adoption of the Thirty-nine Articles, the creation of the Course of Ecclesiastical Studies, the development of a more vigorous pattern of the episcopate, and the formation of theological seminaries helped to create a church more confident of its own identity. The first great test of this new identity was the War of 1812. Episcopalians again had to choose between their English roots and their new republic. While some questioned the wisdom of the war, there were no defections to England.

Church Parties

In the years immediately after the American Revolution, Episcopalians had come very close to forming two different denominational structures—a middle and southern states church and a Connecticut-based New England church. It would not have been unusual had they done so. Other American denominations divided over ethnic and theological grounds during the eighteenth and nineteenth centuries.

Three major differences had separated the two opposing organizational efforts: their attitude toward the Revolution, their understanding of the role of the laity, and the apologetic stance that they took toward other denominations. In general, New England Episcopalians opposed the Revolution, denied the laity a role in the government of the diocese, and stressed the apostolic succession that other Protestants lacked. Middle and southern states Episcopalians were more likely to support the war, accept lay participation in the church hierarchy, and emphasize similarities rather than differences with other Protestants. After 1800, the first two issues became relatively unimportant: it was hard to dispute the success of the Revolution, and after Seabury's death, even Connecticut began to send lay deputies to General Conventions. The apologetic debate continued to be important, however. Was the Episcopal Church to stress its similarities with or its differences from other Protestant churches?

The debate was a critical one, for it involved both the continuing utility of Anglican covenant theology and the Episcopal response to the Great Awakening. The solution that Episcopalians reached involved something of a compromise: an attempt to combine the best of the covenant arguments with the stress on personal faith of the Awakening.

The lines of their argument had been suggested a century before by Samuel Bradford (1652–1731), the Anglican Bishop of Rochester. In his *Discourse Concerning Baptismal and Spiritual Regeneration* (1708), Bradford had called attention to Titus 3, which declared that "[God] saved us . . . by the washing of regeneration and renewal in the Holy Spirit."[23] Bradford understood the lines to say that two elements were necessary for the Christian life: washing (i.e., baptism) and renewal. Nineteenth-century Episcopalians picked up this line of reasoning. In 1826, for example, the House of Bishops unanimously recommended that the following prayer be added to the confirmation office:

Almighty and everliving God, who hast vouchsafed in baptism, to regenerate these thy Servants, by water and the Holy Ghost; thus giving them a title to all the blessings of thy covenant of grace and mercy, in thy Son Jesus Christ, and now graciously confirm unto them, ratifying the promises then made, all their privileges; grant unto them, we beseech thee, O Lord, the renewing of the Holy Ghost. . . .[24]

Episcopalians believed that both entrance into the apostolic covenant and an adult renewal of faith were necessary.

This compromise did not, however, eliminate all theological debate within the Episcopal Church. Given the pairing of regeneration and renewal, Episcopalians still had to decide where to place their emphasis. Quite naturally, those Episcopalians for whom the covenant theology had been most important emphasized baptismal regeneration. Those who had been moved by the Great Awakening placed more emphasis on adult renewal.

Participants in this discussion did not, however, simply preserve the distinction between New England and the middle and southern states. The predictable geographical blocks of the eighteenth century were replaced by two church parties that by the 1820s had representatives in each of the dioceses. Thus, the sometimes heated conflicts between these two groups were a side product of a very important phenomenon—the creation of one national church in the place of the two that had preceded it.

Those Episcopalians who stressed the baptismal covenant referred to themselves as members of the high church party, because they held high the distinctive apostolic succession of their church. Those who stressed adult renewal called themselves evangelicals, the term most often used by other post–Great Awakening Protestants. John Henry Hobart of New York, the bishop who provided a more active model for the episcopate, was the most effective leader of the high church party. Hobart took the episcopacy very seriously and refused to allow clergy in his diocese to participate in benevolent organizations with Christians of denominations that lacked the apostolic succession. He cautioned clergy in his diocese, for example, against participation in the American Bible Society. The bishop formed his own Prayer Book and Bible Society to distribute combined Bibles and prayer books.

Hobart was also wary of participating in the civil government that, in contrast to the government in England, was largely in the hands of non-Anglicans. He refused to vote.[25] In the years before the Civil War, many high church Episcopalians would share his

suspicion. Perhaps they recalled the hostility to a colonial episcopate that many Presbyterian and Congregational legislators
had exhibited before the Revolution. Certainly, they believed
that Christians were sure of only one hierarchy in this
world—the historic episcopate.

Hobart used his considerable persuasive abilities to advance
the fortunes of those who agreed with him. Seven of his assistants at Trinity, and a number of his other associates, would
later themselves become bishops.[26] This influence extended
beyond the New England area in which covenant theology had
been so important. Hobart found supporters, for example, in
North Carolina, where Adam Empie's efforts at revival led to
the election of Bishop John Stark Ravenscroft (1772–1830).
Ravenscroft, though from Virginia, was a committed member
of the high church party. After his death, North Carolinians
elected Hobart's son-in-law, Levi Silliman Ives (1797–1867),
to succeed him.

Arrayed against this high church party was a slightly
younger group of clergy in the Washington, D.C., area. In the
1790s, Congress established a new nation's capital in a square
piece of land that included the existing towns of Alexandria,
Virginia, and Georgetown, Maryland. Though no rival to New
York in size, the political importance of the city made it a
major competitor.

Around 1810, a group of young clergy began to congregate
in this Washington area. Most important among them were
William H. Wilmer and William Meade. Wilmer wrote an
Episcopal Manual (1815) summarizing his understanding of
Episcopal doctrine, ran for General Convention, and by 1820
was elected president of the House of Deputies. Meade joined
with Wilmer in bringing Richard Channing Moore to Virginia
as successor to Bishop James Madison. Wilmer would die
young, but Meade would later follow Moore as Bishop of
Virginia.

Wilmer, Meade, and other evangelicals placed their stress
not upon the apostolic succession in the covenant but upon the
importance of adult renewal of faith. They simplified the

liturgy by separating the antecommunion service from Morning Prayer in order to provide additional time for preaching.[27] They developed a modified form of revivalism, which they called the association, and stressed the importance of a change of conduct in adult believers.[28]

Wilmer, Meade, and other evangelicals began to seek out like-minded clergy, much in the way that Hobart did. This agreement on an evangelical theological approach was often strengthened by a teacher-student connection or a family tie. Alexander Viets Griswold (1766–1843), the Bishop of the Eastern Diocese (Rhode Island, Massachusetts, Maine, New Hampshire, and Vermont) whose high church sympathies were changed by an 1811 revival in his Bristol, Rhode Island, parish, kept in touch with the Washington area through his former theological students John P.K. Henshaw (1792–1852) and Stephen H. Tyng (1800–1885). Elizabeth Channing Moore, a member of a female religious society at Trinity Church, New York that met weekly in parishioners' homes, raised her family with such strong evangelical convictions that her children and grandchildren would include three priests and two evangelical bishops (Richard C. Moore of Virginia and Gregory T. Bedell of Ohio).[29]

Bishop White recognized this development of parties in the church and neatly presided over it in his own parish by choosing pairs of assistants, one of each persuasion. Long after his death he would be looked upon as the patron of both groups. Indeed he was, for both parties used his Course of Ecclesiastical Studies and read his history of the denomination. White presided over the General Convention and took pains to keep from being identified exclusively with either position, much as he had avoided siding exclusively with either Provoost or Seabury.

The existence of the church parties contributed to the formation of the theological seminaries. General Seminary in New York received its charter in 1822 after a protracted fight. Hobart insisted on having control over any seminary in his diocese. The initial efforts to establish a seminary for the whole church in New York that had begun in 1817 had resulted in two conflicting institutions—a diocesan school and a general institution that found the bishop so inhospitable that it moved to New Haven. A generous donor, leaving funds for a *general* seminary *in New York,* solved the problem. The two institutions had to combine to receive the gift. Hobart gained two important concessions. His own assistant was to be the first professor of ecclesiastical polity (thereby guaranteeing a proper stress on the episcopacy that separated the Episcopal Church from other Protestant denominations), and his diocese was to receive representation on the board of trustees proportionate to contributions. General Seminary, while an institution of the church at large, became a successful proponent of Hobartian high church doctrine.

Meade and Wilmer and a host of others founded a seminary near Alexandria, Virginia, that accorded better with their evangelical understanding of the church. As at General Seminary, the students at Virginia used texts from the list prepared by Bishop White, but Wilmer, who served as the first professor of the school, took a very different apologetic stance from his counterparts at General. He stressed the similarities, rather than the differences, between Episcopalians and other Protestants.

Expansion and Missions

At the close of the American Revolution, the Episcopal Church was ill prepared to minister to the rapidly expanding western migration. The Revolution had caused a rapid decline in the number of available clergy, a loss of important revenue sources, and a confusion about organization. The bishops and General Convention deputies may have adopted a constitution and a prayer book in 1789, but not until the 1840s would all of the original thirteen states have diocesan structures and diocesan bishops.

Given this disarray in the East, it was not surprising that Episcopalians concentrated their initial efforts on revitalizing the church on the eastern seaboard. Successive General Conventions carried word of increasing progress in this effort. Delegations joined the convention from Rhode Island (consistent participation in Convention began in 1808), Vermont (1811), New Hampshire (1811), North Carolina (1817), Maine (1820), and Georgia (1823).

Table 2. The Episcopal Church in the Original Thirteen States

State	Represented at General Convention	First bishop	Names of early diocesan bishops[1]
Connecticut	1789	1784	Samuel Seabury (1784–96) Abraham Jarvis (1797–1813) Thomas Brownell (1819–65)
Pennsylvania	1785	1787	William White (1787–1836)
New York	1785	1787	Samuel Provoost (1787–1801)[2] Benjamin Moore (1801–16) John Henry Hobart (1816–30)
Virginia	1785	1790	James Madison (1790–1812) Richard Moore (1814–41)
Maryland	1785	1792	Thomas Claggett (1792–1816) James Kemp (1816–27)
South Carolina	1785/1814[3]	1795	Robert Smith (1795–1801) Theodore Dehon (1812–17) Nathaniel Bowen (1818–39)
Massachusetts	1789	1797	Edward Bass (1797–1803) Samuel Parker (1804–08)
Rhode Island	1808[4]	1811	Alexander Griswold (1811–43)
New Jersey	1785	1815	John Croes (1815–32)
North Carolina	1817	1823	John Ravenscroft (1823–30)
Georgia	1823	1841	Stephen Elliott (1841–66)
Delaware	1785	1841	Alfred Lee (1841–87)
New Hampshire	1811	1844	Carlton Chase (1844–70)

1. The names listed are of diocesan bishops who served before 1820, except in those states in which the first bishop was consecrated after that date. Some of these diocesan bishops had assistant bishops. Among those assistants were: John

Henry Hobart (Assistant Bishop of New York, 1811–16), James Kemp (Assistant Bishop of Maryland, 1814–16), and William Meade (Assistant Bishop of Virginia, 1819–41). All three became diocesan bishops on the death of their predecessors.

2. Bishop Provoost retired in 1801. He tried, however, to resume a more active role in his diocese in 1811. He died in 1815.

3. South Carolina delegations attended the General Conventions between 1785 and 1795. No delegations attended, however, between that year and 1814.

4. Alexander Viets Griswold was resident in Rhode Island. He served, however, as the Bishop of the Eastern Diocese, an area that included all of the New England states that did not have resident bishops. Connecticut was without a resident bishop from 1813 to 1819. The remaining New England states remained under Griswold's care for much longer. Vermont elected its first resident bishop in 1832. Massachusetts elected an assistant bishop to Griswold in 1842. New Hampshire did not choose a separate bishop until after Griswold's death in 1843.

Rhode Island was represented at the General Conventions of 1799 and 1801, but did not send delegations consistently until 1808.

While they concentrated on this effort, Episcopalians adopted a laissez-faire policy toward western and foreign missions. Individual Episcopal laypersons and occasional clerics followed the migration west; of these, some formed western congregations. Others volunteered for interdenominational foreign missionary societies. In the 1830s, the General Convention established a more coherent missionary policy and tried to overcome a late start on the frontier.

During these years, however, a remnant of the ministry to Native Americans, which the SPG had supported during the colonial period, continued on the western frontier, largely as a result of the efforts of Episcopalians in New York. Bishop Hobart designated Eleazar Williams as a catechist to the Oneida in the years following the War of 1812. Williams, who may have been

Fig. 21.
Philander Chase

Fig. 22.
Benjamin Bosworth Smith

of Mohawk heritage but who claimed to be a lost descendant of the King of France, served both in western New York and in Green Bay, Wisconsin, to which he and others urged the Oneida to move in 1823.[30]

Western Dioceses

That some western dioceses were formed before 1830 was a tribute to the rugged individualism of a few exceptional pioneers. Among them were Philander Chase, Benjamin Bosworth Smith, and James Otey. In 1805, after six years of parish ministry in western New York, Chase (1775–1852) decided to move further west. He went first to New Orleans, where as rector of Christ Church he presided over the earliest Protestant congregation in the newly acquired Louisiana purchase.[31] After a brief stint at Christ Church, Hartford, Connecticut (1811–17), he again went west, this time to Ohio. Meeting Episcopal laypersons who included the brother of Bishop Griswold of Rhode Island, Chase called for the formation of a diocesan convention. The convention's second annual meeting unanimously elected Chase bishop. After a trip to the East for consecration (1819), Chase set about building educational institutions that would help train clergy. In 1821, he became the president of Cincinnati College, and in 1824, he used contributions that he secured on an English fund-raising trip to establish Kenyon College, an institution that included a theological department (Bexley Hall, which is now part of the Colgate-Rochester consortium of theological schools). Chase's school was a modest affair over which he exercised total control, choosing the professors and designing the course of studies.[32] When faculty members questioned the bishop's exercise of authority, Chase resigned as both bishop and college president and headed west to found a new diocese (Illinois) and a new school (the unsuccessful Jubilee College). After his resignation the clergy and laity of Ohio elected Charles P. McIlvaine (1799–1873), one of the early members of the Washington, D.C., group of evangelicals, as their bishop.[33]

Fig. 23. James Hervey Otey, St. Andrew's Cathedral, Jackson, Mississippi

Benjamin Bosworth Smith became the first Bishop of Kentucky in 1832. With the exception of the dispute and resignation, his story was much like Chase's. He helped to organize a frontier diocese and worked on both public (state superintendent of public schools) and church education. Smith started the Episcopal Theological Seminary in Kentucky in 1834. (The school closed at midcentury but reopened in 1951.)

James Hervey Otey (1800–1863) moved from North Carolina to Tennessee, where he ministered to congregations in the cities of Franklin, Columbus, and Nashville. Elected bishop in 1834, he founded a school for girls in Columbia and was one of the initial planners for the University of the South.

These three early bishops operated very much like the original commissaries. They went to areas where there were a minimal number of Episcopalians and sought to found basic educational institutions to support a church. They were elected by the small number of clergy and laity they were able to gather, and they received only minimal support from the eastern dioceses. Considering the obstacles that they faced, they made considerable gains. Throughout the 1820s and early 1830s, the number of western states represented at General Convention increased. In addition to Ohio (1823), Kentucky (1829), and Tennessee (1832), delegations arrived from Mississippi (1826), Alabama (1832), and Michigan (1832).

The bishops and deputies at General Convention recognized that a more organized system was needed. In 1835, therefore, they reorganized the Domestic and Foreign Missionary Society. Reorganization was not a new element for the society. From the time it first established it in 1820, the General Convention had continually revised the constitution of the society in order to establish a more secure funding base. It had, in turn, made membership universal for Episcopalians (1820); established a special offering at sessions of General Convention and limited membership to those in the General Convention or those who made contributions of a designated size (1823); dropped the automatic membership of the members of the House of Deputies, and abandoned the General Convention offering (1832). Contributions, most of which came from the Diocese of New York, gradually climbed during this period, and by 1835 the General Convention finally felt sure enough of the financial stability of the society to take two further steps. It returned to the 1820 definition of membership, and it adopted a procedure for election of missionary bishops, who were to be paid out of the

Fig. 24.
Jackson Kemper

society's funds. Such bishops would be consecrated and sent out from the General Convention. Western Episcopalians need no longer wait until they were sufficient in numbers to form their own diocesan conventions and to elect their own bishops.

Jackson Kemper (1789–1870) was the first such missionary

bishop. A former assistant of Bishop White in the United Parishes of Philadelphia, Kemper was consecrated in 1835 as the missionary Bishop of Missouri and Indiana, though at times his cure also included Iowa, Wisconsin, Nebraska, and Kansas. In addition, he visited Alabama, Arkansas, Mississippi, Louisiana, Georgia, and Florida in a grand tour in 1837–38. In 1838, Leonidas Polk (1806–64) followed Kemper as the second missionary bishop. His responsibility included Arkansas and the Indian Territory (Oklahoma).

As the population on the frontier increased and Episcopal congregations grew more numerous, Episcopalians within portions of these large missionary districts organized smaller dioceses and elected their own bishops. Members of the Episcopal Church in Louisiana formed a diocese and convinced Polk to resign his missionary diocese and become their bishop in 1841. Those in Wisconsin formed a diocese and in 1859 elected Kemper to become their diocesan bishop.

Table 3. Dioceses in States Admitted to the Union 1791–1859

State	Joined Union	First bishop	Years later	Bishop's name
Vermont	1791	1832	41	John Henry Hopkins
Kentucky	1792	1832	40	Benjamin Bosworth Smith
Tennessee	1796	1834	38	James H. Otey
Ohio	1803	1819	16	Philander Chase
Louisiana	1812	1841	29	Leonidas Polk
Indiana[1]	1816	1844	28	Jackson Kemper
Mississippi	1817	1850	33	William M. Green
Illinois	1818	1835	17	Philander Chase
Alabama	1819	1844	25	Nicholas H. Cobbs
Maine	1820	1847	27	George Burgess
Missouri[2]	1821	1844	23	Cicero S. Hawkes
Arkansas[3]	1836	1844	8	George W. Freeman
Michigan	1837	1836	(1)	Samuel A. McCoskry
Florida	1845	1851	6	Francis H. Rutledge
Texas	1845	1859	14	Alexander Gregg
Iowa	1846	1854	8	Henry W. Lee

Wisconsin	1848	1859	11	Jackson Kemper
California	1850	1857	7	William I. Kip
Minnesota	1858	1859	1	Henry B. Whipple
Oregon	1859	1854	(5)	Thomas F. Scott

1 From 1835 until 1844, Indiana was combined with Missouri in a missionary district of which Jackson Kemper was bishop.

2. In 1844, Missouri, which had been combined in a missionary diocese with Indiana, formed a separate diocese. Kemper left for Wisconsin, and George Upfold became Bishop of Indiana.

3. From 1838 to 1841 Arkansas and the Indian Territory (Oklahoma) were combined into one missionary district of which Leonidas Polk was bishop.

Not all the frontier diocesan bishops were former missionary bishops, however. Michigan elected Samuel McCoskry (1804–86) bishop in 1836. In 1844,
Alabama elected Nicholas Hamner Cobbs (1796–1861), and the clergy and laity of Missouri elected Cicero Stephens Hawkes (1812–68) in 1844.

As these new dioceses filled in territory in the easternmost dioceses, new missionary territories were established yet further west.

Foreign Missions

Though individual priests had participated in the work of the American Colonization Society before 1820, the Domestic and Foreign Missionary Society of the Episcopal Church did not send out a missionary team on behalf of the whole church until 1830. Contributors in the 1820s had suggested that the society send missionaries to Liberia or Argentina.[34] The missionary team sent in 1830, composed of the Reverend and Mrs. J.J. Robertson, the Rev. John (1791–1882) and Mrs. Frances (1799–1884) Hill, and Mr. Solomon Bingham, went, however, in a different direction—to Greece. The successful Greek war for independence against Turkey had captured the imagination of many in America and England. The missionary team from the United States hoped to help in the difficult task of rebuilding a Christian nation after centuries of Muslim occupation. Like many of the western missionaries in the U. S., the members of the team decided to concentrate their efforts in education. The Robertsons and Mr. Bingham, who was a printer by trade, established a Greek language publishing program. The Hills founded a series of highly successful schools that played an essential role in the creation of a Greek school system.

Conscious of the fact that they were in a Greek Orthodox nation, the members of the team did not seek to proselytize. They hoped rather to invigorate the Greek Church by their educational efforts and Bible teaching. The Hills had a successful ministry that continued into the 1880s.[35] Among those who assisted in their effort was educator Mary Briscoe Baldwin (1811–77), who left a teaching career in the United States for work in both Greece (1833–66) and Syria (1871–77).[36]

The work in Greece was soon followed by missionary efforts in non-Christian countries. The first two missionaries to China left New York in 1835. William Jones Boone (1811–64), who would be consecrated as the church's first foreign missionary bishop in 1844, followed two years later. Three missionaries, including later Bishop John Payne (1815–74), were appointed in 1836 to work in Liberia.

NOTES

1. W.J. Rorabaugh, *The Alcoholic Republic* (Oxford: Oxford University Press, 1979), 8.

2. George Herbert, *The Country Parson, The Temple,* Classics of Western Spirituality (New York: Paulist Press, 1981), 57; and Gilbert Burnet, *A Discourse of the Pastoral Care,* 14th ed. corrected (London: Rivingtons and Cochran, 1821), 182.

3. *Journal of the General Conventions of the Protestant Episcopal Church in the United States, 1785–1835,* ed. William Stevens Perry, 3 vols. (Claremont, N.H.: Claremont Manufacturing Company, 1874), 1:128.

4. Douglass Adair and Marvin Harvey, "Was Alexander Hamilton a Christian Statesman?" *William and Mary Quarterly* (3d series) 12 (April 1955):309. Bishop Moore visited Alexander Hamilton twice after the duel. On his first visit, he refused Hamilton communion. He relented, however, on his second visit.

5. William Meade, *Old Churches, Ministers, and Families of Virginia,* 2 vols. (1857; reprint, Baltimore: Genological Publishing Company, 1966), 1:23.

6. *Journal of the General Conventions,* 1:458.

7. Ibid., 2:494. R. Bruce Mullin has argued in *Episcopal Vision/American Reality* that high church Episcopalians had little interest in public morality. He is correct within the limited framework in which he makes his argument: white, male, high church clergy had little interest in moral campaigns, particularly those involving other Protestants after 1820. All of the high church bishops present at the General Convention of 1817 did, however, vote for the morality resolution. High church females and evangelicals of both sexes were more consistent in their support for moral campaigns. See R. Bruce Mullin, *Episcopal Vision/American Reality: High Church Theology and Social thought in Evangelical America* (New Haven: Yale University Press, 1986), 78–85, and, for a contrasting opinion, Manross, *Episcopal Church in the United States, 1800–1840: A Study in Church Life* (New York: Columbia University Press, 1980), 186–93.

After the 1820s, when a second generation of temperance leaders began to advocate abstinence from alcohol even in the communion cup, Episcopalians became less active in the campaign against drink.

8. Edward T. James, Janet Wilson James, and Paul S. Boyer, eds., *Notable American Women 1607–1950,* 3 vols. (Cambridge, Mass.: The Belnap Press, 1971), 2:202–4, 586–87, 649–50.

9. William Wilson Manross, *The Episcopal Church in the United States,* 189–90.

10. Linda K. Kerber, *Women of the Republic: Intellect and Ideology in Revolutionary America* (Chapel Hill: University of North Carolina Press, 1980), 193.

11. White parishioners interrupted Jones and Allen during their private devotions before worship and asked them to move to a segregated balcony. The event, which occurred at some point after the creation of the Free African Society and before the beginning of construction on a separate building (1792), was probably not the only example of discrimination against blacks, but it was the symbolic event to which Richard Allen would later refer in his explanation of the departure from St. George's. In his old age Allen remembered the balcony incident as occurring in 1787, but construction records at St. George's would date it later, perhaps in 1792, for that is the year the balcony to which they were asked to move was completed. See Milton C. Sernett, *Black Religion and American Evangelicalism: White Protestants, Plantation Missions and the Flowering of Negro Christianity, 1787–1865* (Metuchen, N.J.: Scarecrow Press and the American Theological Library Association, 1975), 116–19.

12. Dorothy Sterling, *We Are Your Sisters: Black Women in the Nineteenth Century* (New York: W.W. Norton, 1984), 105; *Journal of the 29th Convention of the Protestant Episcopal Church in the State of Pennsylvania* (1815), 16.

13. Rayford W. Logan and Michael R. Winston, eds., *Dictionary of American Negro Biography* (New York: W.W. Norton, 1982) s. v. "James Varick" by W. Logan and "Peter Williams, Jr.," by J. Carleton Hayden.

14. Carleton Hayden, "The Black Ministry of the Episcopal Church: An Historical Overview," in *Black Clergy in the Episcopal Church: Recruitment, Training, and Deployment,* ed. Franklin D. Turner and Adair T. Lummis (New York: Office of Black Ministries of the Episcopal Church, n.d.), 7.

15. H. Shelton Smith, *In His Image, but . . .* (Durham: Duke University Press, 1972), 23–72.

16. P.J. Staudenraus, *The African Colonization Movement, 1816–65* (New York: Columbia University Press, 1961), 180–84.

17. Randall K. Burkett, "Elizabeth Mars Johnson Thomson (1806–1864): A Research Note," *Historical Magazine of the Protestant Episcopal Church* 55 (March 1986):21–30.

18. William White, "The Case of the Episcopal Churches Considered," in *Readings from the History of the Episcopal Church* ed. Robert W. Prichard (Harrisburg, PA: Morehouse, 1986), 62.

19. For a discussion of the contents of the reading list, see George Blackman, *Faith and Freedom: A Study of Theological Education and the Episcopal Theological School* (New York: Seabury Press, 1967), 7–17 and Robert W. Prichard, "Theological Consensus in the Episcopal Church, 1801–1873" (Ph.D. diss., Emory University, 1983), 19–51.

20. Edwin Augustine White, *Constitution and Canons for the Government of the Protestant Episcopal Church in the United States of America Adopted in General Convention, 1789–1922, Annotated etc.* (New York: Edwin S. Gorham, 1924), 698.

21. Mullin, *Episcopal Vision,* 54. Mullin noted that in 1815 Hobart became the first American bishop to issue a pastoral letter to his diocese. In 1808, however, Bishop White began to write national pastoral letters for the House of Bishops. Hobart was the secretary of the House of Deputies in that year.

22. Lawrence Foushee London and Sarah McCulloh Lemmon, eds., *The Episcopal Church in North Carolina, 1701–1959* (Raleigh: Episcopal Diocese of North Carolina, 1987), 94–99.

23. Titus 3:6, RSV.

24. William McGarvey, ed., *Liturgiae Americanae or the Book of Common Prayer as Used in the United States of America Compared with the Proposed Book of 1786 and with the Prayer Book of the Church of England* (Philadelphia, 1895), appendix II, 88.

25. Mullin, *Episcopal Vision,* 86.

26. Michael Taylor Malone, "Levi Silliman Ives: Priest, Bishop, Tractarian, and Roman Catholic" (Ph. D. diss., Duke University, 1970), 10.

27. During the early nineteenth century, most Episcopal parishes celebrated the eucharist four times a year. On the remaining

Sundays, parish clergy or lay readers read Morning Prayer and antecommunion (the first half of the eucharistic liturgy). Meade and others dropped the reading of antecommunion. Hobart protested to the General Convention of 1826 but was unable to stem the practice.

28. For a description of the association, see John Johns, *A Memoir of the Life of the Right Rev. William Meade, D.D.* (Baltimore: Innes and Company, 1867), 101–2.

29. Gregory T. Bedell, *Sermons by the Rev. Gregory T. Bedell, Rector of St. Andrew's Church, Philadelphia with a Biographical Sketch of the Author by Stephen H. Tyng*, 2 vols. (Philadelphia: William Stavely, John C. Pechin, 1835), 1:ii; C.I. Gibson, "Sketch of Our First Four Bishops," *Addresses and Historical Papers before the Centennial Council of the Protestant Episcopal Church in the Diocese of Virginia, etc.* (New York: Thomas Whittaker, 1885), 145.

30. Owanah Anderson, *Jamestown Commitment: The Episcopal Church and the American Indian* (Cincinnati: Forward Movement, 1988), 32–37.

31. "Christ Church Cathedral" (New Orleans: Christ Church Cathedral, n.d.).

32. Henry Caswall's *America and the American Church* (London: J.G. and F. Rivington, 1839) contained a firsthand description of life at Kenyon. See pp. 33–40.

33. Richard M. Spielmann, *Bexley Hall: 150 Years, A Brief History* (Rochester: Colgate Rochester Divinity School/Bexley Hall/Crozer Theological Seminary, 1974), 14–17.

34. White, *Constitutions and Canons*, 903.

35. Wallace E. Rollins, "The Mission to Greece," in *History of the Theological Seminary in Virginia and Its Historical Background,* ed. W.A.R. Goodwin, 2 vols. (Rochester: Du Bois Press, 1924), 2:252–70.

36. Joanna B. Gillespie, "Mary Briscoe Baldwin (1811–1877): Single Woman Missionary and 'Very Much My Own Mistress,'" *Anglican and Episcopal History* 57 (March 1988):63–92. Mary Briscoe Baldwin's cousin Mary Julia Baldwin (1829–1897) was the educator after whom the college in Staunton, Virginia was named.

6
Romantic Reaction
(1840–80)

Episcopalians in the first third of the nineteenth century had made great progress in putting the chaos and confusion of the Revolutionary War years behind them. They had found a new, more aggressive model for the episcopate, had adopted both the Thirty-nine Articles and a uniform Course of Ecclesiastical Studies, and had begun to send bishops to the West. Unlike the generation that had preceded them, Episcopalians maturing after 1800 knew where their church stood on a variety of issues and could be quite explicit about that stance.

This increasingly confident orthodoxy served Episcopalians well in the first third of the century. By 1840, however, America was changing, and many Americans found that the rational approach to theology and the church no longer met their needs. The enlarged textile factories in Lowell, Massachusetts (1813), the newly opened Erie Canal (1825), and the Baltimore and Ohio Railroad (1828) all heralded a more sophisticated, industrialized nation.[1] The triumph of an industrial North over an agricultural South in the American Civil War made it all the more clear. Americans were no longer citizens of a frontier agricultural nation. The values of the new industrializing nation were different, and many Americans looked to Christianity to preserve the virtues—a closer connection with nature, the intimacy of the frontier family, a sense of awe in creation, and a more spontaneous and expressive way of life—that they attributed to their past. Once Americans began this search for such a past, they were not content, however, simply to examine their own recent history. Many looked beyond it to Greece and Rome.

Greek Christians, subjects of the Muslim Ottoman Empire since the mid-fifteenth century, had rebelled and gained their independence from Turkey in 1829. The victory caught the imaginations of Americans. They followed the exploits in Greece of British poet George Gordon Byron (1788–1824). They read the "Ode on a Grecian Urn" by John Keats (1795–1821) and built homes in Greek revival styles. American college students formed Greek letter fraternities. It was this excitement over things Greek that had led the Episcopal Church to send its first official missionary team to Greece in 1830. In 1844, it would lead the House of Bishops to approve the consecration of a missionary bishop (Horatio Southgate, 1813–94) for what would prove to be an unsuccessful attempt to establish a missionary diocese in Turkey itself. (Southgate halted his work in 1849.)

The Greek invasion was one of culture and imagination; the Roman invasion was of another sort. The vast majority of American colonists in the seventeenth and eighteen centuries were Protestant. They reflected the overwhelmingly Protestant character of the nation from which they came; at the time of the American Revolution, Roman Catholics accounted for less than 1 percent of the population of England or America.[2] By the 1830s, however, the situation had changed. No longer a colony, the United States welcomed immigrants from predominantly Roman Catholic areas of Europe, who would have been excluded by the British. In addition, a series of poor potato harvests send waves of Irish Roman Catholics both to England and to the United States. In England, the Roman Catholic population increased to perhaps 10 percent of the population. In the United States, Roman Catholics would be by 1926 more than twice as numerous as the members of the largest Protestant denomination.[3]

Protestant Americans reacted in two ways to this increased Roman Catholic presence. Some responded with suspicion and anger. In 1844, for example, Protestant mobs attacked Roman Catholic churches in Philadelphia. Others found in Roman Catholicism the past for which they yearned and either brought more catholic perspectives to the churches of which they were part or—as 700,000 Americans would do during the nineteenth century—converted to the Roman Catholic Church.[4]

This attraction of a Greek and Roman past and the nostalgia produced by the industrialization of America challenged the rational orthodoxy of the earlier part of the century. Many Americans at midcentury no longer looked to their churches for a clear exposition of doctrine. Rather, they looked to them for mystery, beauty, and a sense of permanence. Episcopalians were as successful as any Protestant church in coming to terms with the new American mood, yet even for them the transition was a difficult one.

The General Convention of 1844

Rational orthodox Episcopalians of the early nineteenth century had assumed that two elements were necessary for salvation: baptism into the apostolic covenant community and adult renewal of that covenant. By the time bishops and deputies gathered in Philadelphia for the 1844 General Convention, both premises were under attack. Roman Catholics challenged the Episcopal monopoly on apostolic orders, and the Oxford theologians, leaders of a romantic Anglican theological party that was attracting increasing attention in England and the United States, questioned the necessity of adult renewal. The bishops and deputies at the Convention, and Episcopalians in general, were, as a result, forced to rethink some of their basic theological assumptions.

Since the colonial days of the Society for the Propagation of the Gospel (SPG), Episcopalians had stressed the apostolic succession of their clergy. Such an argument distinguished the Episcopal Church from other Protestant denominations, but it did little to separate it from the growing Church of Rome. The issue was difficult to ignore; the city in which the bishops and deputies met in October 1844 (Philadelphia) was still recovering from the anti-Roman riots of the previous May. In addition, the Roman Catholic Bishop Coadjutor of Philadelphia, Francis

Patrick Kenrick (1796–1863), was at the time of the Convention carrying on a literary debate with the Episcopal Bishop of Vermont, John Henry Hopkins [Sr.] (1792–1868). Kenrick, a former seminary professor who would later become Archbishop of Baltimore, argued that the increasingly larger Roman Catholic Church preserved apostolic succession in a form unsullied by the Protestant Reformation. He had written the members of the Episcopal House of Bishops in 1838 urging them as individuals to join the Roman Catholic Church. The bishops should convert, he warned, before all their parishioners joined Rome. Kenrick had also written specifically to Hopkins in 1837 in order to criticize the Episcopal bishop's work on church history (*The Primitive Church*, 1835). Hopkins responded as an individual and on behalf of the church by suggesting that the Episcopal Church's English language doctrine and liturgy were more appropriate to the American setting than the Latin used by the Roman Catholic Church.[5]

Hopkins suggested a theme that would be sounded frequently by Episcopal authors as the century progressed. The reply, however, was not a sufficient answer to the rising interest in the Roman Catholic Church of some Episcopalians. Indeed, a number of them, including at least twenty-nine priests and deacons, and one bishop, joined the Roman Catholic Church in the three decades after 1840.[6] Their number included some prominent figures: Levi Silliman Ives (1797–1867), Bishop of North Carolina and son-in-law of John Henry Hobart; George Hobart Doane (1830–1905), the eldest son of Bishop George Washington Doane of New Jersey; and James Kent Stone (1840–1921), a former Kenyon professor whose father (John S. Stone, 1795–1882) would later serve as the first dean of the Episcopal Theological School (now the Episcopal Divinity School) in Cambridge, Massachusetts.

Roman Catholicism was not the only challenge to the rational orthodoxy of the Episcopal Church. The bishops and deputies at the 1844 General Convention were also beginning to grasp the implications of the English Oxford movement. The movement was in part a product of the British political situation in the 1830s. In that decade the British Parliament began to reorder the state church, adjusting the size of dioceses to conform to population shifts and transferring some functions that had been previously performed by the church to the civil service.

In keeping with this policy, the Parliament decreased the number of dioceses and bishops in Ireland in 1833. A group of scholars at Oriel College, Oxford that included John Keble (1792–1866), John Henry Newman (1801–90), Richard Froude (1803–36), and Edward Pusey (1800–82) objected, not to the decision itself, but to the way in which it was made. The action of the Parliament was all wrong, for it made the church little more than an arm of the secular government. Only the church could initiate such a reform.

Keble preached a rousing sermon in 1833 in which he called the Parliament's action "National Apostasy." Newman, Pusey, and Froude followed with a series of *Tracts for the Times* (1833–41) in which they examined the history and theology of the church. Their initial complaint was political and had little bearing on the American situation. As the tracts progressed, however, the Oxford theologians, or "Tractarians" (i.e., the authors of the tracts), began also to critique the prevailing patterns of Anglican theology of their day. The same patristic, pre-Reformation, and Reformation history of the church that provided examples of the independence of the church from the state also suggested theological and liturgical formulae that predated the Great Awakening and its stress upon adult experience. The Oxford theologians, finding little precedent for the renewal about which most rational orthodox Anglicans taught, complained that adult change of heart had become a new kind of works-righteousness. Christians, they warned, believed that a simple mental exercise would bring salvation. To avoid this danger they stressed the importance of baptismal regeneration and denied any separate integrity to adult renewal.[7]

Members of the evangelical party at the 1844 Convention, anxious to protect the adult renewal that they had always stressed in the baptismal covenant–adult renewal formula, proposed a blanket condemnation of both Roman Catholic and

141

Oxford theology. Bishop Charles P. McIlvaine of Ohio, whose commitment to evangelical doctrine was similar to that of his college classmate and long-time friend Charles Hodge (1797–1878), laid the groundwork for such an action in his *Oxford Divinity* (1841).[8] He charged that Oxford divinity was identical to that of the Roman Catholic Church and suggested further that both undermined the Protestant doctrine of justification by faith alone by questioning adult religious experience.

The senior high church leaders in the House of Bishops agreed to only a limited extent. The Tractarians, after all, had not directly attacked the baptismal element that they had always emphasized in the baptismal covenant–adult renewal pairing. High church leaders did, however, accept a pastoral letter composed by Presiding Bishop Philander Chase that reversed the mild tone of Bishop Griswold's 1838 pastoral. In the place of Griswold's call for "kindness and love" toward Roman Catholic immigrants, Chase warned of the "dreadful perversions" of Rome that undermined the "evangelical covenant."[9] The high church bishops were also willing to support an investigation of

Table 4. Response to the Oxford Movement in the House of Deputies (1844)

Dioceses voting for anti-Oxford Resolution[1]	Divided Dioceses[2]	Dioceses voting against Resolution[3]
Georgia	Kentucky	Alabama
Illinois	Louisiana	Connecticut
Maine	Massachusetts	Delaware
Michigan	Missouri	Florida
Mississippi	Pennsylvania	Indiana
New Hampshire	South Carolina	Maryland
Ohio		New Jersey
Rhode Island		New York
Virginia		North Carolina
		Tennessee
		Vermont
		Western New York

1. The resolution noted that "the minds of many of the Members of this Church . . . are sorely grieved and perplexed, by the alleged introduction among them of serious errors in doctrine and practice, having their origin in certain writings emanating chiefly from members of the University of Oxford," and asked the House of Bishops "to communicate with [the Deputies] . . . and to take such order thereon, as the nature and magnitude of the evil alluded to may seem to them to require." The motion failed for lack of a majority in either order. In the lay order, Eleven delegations voted in favor, eleven voted against, and one divided. In the clerical order, eight delegations supported, fifteen delegations opposed, and four delegations divided on the motion. See *Journal of the Proceedings of the Bishops, Clergy and Laity of the Protestant Episcopal Church in the United States of America in General Convention, . . . 1844* (New York: James A. Sparks, 1845), 63–64.

The vote for the resolution was unanimous in five states (Georgia, Maine, Ohio, and Virginia; and in Illinois in which only a clerical delegation voted). In Michigan and Rhode Island the laity voted for the resolution, but the clergy divided.

2. In Kentucky and South Carolina the clergy supported the resolution and the laity opposed. The reverse was true in Massachusetts and Missouri. In Louisiana the clerical delegation, which was the only one present, divided, as did both orders in Pennsylvania.

3. The vote was unanimous in both orders except in Florida and Tennessee, in which no laity voted, and in Indiana, in which the decision was decided by a plurality.

the faculty of General Theological Seminary that led to the departure of Professor John David Ogilby (1810–51).[10] They would not agree, however, to a total condemnation of the Oxford movement. There was too much in the tracts—particularly, the strong emphasis on the institution of the episcopacy—of which they approved.

Much the same thing happened in the House of Deputies, where evangelicals found that they had too few votes to adopt a resolution that alluded to "the alleged introduction . . . of serious errors in doctrine and practice, having their origin in certain writings emanating chiefly from members of the University of Oxford."[11] After a prolonged debate, evangelicals eventually agreed to a watered-down resolution that declared that the

> Liturgy, Offices, and Articles of the Church [were] sufficient exponents of her sense of the essential doctrines of Holy Scripture . . . and . . . that the General Convention [was] not a suitable tribunal for the trial and censure of . . . the errors of individuals.[12]

The deputies and bishops at the 1844 General Convention were unwilling to rule on the validity of the Oxford movement.

The convention's inaction did not, of course, resolve the debate about Oxford theology. The debate simply moved to other fora. During the next two decades, episcopal elections (the 1859 election of a missionary bishop for the Northwest), disciplinary trials (for bishops H.U. and B.T. Onderdonk in 1844 and George Washington Doane in 1852–53), and diocesan visitations (the much-postponed visit of evangelical Bishop Manton Eastburn of Massachusetts to Tractarian Church of the Advent in Boston) all became occasions for party wrangling between those who opposed the Oxford movement and those who gave it some measure of approval.

The continuing debate also contributed to the creation of new institutions. A trio of new seminaries shared the high church orientation of General Seminary. Three General students from the class of 1841 founded the first of these, Nashotah House (Wisconsin). In 1854, Connecticut bishop John Williams (1817–99) created Berkeley Divinity School (Berkeley-at-Yale Divinity School since 1971) from the theology department of Trinity College (Hartford). Six years later, James Lloyd Breck (1818–76), one of three General graduates to found Nashotah, created Seabury Divinity School (Seabury-Western after a 1933 merger with Chicago's Western Seminary) in Faribault, Minnesota. The energetic Mr. Breck, who was also a missionary to the Ojibwa (Gull Lake, Minnesota) and a founder of six parishes in California, was unsuccessful in his attempt to found a fourth new seminary on the West Coast (Benicia, California).

Evangelicals founded two new seminaries and several societies of their own. In 1862, Philadelphia evangelicals, unable to send students to Virginia during the Civil War, formed the Philadelphia Divinity School. In 1867, New England evangelicals followed suit, creating the Episcopal Theological School in Cambridge Massachusetts (now the Episcopal Divinity School in Cambridge as a result of a 1974 merger with Philadelphia). The new societies included the Evangelical Knowledge Society (1847), the Missionary Society for the West (1851), and the American Church Missionary Society (1859).

The Civil War and the Changing Character of the Church

During the American Civil War (1861–65) Episcopalians met in two separate bodies: the General Convention of the Protestant Episcopal Church in the United States of America and the General Council of the Confederate States of America. The latter body, organized largely as a result of the efforts of Bishop Leonidas Polk of Louisiana and Bishop Stephen Elliott (1806–66) of Georgia, met from 1861 to 1865. When the fighting ended, the church reunited (1865).[13] It soon became evident, however, that the war had changed the church in important ways. The character of the church's ministry to black Americans changed, particularly in the South. In addition, the war affected the church's theological parties.

The Protestant Episcopal Freedman's Commission

The number of black members of the Episcopal Church had been rapidly rising in the years immediately preceding the Civil War, largely due to ministry to slaves in the southern states. Early in the century, southern Episcopalians had provided religious instruction for small numbers of house servants

145

who attended church with them, though often in segregated balconies. It was not until the 1840s and 1850s that slave holders began a major effort to evangelize the larger number of slaves engaged primarily in agriculture. Slave owners, particularly in the lower regions of South Carolina, constructed approximately one hundred plantation chapels. As a result, the number of black communicants in the South rose rapidly from 489 in 1830 (as compared to to 5,992 whites) to 5,828 (as compared to 22,051 whites) in 1860, and the number of black baptized persons reached approximately 35,000. By 1860, black communicants were more numerous in the Diocese of South Carolina than white.[14]

The Civil War both ended the institution of slavery on which much of the church's work was predicated and destroyed the financial base for new forms of evangelism. The percentage of black Episcopalians fell, therefore, in the years immediately following the war.

The General Convention tried to address the changed circumstances in the South by establishing the Protestant Episcopal Freedman's Commission (1865–78). The body, a department of the Domestic and Foreign Missionary Society also referred to as the Commission of Home Missions to Colored People, initially concentrated on founding schools. In 1868 it reported to the General Convention that it had established sixty-five institutions with 5,500 students. The number of students fell to about 2,500, however, as contributions declined ($75,033 in 1865–68, approximately $50,000 in 1869–71, $43,944 in 1872–74, and $43,949 in 1875–77), and the commission turned its primary focus to congregational development. By 1877, it noted that there were thirty-seven congregations, fifteen black clergy, and fourteen candidates for ordination in the old slave states.[15] In 1878, the year after Congress ended Reconstruction, the Missionary Society dissolved the Freedman's Commission and transferred continuing efforts to its committee on domestic missions.

Church Parties

The war had distracted Episcopalians from the church party wrangling that had preoccupied them since 1844. When it concluded, however, it became obvious to many that the fighting had done more than simply interrupt the dispute. It had accelerated the demise of rational orthodoxy and the alteration of the party character of the Episcopal Church.

On the high church side, the war had led many to rethink one of the central principles laid down by Bishop Hobart. Hobart had carefully distinguished religious responsibility from civic duty. Believing that the apostolic tradition provided the church with a deeper kind of truth than that produced by the political process, he had refused to vote and tried to keep his church apart from secular moral campaigns. Hobart's successors in the North simply could not, however, remain aloof of a war that claimed the lives of many of their children. Hobart's old parish, Trinity Church, New York, began to fly the American flag, and the House of Bishops in the northern states began to issue pastoral letters endorsing the Union cause.[16] By the war's end, Hobart's rational high church principles no longer rang true. It would take more than the ideal of apostolic succession to capture the hearts of the postwar generation.

The evangelical party was affected as well. While much of the high church strength had been concentrated in the North, evangelical leadership had come from both North and South. The war divided and, therefore, weakened the movement. At the same time, the war's outcome undermined the rational orthodox presumptions of the southern evangelicals. Before the war, Episcopalians had been a part of the cultural leadership in the South. In southern cities, their clergy, who were well educated, were second in number only to the Methodists.[17] Robert E. Lee (1807–70) and other southern leaders were members of the denomination. Southern Episcopalians supported the Confederacy and enlisted in its armed forces. In North Carolina the Episcopal Church provided fifteen chaplains for the Confederate army; in Virginia, it sent twenty-nine.[18] Bishop Leonidas Polk of Louisiana served as a major general and died in battle.

With the southern defeat, evangelical Episcopalians lost prestige, financial resources, educational structures, and, to some degree, the very conviction that their own process of reasoning led to truth. After the war, the most aggressive leadership in the evangelical party came from northern and border states. Within a decade of the war's end, however, evangelical leadership in those areas was weakened as well. Frustrated by their church's inability to root out Oxford theology, a small number of evangelicals, led by Bishop George David Cummins (1822–76) of Kentucky and Chicago priest Charles E. Cheney (1836–1916), formed a separate Reformed Episcopal Church (1873).[19]

New Options for the Episcopal Church: Evangelical Catholics and Anglican Catholics

In the years immediately before and after the Civil War, Episcopalians began to search for alternatives to the fading high church and evangelical parties. The two most important of these new alternatives were evangelical catholicism and Anglican catholicism. The two approaches shared common elements; advocates of both claimed the word *catholic* for the Episcopal Church, introduced more ornate forms of worship, and distanced themselves from American revivalism. There were, however, significant differences between them, particularly in their understanding of justification by faith alone and ecumenism.

In matters liturgical, both groups drew much of their inspiration from the Cambridge University. At a time when the advocates of the Oxford movement had been primarily concerned about theology and the relationship of the church and the state, John Mason Neale (1818–66) and others at Cambridge had formed the Cambridge Camden Society. Members of the society initially encouraged walking tours of English churches.

When, however, their tours revealed pews that faced away from the altar, chancels that had been closed off, and even a senior warden who climbed upon an altar to open windows during worship services, they began to campaign for liturgical reform. Within two years after its incorporation in 1839, the society's membership included sixteen bishops, and its finances were on firm enough a footing to justify publication of a regular magazine, *The Ecclesiologist*.[20]

The members of the Cambridge Society favored a careful examination of the ritual and architecture of the Church of England. Out of their examination came a new appreciation for elements of liturgical worship that had in many cases been abandoned by Anglicans in the sixteenth or seventeenth centuries. Society members advocated, for example, the use of surplices (in disuse in parts of England since the seventeenth century) and cassocks (rare since the eighteenth). They advocated wearing the surplice, rather than the more usual gown, in the pulpit and also introduced surplices for use by choirs. Occasionally, their efforts touched off popular animosity, as in the Exeter surplice riots of 1840.[21]

The Cambridge Society's liturgical revival quickly crossed the Atlantic. Advertisements in the *Church Almanac*, the nineteenth-century Episcopal handbook, indicated, for example, a gradual acceptance of English innovations in clerical dress. In 1851, *Almanac* advertisements by Nelson Jarvis, merchant tailor of New York, listed cassocks and surplices along with clerical frock coats, waistcoats or vests, gowns, scarfs, and bands that were more typical of Protestant clergy and had been worn by Episcopalians earlier in the century.[22] By 1864, Mr. Jarvis had expanded his line of goods to include bishop's robes, clerical and cassock vests, and stoles.[23] Two years later, an English firm further expanded the line of goods available by advertising "chasubles, dalmatics, copes etc., made in accordance with Anglican Patterns of the 12th and the 13th centuries."[24] Presiding Bishop (1865–68) John Henry Hopkins [Sr.], gave a nod of approval to this and other liturgical innovations in his *Law of Ritualism* (1866), which suggested that there were

usable, but not mandatory Old Testament models for sung services, incense, altar candles, and eucharistic vestments.

As the title of a second book by Hopkins indicated (*Essay
on Gothic Architecture,* 1836), a rising interest in gothic architecture crossed the Atlantic as well. The New York
Ecclesiological Society (1848–55), formed at General
Theological Seminary, popularized gothic style, and such
architects as Richard Upjohn (1802–78) and Henry Congdon

Fig. 25. Trinity Church, Portland, Connecticut (1873–88),
designed by Henry Congdon.

(1834–1922) applied it in the design of specific churches.
Upjohn, a founder and early president (1857–76) of the
American Institute of Architecture, planned a number of
churches, including a new building for Trinity Church, New
York (1841–46).[25] Congdon was responsible for the construction or redesign of more than twenty-five churches between
1860 and 1900.[26]

William Augustus Muhlenberg (1797–1877), the prototypi-
cal evangelical catholic, introduced daily (rather than weekly)
offices, weekly (rather than quarterly) celebrations of the
eucharist, and the first vested boy's choirs in New York City in
his Church of the Holy Communion.[27] Muhlenberg retained,

however, the emphasis on personal experience that had been typical of Protestant theology since the Great Awakening; the church was the institution that enabled individuals to embrace and lay hold of a saving faith in Jesus Christ.[28] What marked the Episcopal Church as different from other Protestant denominations was not this premise but the means by which it pursued it; it fostered personal faith with ritual worship, rather than

Fig. 26.
William Augustus Muhlenberg

with the "new measure" revival techniques introduced by Presbyterian Charles Grandison Finney (1792– 1875).

Like members of the evangelical party earlier in the century, Muhlenberg was an advocate of ecumenical relations with other Protestants. When, for example, the Episcopal *Church Review* criticized John Williamson Nevin (1803–86) of Mercersburg German Reformed Seminary for suggesting that the historical development of the church involved more than the apostolic succession that the Episcopal Church had pre-served, Muhlenberg came to Nevin's defense. Elsewhere, Muhlenberg held out the hope of what he called "the church idea"—the idea that a single more catholic institution might one day embrace all Christians.[29]

Muhlenberg never formed a church party in the narrow sense of the word. He was, nonetheless, a tireless proponent of evangelical catholicism. He used the term, which he had coined, as the title of a periodical that he began to publish in 1851. Two years later he tested some of his ideas with a memorial (resolution) to the House of Bishops. In it, Muhlenberg suggested that the Episcopal Church both relax "somewhat the rigidity of her Liturgical services" and create a comprehensive (Protestant) church institution for which the Episcopal Church would provide apostolic succession.[30] Though the only actions that the General Convention took on

Muhlenberg's proposal were the appointment of a commission and the publication of their deliberations (*Memorial Papers*), the memorial proved an effective means of propagating Muhlenberg's evangelical catholicism. Among the many who came to share his general perspective were Alonzo Potter (1800–1865) and James Craik (1806–86). A former professor at Union College, Schenectady, New York, Potter had been elected Bishop of Pennsylvania in 1845. Craik, the son of George Washington's doctor, was a rector of Christ Church, Louisville, Kentucky who would later serve as the president of the House of Deputies (1862–74). Potter was a member of the commission that investigated the memorial; both contributed to the *Memorial Papers*.[31]

Potter, who entered the Episcopal Church while working in Philadelphia soon after his graduation from college, had a thoroughly ecumenical background. His parents were Quakers; his wife (Sarah Maria Nott), the daughter of a Congregational clergyman (Dr. Eliphalet Nott, president of Union College); and a good friend (Francis Wayland, 1796–1865), the Baptist president of Brown University. Potter heartily endorsed, therefore, Muhlenberg's interest in ecumenism and rejected the high church (and Anglican catholic) insistence upon apostolic succession for the validity of the church. By the same token, however, he believed that evangelicals erred when they resisted the tide of liturgical change. As Potter explained in the chapter that he contributed to the *Memorial Papers,* "too stringent a demand for uniformity in doctrine and worship" only created unnecessary divisions in the church.[32]

Like Muhlenberg, Potter believed the focus on personal morality, which had been typical of Episcopalians earlier in the century, was also too narrow. For him, the Christian faith had to have impact on all of human life. He spoke out against slavery, helped organize a church hospital, encouraged prison visitation, and supported a parish (St. Mark's, Frankford) visitation of unchurched working-class families.[33] He was also mindful of the need for the church to expand beyond its geographical limits; his visit to an Episcopal parish in Aspinwall (later Colón), Panamá, was the first by an Episcopal bishop to Central America.[34] Potter died in 1865, but his family continued to play an important role in the church long afterward. His brother (Horatio Potter, 1802–87) and son (Henry Codman Potter, 1835–1908) were successive bishops of the Diocese of New York.

James Craik shared Muhlenberg and Potter's vision of a broader ministry for the church. He supported, for example, the free church movement—the attempt by Muhlenberg to substitute voluntary offerings for the renting of pews that was the general rule in nineteenth-century Protestant churches.[35] Craik's most interesting contribution, however, may have been his attempt to provide a theological grounding for the evangelical catholic vision. Well read in English theology, he was one of the first American Episcopalians to work with the incarnational themes developed by F. D. Maurice (1805–72).

Maurice had argued in *The Kingdom of Christ* (1837) that the incarnation provided a key to escaping a narrow personal understanding of faith. For Maurice, Christ's coming into flesh changed not only the character of people, but human relationships and institutions, and nature itself. Christian efforts to deal seriously with the corporate problems of modern society were, therefore, not just a working out of the logical implication of a renewed soul; they were a participation in the Incarnation. Craik suggested to American readers in his *The Divine Life and the New Birth* (1869) that such a perspective would free the church from doctrinal debates on the chronology of personal salvation (Was baptism or adult renewal more important?) and focus new attention on the work of the church in the world.

Leading Anglican catholics (who also referred to themselves as "advanced" members of the high church party, "ritualists," or, somewhat later, "Anglo-Catholics") included James DeKoven (1831–79), the warden of Racine College, Wisconsin, and the party's floor leader in General Convention; Ferdinand C. Ewer (1826–83), the rector of Grace Church, San Francisco, Christ Church, New York, and St. Ignatius', New

York, and the party's most prolific author; John Henry Hopkins, Jr. (1820–91), the priest and musician best known for his "We Three Kings"; and Charles C. Grafton (1832–1912), rector of the Church of the Advent, Boston, and the second Bishop of Fond du Lac. While they shared some basic convictions with the evangelical catholics, they disagreed with them rather strongly on some points. (Craik and DeKoven,

Fig. 27. James DeKoven

for example, carried on an extended debate.) Similarly, though the Anglican catholics shared some sympathies with the older high church party, they parted company at many points and referred to the older party at times as "high and dry."[36]

The Anglican catholics rejected ecumenism with other Protestants in favor of a vision of the basic identity of the Episcopal Church with Roman Catholicism and Eastern Orthodoxy. For the older high church party, it had been enough for the Episcopal Church to guard apostolic succession in a Protestant nation in which it was not properly appreciated. For Anglican catholics, in contrast, the apostolic succession was only the starting point. For them the basic catholic identity of the Episcopal Church had been obscured by Protestant errors, which had to be removed if the church were to have life. Ewer explained in his *Catholicity in its Relationship to Protestantism and Romanism* (1878) that:

> a sect, from the time it is cut off from the Catholic Church, never recovers; it withers; its career is always downward to death. But the Anglican Church shows that it has Catholic life. For even after having been overwhelmed with Protestants in pulpit, Episcopal throne, Theological Seminary, and pew, she is nevertheless recovering; for she is rooted in the Catholic Tree; and against no part of the Catholic Church can the gates of Hell prevail.[37]

The church's very life depended on its connection with a tradition that it was in danger of losing.

Like the evangelical catholics, the Anglican catholics found English incarnational theology a useful tool in interpreting their tradition. They relied, however, on Oxford author Robert Isaac Wilberforce (*The Doctrine of the Incarnation,* 1848). Parting company with F.D. Maurice's *Kingdom of Christ,* Wilberforce had linked the Incarnation with the catholic sacramental system. The benefits of the Incarnation were, he suggested, transmitted through the baptism, the eucharist, and priestly absolution. It was for that reason that the Anglican catholics regarded the reintroduction of weekly (or daily) celebration of the eucharist and of private confession as so important. They were literally the channels by which Christ redeemed the world.

Evangelicals and evangelical catholics, who treasured their ties to other Protestant churches, and high church Episcopalians, who had never understood themselves as surrendering their catholic principles, were all somewhat uneasy with this Anglican catholic approach. Weakened as the parties were, however, they were unable to dislodge the Anglican catholic party from the church. Evangelicals, evangelical catholics, and the older high church party did compromise at the General Convention of 1871 on a statement (drafted by high church Bishop William R. Whittingham of Maryland and evangelical Charles P. McIlvaine) that rejected the tenet that "moral change" took place in infant baptism.[38] Three years later, the convention condemned "any actions of adoration of or toward the Elements."[39] In addition, individuals—often high church leaders irked by the imputation that they did not understand catholic principles—took actions against Anglican catholics. The faculty of Nashotah House, for example, successfully blocked the approval of James DeKoven's election as Bishop of Wisconsin (1874) and Illinois (1875).

Despite such efforts, however, the Anglican catholics were able to establish beachheads in Baltimore (Mt. Calvary), Philadelphia (St. Mark's and St. Clement's), Boston (Church

155

of the Advent), and New York (St. Mary the Virgin and St. Alban's), and establish an Anglican catholic stronghold in the Midwest, in such areas as the new Diocese of Fond du Lac (1874) in northern Wisconsin.

An Anglican Tradition

One consequence of the continuing discussion about the Episcopal Church and its faith was that Episcopalians increasingly came to see their church as in a category by itself.

Early in the nineteenth century, most Episcopalians would have agreed with John Lawrence Mosheim's *Ecclesiastical History*. The text, suggested by Bishop White and used in Episcopal seminaries, classified the Anglican Church as part of the Reformed tradition.[40] As the century progressed and Episcopalians became more confident of their own denomination, however, some began to search for alternative ways of understanding their relationship to other churches. In the 1840s, Bishop John Williams of Connecticut prepared an American edition of Edward Harold Browne's *Exposition of the Thirty-nine Articles*, which suggested Episcopal views on predestination were more Lutheran than Reformed. In 1862, the General Convention established a standing committee on intercourse with the Church of Sweden exploring the relationship of the Episcopal Church with that branch of Lutheranism that had preserved the historic episcopate. Other Episcopalians suggested common ties with the Orthodox churches; the 1862 General Convention also created a joint committee to communicate with what it called the "Russo-Greek Church." Yet others were attracted by James DeKoven's suggestion that the Episcopal Church affirm its basic catholic identity by dropping the word *Protestant* from its official title.

The question as to whether the Episcopal Church was more like the Lutheran, Orthodox, or Roman Catholic churches than like the Reformed was answered in part by the council of bishops summoned to Lambeth Palace in England in 1867 by Charles Longley (Archbishop of Canterbury, 1862–68).

Seventy-six of the one hundred forty-four bishops in the Anglican Communion accepted Longley's invitation. Longley's rationale for the gathering was occasional; the bishops discussed a dispute over the interpretation of Genesis between Archbishop of Capetown Robert Gray (1809–72) and Bishop of Natal John Colenso (1814–83). Those who participated, however, recognized the value of scheduling such meetings on a regular basis. With the exception of an interruption during World War I, and another during World War II, Lambeth Conferences have met in every decade since.

Buoyed by the fellowship at such events, American Episcopalians increasingly saw their denomination as a tradition in its own right. They were no longer part of a Reformed, Lutheran, Roman Catholic, or Orthodox expression of faith. Though small in the American setting, the Anglican Church was itself a major religious tradition. In the 1880s, copies of the *Church Almanac* made this point clear by including "Statistics on the Anglican Communion" that showed a world wide denomination with 205 bishops, 28,000 clergy, and a ministry to a huge population that the *Almanac's* editors creatively figured by totaling the entire populations of England, Wales, Scotland, Ireland, India, and the United States.[41]

William I. Kip (1811–93) captured this new Episcopal self-understanding in his *Double Witness of the Church* (1843). Apologies earlier in the century, such as John Henry Hobart's *Apostolic Order,* had identified the Episcopal Church chiefly in terms of the apostolic succession and the latitude on the Arminian-Calvinist debate that distinguished it from the Congregationalist and Presbyterian churches. By midcentury, however, Kip felt it necessary to contrast the Episcopal Church not only with Protestantism but with Roman Catholicism as well. For him, the Episcopal Church was a separate entity that had a witness to make to both traditions. Running through twenty-four editions by 1898, *Double Witness* became the best selling Episcopal tract of the late nineteenth century. Its immediate popularity contributed to Kip's election as first Missionary Bishop of California (1853).

Changing Roles for Women

The lot of women in the eastern states, and particularly in New England, was rapidly changing in the years around 1840.[42] In the colonial period, most nonfarming enterprises had been carried on in the home. Men and women worked together in a variety of endeavors. Those businesses large enough to employ nonfamily members took in apprentices who lived in the household like members of an extended family. By the nineteenth century, however, the British industrial revolution had begun to reach America. Factory capitalism began to replace cottage industries.

Fig. 28. Confirmation by Levi Silliman Ives Bishop of North Carolina 1831-53

The new factories influenced American home life in two ways: they took men out of the homes as factory workers, and they produced goods inexpensively enough to make certain home production techniques uneconomical. Married women were left at home with little demand for some of their traditional activities. Unmarried women, a group whose numbers swelled after the Civil War drastically reduced the number of eligible males, did enter the marketplace in increasing numbers. Often, however, they did not find the employment available to them particularly rewarding. Both groups of women, therefore, turned to the church, hoping to find within it an avenue for meaningful work and an assurance of their value. They found that evangelical catholics, who were anxious to cooperate with others in ministry to the social order, and Anglican catholics, who were attracted to medieval monasticism, were among their most eager allies.

In 1855, Mary Black and Catherine Minard accepted the offer of Baltimore clergyman Horace Stringfellow and entered the female diaconate. Stringfellow, the rector of St. Andrew's Church in Baltimore, had been in England earlier in the year, where he had spoken with participants in the European revival of the female diaconate.[43] Stringfellow became convinced that deaconesses were the best solution to the increasing demand for a social ministry that confronted him in his community. Black and Minard answered his appeal for interested candidates, and with the support of Bishop Whittingham of Maryland, they began a nursing ministry at what they soon called Saint Andrew's Infirmary. Others in the Episcopal Church would follow. Bishop Richard H. Wilmer (1816–1900) of Alabama supported an effort by deaconesses to found an orphanage in 1864. Three years later, Mr. and Mrs. William Welsh of Philadelphia spearheaded an effort to found a training school for women (Bishop Potter Memorial House), which by 1872 had trained thirty-seven persons. In that year, Bishop Abram Littlejohn (1824–1901) set apart seven women as deaconess in Long Island.[44]

The bishops and deputies at General Convention began to discuss the female diaconate in 1868 but did not finally adopt a canon on the diaconate until 1889.[45] The new canon covered qualifications (a devout, unmarried communicant of twenty-five or older with recommendations of two presbyters and twelve laypersons), work (assisting in the care of the poor and sick, religious training of the young and others, and working for moral reformation), administration (appointed and given a specific assignment by a bishop, and serving under his authority or that of a rector), resignation (at any time), discipline (for cause by a bishop after a hearing), and liturgy (the form of induction to be specified). Soon after, Episcopalians established training schools for deaconesses in New York (New York Training School for Deaconesses, 1890), Philadelphia

(Church Training and Deaconess School of the Diocese of Pennsylvania, 1891), and Berkeley, California (Deaconess Training School of the Pacific, 1908).[46]

While most Protestant churches accepted the revival of the female diaconate, the Episcopal Church stood alone among Protestant churches in reviving monastic orders for women. On All Saints' Day 1845, Anne Ayres (1816–96), an English-born parishioner of William Muhlenberg's Church of the Holy Communion in New York City, dedicated herself to monastic vows, becoming the first American nun in the Anglican tradition.[47] Others joined her, forming the Sisterhood of the Holy Communion (1852), which had an active ministry to the sick at St. Luke's Hospital.

The charitable efforts in which deaconesses and nuns were engaged were often made possible by female philanthropists. Many projects at the Church of the Holy Communion were made possible, for example, by Muhlenberg's sister, Mary A. Rogers, who was a wealthy widow. Her contributions made it possible for the congregation to function without pew rents.[48] With Rogers, moreover, Ayres had first come to the Church of the Holy Communion.

Fig. 29. Constance and Companions, Church of the Ascension, Knoxville, Tennessee

Some Episcopalians felt that female monasticism was a Roman Catholic institution that did not belong in their church. The valiant actions of the sisters of the Community of St. Mary did much, however, to quiet such criticism. The community, formed in New York City in 1863 by Harriet Starr Cannon (1823–96) and other women who wanted a more intense community life than that which they had found in Ayres's Sisterhood of the Holy Communion, had a branch house in Memphis, Tennessee, at the time of the city's 1878 yellow fever epidemic. The sisters and their lay associates, disregarding dangers to their own health, cared for the sick and both black and white children who were orphaned by the disease. Sister Constance, three other sisters, and one lay associate died as a result. Such heroism won over many critics.[49]

Two years after the Memphis epidemic, the *Church Almanac* listed thirteen Episcopal sisterhoods. Of these four were in New York City, and two were in Baltimore. The remaining seven orders were located in Washington, D.C.; Newark; St. Louis; Albany; Boston; New Orleans; and Louisville. The sisters in these institutions worked in hospitals, schools, and institutions for the poor.[50]

In contrast to these women's orders, monastic institutions for men were fewer in number and were later in organization. The English Cowley Fathers (Society of St. John the Evangelist), for example, established their first American branch in 1872, twenty-seven years after Anne Ayres took her monastic vows. Men interested in monastic orders often looked to the female example for guidance. Father James O.S. Huntington (1854–1935) modeled his Order of the Holy Cross (1881), the first American Episcopal religious order for men, after the example of the Sisters of St. John the Baptist (of New York City).[51]

As was the case with deaconesses, the General Convention followed, rather than led, in the formation of monastic orders. Not until 1913 did the Convention adopt its first canon on the subject.[52]

Frontier Missions

In 1858 prospectors found gold in the area around Pikes Peak in what was then western Kansas. As the news spread, settlers headed to the area that is now Colorado. Among them was a sixty-three-year-old widower named John Henry Kehler. He had heard of the area from his son, then the sheriff of a western Kansas county. Kehler was an Episcopal priest with twenty years of experience in Virginia and Maryland. Reaching the town of Denver, he helped organize the first Episcopal congregation, serving it until he was recruited as an army chaplain.

At the same time that Kehler was moving west, Joseph C. Talbot (1816–83) was also moving. Elected Bishop of the Missionary District of the North West, he referred to himself as the "Bishop of All Outdoors." His territory included Nebraska, North Dakota, South Dakota, Wyoming, Colorado, New Mexico, Arizona, Utah, Montana, and Idaho.

Both Kehler and Bishop Talbot noted the importance of female participation in the frontier congregations. Talbot's first seven confirmands in Colorado were all women. Kehler noted that one of the important sources of financial support for his parish was a group of "devout women always given to good works" who had "secured $165" through a mite society.[53]

Their experience was not unusual. Women often exercised the real power in frontier parishes, leaving male parishioners in figurehead vestry positions. The women of All Saints Parish in Northfield,

Fig. 30. Enmegahbowh

Minnesota, for example, organized the parish, recruited men to serve in the vestry, raised funds for a church building and rectory, taught in the Sunday school, and provided for congregational music. Their experience was repeated in numerous frontier parishes.[54]

Episcopalians on the frontier attempted to recapture some of the leadership in the ministry to Native Americans that SPG clergy had provided before the Revolution. Enmegahbowh, an Ottawa Indian ordained a deacon by Bishop Kemper in 1859, joined with Bishop Henry Benjamin Whipple (1822–1901) in establishing an active ministry for the Episcopal Church in native American communities in Minnesota. After eight years in the diaconate, Enmegahbowh was ordained a priest by Bishop Whipple (June 20, 1867). Two years later Paul Mazakute would become the first Dakota (Sioux) priest. In 1881, Oakerhater (literally "Making Medicine," d. 1931) became the first Cheyenne deacon. His conversion was the result of contact with a circle of Episcopalians (many of them vacationing) in St. Augustine, Florida, where he was imprisoned at Fort Marion for his role in the 1874 battle of Adobe Walls. Alice Pendleton, daughter of Francis Scott Key, visited Oakerhater regularly in order to talk about the Christian faith. Captain Pratt of the military prison encouraged Bible study and allowed Oakerhater and other Indian prisoners to give archery lessons to women in the community. (Pratt became so

Fig. 31. Indian Prisoners and Ladies Archery Club by Oakerhater

interested in the American Indians that he later served as the first superintendent of the Carlisle Institute in Pennsylvania, a school for Indians that Alice Pendleton's husband, Ohio senator George Hunt Pendleton, was instrumental in establishing.) When Oakerhater expressed interest in sharing his Christian faith with others of his tribe, Deaconess Mary Douglass Burnham (1823–1904) arranged for theological study in New

York. Oakerhater, who took the English name David Pendleton, was one of the first Christian missionaries in the Indian Territory (Oklahoma).[55]

By 1880, the Episcopal Church was a very different institution than it had been in 1840. The rational approach of earlier in the century had given way, and for many the Episcopal Church became more identifiable for its focus on worship and social ministry than for its doctrine. When Harriet Beecher Stowe (1811–96), an author with a continuing interest in the Episcopal Church despite the fact that her father and husband were Congregational clergymen, wrote in *The Minister's Wooing* (1859) that the friend of a bride-to-be "dress[ed] the best room . . . [with] evergreens and . . . wreathes, and . . . green boughs over the pictures, so that the room looked just like the Episcopal church at Christmas," most of her readers understood.[56]

NOTES

1. E. Brooks Holifield, *A History of Pastoral Care in America: From Salvation to Self-Realization* (Nashville: Abingdon Press, 1983), 113.

2. Sydney E. Ahlstrom, *A Religious History of the American People* (New Haven: Yale University Press, 1972), 517; Robert Currie, Alan Gilbert, and Lee Horsley, *Churches and Churchgoers: Patterns of Church Growth in the British Isles since 1700* (Oxford: Clarendon Press, 1977), 4.

3. Ahlstrom, *Religious History,* 518; Currie, *Churches,* 4.

4. Ahlstrom, *Religious History,* 548.

5. The debate between Hopkins and Kenrick lasted over thirty years. Hopkins followed his *The Church of Rome Contrasted* (1837) with a series of letters to Kenrick, which were published collectively as *The End of the Controversy Controverted* (1854). A decade later he wrote *A Candid Examination of the Question of Whether the Pope of Rome is the Great AntiChrist,* which appeared posthumously in 1868. Kenrick replied with *The Primacy of the Apostolic See* (1838), *A Review of the Second Letter . . . of the Right Rev. John Henry* [Hopkins] (1843), and *A Vindication of the Catholic Church* (1855). For Hopkins's argument on the superiority of the Episcopal Church in American culture, see *The End of Controversy Controverted,* 2 vols. (New York: Pudney & Russell, 1854), 1:17. For an account of the controversy from a Roman Catholic perspective, see Margaret Mary Reher, *Catholic Intellectual Life in America* (New York: Macmillan, 1989), 38–39.

6. E. Clowes Chorley, *Men and Movements in the American Episcopal Church* (New York: Charles Scribner's Sons, 1946), 224.

7. Robert W. Prichard, "Theological Consensus in the Episcopal Church" (Ph.D. diss., Emory University, 1983), 258–69.

8. Charles Hodge, *The Way of Life,* ed. Mark A. Noll (New York: Paulist Press, 1987), 8.

9. *Pastoral Letters from the House of Bishops etc.* (Philadelphia: Edward C. Biddle, 1845), 229, 264–66.

10. Rumors had reached the General Convention of conversions to Rome from the student body at General. Fearing that improper teaching may have been the cause of the conversions, a group of vis-

itors appointed by the House of Bishops addressed a series of questions to the faculty. The bishops soon narrowed their interest to one man, John David Ogilby. Ogilby, the professor of ecclesiastical history, was the heir apparent to Bird Wilson (1777–1859), the aging professor of divinity. The bishops learned that Ogilby used Newman's *History of Arianism* (the only text by an Oxford movement theologian on any Episcopal seminary course list) and that he was unwilling to condemn the Roman Catholic Church as heretical "in the strictest sense." They took no formal action against him, but their investigation so discredited Ogilby that the Board of Trustees convinced Bird Wilson to delay retirement until they found someone other than Ogilby for the chair of divinity. Ogilby pled ill health and resigned. See the *Journal of the General Convention . . . 1844*, 239–242.

11. *Journal of the General Convention of the Protestant Episcopal Church in the United States . . . 1844* (printed for the Convention, 1844), 64.

12. Ibid, 64–65.

13. After the fighting ended, Presiding Bishop John Henry Hopkins (Vermont) wrote to Bishop Atkinson (North Carolina), inviting him to the October 1865 General Convention. Atkinson, who among the southern bishops had been the least enthusiastic about the formation of a separate church, attended the Convention along with his nephew, Henry Lay (Bishop of Arkansas). Some southern bishops were more hesitant about reunion. Bishop Wilmer of Alabama, for example, directed his congregations not to pray for the president. By May 1866, however, all the Southern dioceses had indicated their return to the General Convention. See D. Murphey, "The Spirit of Primitive Fellowship: The Reunion of the Church," *Historical Magazine of the Protestant Episcopal Church* 17 (December 1948):435–448; and Edwin S. Gaustad, ed., *A Documentary History of Religion in America Since 1865* (Grand Rapids: Eerdmans, 1983), 6–8.

14. Stiles Bailey Lines, "Slaves and Churchmen: The Work of the Episcopal Church among Southern Negroes, 1830–1860" (Ph.D. diss., Columbia University, 1960), i, 240–2.

15. *Journal of the Proceedings of the Bishops, Clergy, and Laity of the Protestant Episcopal Church in the United States of American, Assembled in a General Convention . . . 1865* (Boston: William A.

Hall, 1865), p. 189; *Journal . . . 1818,* 369; *Journal . . . 1871,* 215; *Journal . . . 1878,* 493–4.

16. Robert Bruce Mullin, *Episcopal Vision/ American Reality: High Church Theology and Social Thought in Evangelical America* (New Haven: Yale University Press, 1986), 195–211.

17. E. Brooks Holifield, *The Gentlemen Theologians: American Theology in Southern Culture, 1795–1860* (Durham, N.C.: Duke University Press, 1978), 26.

18. Lawrence Foushee London and Sarah McCulloh Lemmon, eds., *The Episcopal Church in North Carolina, 1701–1959* (Raleigh: Episcopal Diocese of North Carolina, 1987), 245–6.

19. The immediate cause of the division was a fight over the language of the baptismal office. Cheney, the rector of Christ Church, Chicago, was one among a number of evangelical clergy who had begun to omit the word *regeneration* from the baptism of infants. In 1869, Cheney's bishop, Henry John Whitehouse (1803–74) of Illinois, brought charges against him for the omission. Bishop McIlvaine of Ohio and eight other evangelical bishops drafted an appeal for leniency; Whitehouse responded by suspending Cheney from the ministry. McIlvaine and high church Bishop William Whittingham of Maryland worked out a compromise statement on baptism at the 1871 General Convention that quieted some evangelical complaints. After McIlvaine's death in 1873, however, Cheney and Bishop Cummins led the way in the formation of a separate denomination. Cummins shared Cheney's concern about baptismal language. While he had not been one of the original nine bishops to sign the McIlvaine plea for leniency, he had later added his name to the statement. The Reformed Episcopal Church adopted a new prayer book, which was modeled after the 1785–86 *Proposed Book.* It did not include the word regeneration in the baptismal office.

20. James McAllister, "Architectural Change in the Diocese of Virginia?" *Historical Magazine of the Protestant Episcopal Church* 65 (September 1976):297–323.

21. Janet Mayo, *A History of Ecclesiastical Dress* (New York: Holmes & Meier, 1984), 84, 88, 96–99.

22. *The Church Alamanac for the Year of Our Lord 1851* (New York: The Protestant Episcopal Tract Society, 1851), n.p.

23. *Church Almanac . . . 1864,* 65.

24. *Church Almanac . . . 1866,* 78.

25. Dumas Malone, ed., *Dictionary of American Biography,* (New York: Charles Scribner's Sons, 1953), s.v. "Richard Michell Upjohn" by Talbot Faulkner Hamlin.

26. Anne Pettit, "The Architecture of Henry Martyn Congdon (1834–1922)" (master's thesis, George Washington University, 1990).

27. Anne Ayres, *The Life and Work of William Augustus Muhlenberg* (New York: Harper & Brothers, 1880), pp. 223–25.

28. After reading the Oxford theologians, Muhlenberg reflected that his faith rested on "the solid rock of Evangelical truth, as republished by the Reformers." See Ayres, *Muhlenberg,* 173.

29. Ibid., 239; John F. Woolverton, "John Williamson Nevin and the Episcopalians: The Debate on the 'Church Question,' 1851–1874, *Historical Magazine of the Protestant Episcopal Church* 49 (December 1980): 374.

30. Alonzo Potter, introduction to *Memorial Papers: The Memorial etc.* (Philadelphia: E.H. Butler, 1857), vi.

31. Neither Potter nor Craik adopted the use of the "evangelical catholic" label. Both, however, chose language that conveyed much the same idea. In pastoral addresses to the clergy of Pennsylvania, Bishop Potter tried to distinguish the "spurious Catholicism of Rome" from a broader "Catholicism of all ages and of all people," which he identified with the Bible and believed to be compatible with the Reformation (M.A. DeWolfe Howe, *Memoirs of the Life and Services of the Rt. Rev. Alonzo Potter* [Philadelphia: J.B. Lippincott, 1871], 173, and Alonzo Potter, *Third and Fourth Charges to the Clergy of the Diocese of Pennsylvania . . . May 1851, 1852* [Philadelphia: King and Baird, 1852], 31.) In his *Divine Life and New Birth* (1869), Craik suggested that it was possible to claim the best insights of the catholic and evangelical traditions.

32. Potter, *Memorial Papers,* 107.

33. Howe, *Alonzo Potter,* 206–21.

34. The Church in Aspinwall was the first Protestant congregation in Panamá. The town was named after William H. Aspinwall (1807–1875), a New York merchant. Aspinwall and his brother John married Anna and Jane Breck, sisters of James Lloyd Breck. The Aspinwalls supported Breck's missionary efforts and also donated

the funds to build the principal building at Virginia Seminary. William Aspinwall's company, which constructed a rail line across Panamá, paid for the construction of a church building and until 1872 provided support for its clergy. Bishop Potter consecrated the church at the midpoint of an 1865 visit to California. He died before the ship landed in San Francisco. For details, see John L. Kater, Jr., "The Beginnings of the Episcopal Church in Panama," *Anglican and Episcopal Church History* 57 (June 1988):147–158.

35. James Craik, "The Financial Question in the Church," *American Church Review* 39 (1882):57–66. Muhlenberg's Church of the Holy Communion in New York City may have been the first "free church" in nineteenth-century America. See Esther Barnhart McBride, *Open Church: History of an Idea* (U.S.A.: n. p., 1983), for details of the Episcopal Church's leadership in the free church movement.

36. John Henry Hopkins, [Jr.], introduction to *The Collected Works of the Late Milo Mahan,* 3 vols. (New York: Pott, Young and Company, 1875), 1:xxxvii.

37. Ferdinand C. Ewer, *Catholicity in its Relationship to Protestantism and Romanism* (New York: G.P. Putnam's Sons, 1878), 165.

38. *Journal of the General Convention of the Protestant Episcopal Church in the United States . . . 1871* (printed for the Convention, 1871), 283.

39. *Journal of the Proceedings of the Bishops, Clergy, and Laity of the Protestant Episcopal Church in the United States of America, Assembled in a General Convention . . . in the Year of Our Lord 1874* (Hartford, Conn.: printed for the Convention by M. H. Mallory, 1875), 185.

40. John Lawrence Mosheim, *An Ecclesiastical History, Ancient and Modern,* trans. Archibald MacLaine, 4 vols. (New York: Collins & Hannay, 1821).

41. *Protestant Episcopal Church Almanac . . . 1880,* 24.

42. Ann Douglas, *The Feminization of American Culture* (New York: Alfred A. Knopf, 1977), 44–79.

43. The revival of the biblical office of deaconess began in 1836 in the Lutheran Church in Germany with Gertrude Reichardt. In that year, she dedicated herself to the female diaconate with the support

of Pastor Theodore (1800–1864) and Mrs. Frederica (1800–1842) Fliedner. Other nations and denominations quickly followed the Kaiserswerth example. The first deaconesses in America may have been two Lutheran deaconesses sent to Pittsburgh from Kaiserswerth in 1849.

44. Mary Sudman Donovan, *A Different Call: Women's Ministries in the Episcopal Church, 1850–1920* (Harrisburg, PA: Morehouse, 1986), 61–63.

45. The delay in the adoption of a canon on deaconesses was a result of a prolonged debate about the difference between deaconesses and nuns. The early supporters of women's ministries in the Episcopal Church often used the term *sisterhoods* and appealed to the precedent of both the female diaconate and female monasticism. As Episcopalians later came to understand it, however, deaconesses were different from nuns. Deaconesses did not take vows of celibacy and were, therefore, free to leave their orders in order to marry. They did not take vows of poverty and often supported their efforts with their own personal income. They generally participated in the worship life of the parishes in which they worked, rather than observing their own monastic offices.

The General Convention adopted its canon on deaconesses at roughly the same time as the Methodists (Methodist Episcopal Church, 1888; Methodist Episcopal Church South, 1902; and the Methodist Protestant Church, 1908). In addition to the Lutheran, Episcopal, and Methodist churches, deaconesses would eventually be active in Baptist, Congregational, and Evangelical and Reformed Churches. For more details on the ecumenical character of the deaconess movement, see Jackson W. Carroll, Barbara Hargrove, and Adair T. Lummis, *Women of the Cloth: A New Opportunity for the Churches* (San Francisco: Harper & Row, 1981), 28.

46. Donovan, *A Different Call,* 106–117.

47. Marion Hughes had made monastic vows before Edward Pusey in England in 1841. In 1845, she formed the Park Village Sisterhood. See Donovan, *A Different Call,* 30.

48. Anne Ayres, *Muhlenberg,* 178.

49. Donovan, *A Different Call,* 41.

50. *The Protestant Episcopal Almanac for the Year of Our Lord 1880* (New York, 1880), 29–30.

51. Donovan, *A Different Call,* 11.

52. Edwin Augustine White and Jackson A. Dykman, *Annotated Constitution and Canons of the Protestant Episcopal Church in the United States of America,* 2d ed. revised, 2 vols. (New York: Seabury Press, 1954), 2:952.

53. Allen Du Pont Breck, *The Episcopal Church in Colorado* (Denver: Big Mountain Press, 1963), 5–24.

54. Joan R. Gundersen, *"Before the World Confessed:" All Saints Parish, Northfield, and the Community* (Northfield, Minn.: Northfield Historical Society, 1987), 5–23.

55. Henry Benjamin Whipple, *Lights and Shadows of a Long Episcopate* (New York: Macmillan, 1899), 31; Robert H. Keller, Jr., *American Protestantism and U. S. Indian Policy 1869–1882* (Lincoln: University of Nebraska Press, 1983); Sandra Boyd, "Mary Douglass Burnham" (Lecture given at the third Biennial Conference on the History of the Episcopal Church, New Orleans, Louisiana, 22 June 1988); Lois Clark, *David Pendleton Oakerhater: God's Warrior* (Oklahoma City: Episcopal Diocese of Oklahoma, 1985), 6–9.

56. Harriet Beecher Stowe, *The Minister's Wooing* (Hartford: Stowe-Day Foundation, 1978), 560.

7

A Broad Church
(1880–1920)

When the bishops and deputies gathered in Chicago in 1886 for the thirty-fifth General Convention, they must have been aware of the great change that was taking place in their nation. America was no longer a nation of farmers and small factories; it was rapidly becoming an industrial giant. Chicago's Home Insurance Company building—America's first skyscraper, completed the year before the convention—was an indication of things to come. Newer high-rise cities were growing up to preside over a vast economic system, linked together by the transcontinental telegraph lines (first completed in 1861) and railroads (completed 1869). Eight new western states would soon join the Union (Washington, North Dakota, South Dakota, and Montana in 1889; Idaho and Wyoming in 1890; New Mexico and Arizona in 1912), completing the forty-eight contiguous states. The great industrialists and financiers, such as Presbyterian Andrew Carnegie (1835–1919), Episcopalian J.P. Morgan (1837–1913), and Baptist John D. Rockefeller (1839–1937), were creating huge economic empires.

In the years from 1880 to 1920, the American population would swell from 50 million to 105 million. By the 1920 census, a majority of Americans would be living in towns or cities rather than on rural farms. America was more complicated, and more efficient means of organization were needed to coordinate the complicated financial, political, and social life of the nation.

The Episcopal Church was growing as well. Copies of the *Living Church Annual* in the first decade of the twentieth century began to carry a confident chart indicating the steady growth of the church as a percentage of the national population. The "Ratio of Communicants" chart showed that while 1 in 416 Americans was an Episcopalian in 1830, 1 in 95 was a member of the church in 1906.[1] As the church reached across the country, it needed new western seminaries (Western Theological Seminary in Chicago, 1883; Church Divinity School of the Pacific in San Mateo, California, 1893). That western movement combined with a continued growth in the

Fig. 32. The House of Bishops in 1892

East to increase the number of dioceses or missionary districts in the United States from fifty-eight in 1880 to eighty-seven in 1910.

Episcopalians recognized that such growth required adoption of more sophisticated systems of organization. The bishops and deputies at General Convention gradually reshaped the church into a more efficient, modern institution. Realizing that the church was too large to be run out of the offices of the various clergy and bishops who were chosen for national office, they established the church's national headquarters at 281 Fourth Avenue in New York City (1894). The General Convention grouped the dioceses into provinces (1913) and adopted a canon on business methods that standardized parish accounting procedures (1916). The major independent missionary society (American Church Missionary Society) gradually merged with the official Domestic and Foreign Missionary Society (1904–1930). In 1919 the General Convention adopted the Nation-Wide Campaign (a national every member canvass that effectively replaced the lingering pew rent system with individual pledging) and created the National Council (an executive body that was renamed the Executive Council in 1964, which has authority to act for the church between sessions of General Convention). In the same year the Convention altered the method in which presiding bishops had been chosen. Since the time of Bishop White, the bishop who was senior in terms of date of consecration had presided over the House of Bishops. After 1919, the position became an elective with a six-year term.[2] General Convention first exercised this provision with the election in 1925 of John Gardner Murray (1857–1929), Bishop of Maryland.

Social Needs of Industrial America

The new industrial America was not without its problems, however. Industrialization had brought great fortunes to a few but a hard life for many. This was particularly true for the new immigrants who worked in many of the factories and for the farmers who increasingly discovered that large industries controlled the prices that their produce would bring.

Episcopalians, still deeply affected by the belief that they had a responsibility not only to their own parishioners but to society at large, saw the need for actions. Their reaction was not always immediate, but collectively as a denomination they responded more quickly than any other American religious body.[3] The experience in Trinity Church, New York, may have been typical. In the 1880s, the members of the vestry noticed a change in use in the parish real estate holdings. Trinity Parish owned large tracts of land in New York City, much of which was leased to builders who had constructed apartment houses. As the downtown area changed from residential to business, the builders saw little advantage in spending money in improving their property. They squeezed more and more tenants in the decaying buildings, while waiting for the time in which the land could be converted to more profitable commercial use. Shocked by charges that the parish was a "slumlord," the vestry called for an investigation and began a program to improve the housing conditions in the city.[4]

The immigration that the vestry at Trinity discovered was radically changing the character of the nation. At the time of the American census of 1790, 78 percent of the white Americans were of British stock. Waves of Irish, German, Scandinavian, eastern and southern European, and Asian immigration altered that percentage so that by 1920 only 41 percent of the population came from British or northern Irish background.[5]

The problems facing new immigrants were not limited to their housing. Often, for example, they found the kind of dangerous employment in heavy industries that Upton Sinclair (1878–1968) and other turn-of-the-century, muckraking authors would dramatize as a national scandal. Parishes needed, therefore, to go beyond Trinity Church's initial concern for real estate to address a whole series of related social and economic problems.

St. George's Church in New York City was a leader in this more comprehensive effort. Its ambitious social program, begun in 1883, included a boys' club, a trade school, a cadet battalion, girls' and women's organizations, a men's club, and a gymnasium.[6]

The girls' and women's organizations at St. George's were linked to national bodies. Women united to

Fig. 33.
Mary Abbot Emery Twing

form a whole series of these to provide vehicles both for mission and for fellowship. Four sisters—Mary Abbot Emery Twing (1843–1901), Julia Chester Emery (1852–1922), Susan Lavinia

Emery, and Margaret Theresa Emery—provided much of the leadership for the earliest, the Woman's Auxiliary to the Board of Missions (organized, 1871; first triennal meeting, 1874). Mary Abbot (national secretary 1872–74; honorary secretary 1882–1901) supplied the initial impulse; Julia Chester (national

Fig. 34.
Julia Chester Emery

Fig. 35.
Margaret Theresa Emery

secretary 1874–1916), the long-term leadership, Susan Lavinia (editor of *The Young Christian Soldier*, the Board of Mission's youth magazine) supplied the needed editorial skills; and Margaret Theresa (coordinator for "box work," the auxiliary's collection of supplies for missionaries), supplied an organizational know-how.[7] Under the Emery sisters' guiding hands, the auxiliary proved to be an extremely valuable agency for domestic and foreign missions. Of the trust funds available to the Board of Missions in 1900, for example, almost one-half of those for which the sex of the donor was known came from women. Female support was not only financial, however. By 1916 the proportion of Episcopal missionaries who were female was 39 percent, a figure that did not include the large number of unpaid spouses of male missionaries. The auxiliary also proved to be an effective advocate for women within the Episcopal Church. When women gained their first representation in the Episcopal Church's national government, it was through the auxiliary. A postwar reorganization (1919) reclassified the

Women's Auxiliary as an auxiliary to the National Council, to which a subsequent General Convention (1934) gave the auxiliary the right to nominate four of thirty-two members.[8]

Other new organizations and programs for women followed after the Women's Auxiliary: the Girls' Friendly Society (1877), which devoted attention to the needs of female factory workers; the Church Periodical Club (1888), which purchased Christian literature for parishes in the American West; the Daughters of the King (1885), which was devoted to prayer and evangelism; and the United Thank Offering (1889), which provided funding for female missionaries.[9]

During the same period that the Emery sisters guided the organizational effort for Episcopal laywomen, Susan Knapp (d. 1941) became the chief spokeswoman for the deaconess movement. Dean of the New York Training School for Deaconesses from 1897 to 1916, she campaigned for higher academic standards and greater professional recognition.[10] The number of Episcopal women in the diaconate would continue to grow to a high of two hundred twenty-six in 1922.[11]

Mary Kingsbury Simkohvitch (d. 1951) and other female Episcopalians were also active in the settlement house movement. Eleven of the 38 settlement houses begun before 1900 were begun by Episcopalians.[12]

In addition to these female organizations, there were all-male groups, such as the Order of the Holy Cross and the Brotherhood of St. Andrew, that exercised social ministries. Father James O.S. Huntington began the Order of the Holy Cross (1881) in the slums of New York City's East Side, and James Houghteling created the Brotherhood of St. Andrew (initial meeting November 30, 1883) at St. James's Church in Chicago to evangelize and provide social services to unchurched men.

More numerous were the large number of agencies which were neither explicitly male nor female. The 1910 *Living Church Annual* listed ten such organizations: four organizations ministering to the deaf, three temperance societies, one for the advancement of Labor, one that continued Mary Rogers and

William Muhlenberg's campaign for "free and open churches," and one for those who worked among the "Colored People."[13]

The latter organization, the Conference of Church Workers Among the Colored People, was formed by John Peterson (a deacon from St. Philip's Church in New York) and other opponents of segregation. Alexander Crummell (1819-98), a black priest who had returned to the United States after twenty years in Liberia to become rector of St. Luke's, Washington, D.C., served as the organization's first president. The conference was formed in 1883 in response to a proposal made by a group of white bishops and clergy who met in Sewanee, Tennessee, in preparation for the General Convention. They drafted a canon (the "Sewanee Canon") which, if adopted, would have separated black Episcopalians into non-geographical racial dioceses. The proposal was not a new one; the Methodist Episcopal Church, South, had adopted a similar strategy in 1870. The conference sent representatives to the Convention who successfully lobbied against the canon.[14]

The defeat of the Sewanee canon did not, however, end the threat of segregation in the church. Beginning in the 1880s, individual southern dioceses took the action that they were unable to persuade the General Convention to make a national policy. They limited black participation in diocesan conventions. The usual mechanism that they employed was the colored convocation. Rather than sending delegates directly to diocesan conventions, black parishes would elect representatives for a separate convocation, which would, in turn, be allotted a fixed number of seats—usually four—at diocesan convention.

The Episcopalians who organized denominational agencies were often active in interdenominational social efforts as well. Alexander Crummell, for example, formed the American Negro Academy, the forerunner of the National Association for the Advancement of Colored People (NAACP). Members of the Brotherhood of St. Andrew participated in the formation of the interdenominational Brotherhood of Andrew and Philip.[15] A trio of social reformers—Wellesley professor Vida Scudder (1861–1954), Church of the Carpenter (Boston) rector

William Dwight Porter Bliss (1856–1926), and economist Richard T. Ely (1854–1943)—played major roles in the cause of unionism and of Christian Socialism. Bliss founded or helped lead the Church Association for the Advancement of the Interest of Labor (1887), the Society of Christian Socialists (1889), the Christian Social Union (1891), and the Union Reform League. Scudder, a cofounder of the Society of Christian Socialists and a member of Bliss's Church of the Carpenter, was active in the Church League for Industrial Democracy and the Christian Socialist Fellowship presidential campaign of 1912. Ely served as an officer of the Christian Social Union and founded the American Economic Association (1885) to challenge the conservative economic theory then prevalent, according to which union demands for salary increases were immoral attempts to alter just compensation levels set by natural law.[16]

The new emphasis on social ministry was reflected in the new church school materials being used in Episcopal parishes. The Christian Nurture Series, produced in 1916 by William E. Gardner (1872–1965) and Lester Bradner (1867–1929) included an emphasis on social service so that children who grew up in the church would be aware of the needs of others.

New Congregations

The multiple special ministries in which Episcopalians were involved gave turn-of-the-century congregations a different character from many of those which had been founded earlier in the century. Those earlier congregations reflected the various strata of membership in the Episcopal Church. Black and white, rich and poor had worshiped together, though often in circumstances that underlined their social differences rather than their unity in Christ. (It had been common, for example, for blacks and whites in southern churches to enter by separate entrances.) By the century's end, however, advocates of special ministries routinely created congregations composed of members of a single economic or racial group.

The church school often played a central role in the formation of these new congregations. Episcopalians organized classes in outlying geographical areas for target groups such as industrial workers, the deaf, blacks, Asians, or the rural poor. When classes reached a certain size, they were organized as separate congregations.

Southern dioceses coupled this strategy with an emphasis on education in an attempt to reclaim a ministry to black Americans. Three new Episcopal colleges (St. Augustine's in Raleigh, North Carolina, 1867; St. Paul's in Lawrenceville, Virginia, 1882; and Voorhees, in Denmark, South Carolina, 1897) and a seminary (Bishop Payne Divinity School in Petersburg, Virginia, 1878) created a pool of educated people from which black clergy could be drawn. In most southern dioceses, clergy working in black parishes and the parishioners they served were grouped together in "Archdeaconries for Colored Work." Special archdeacons, of whom Florida's Ernest McGill (appointed in 1890) may have been the first, coordinated and directed the work on a diocesanwide basis. Other dioceses that employed the archdeaconary system included South Carolina (1892), North Carolina (1901), Virginia (1901), Arkansas (1914), and Georgia (1918).

Episcopalians hoped that this system of missionary archdeaconries would have a positive effect on the size of black membership in the church. That membership had risen sharply as a result of a seriousness about the evangelization of slaves in the 1850s, even to the point that black parishioners outnumbered white in the Diocese of South Carolina. It had, however, fallen sharply with abolition, the erosion of financial support for clergy in black chapels, and the new competition of all-black denominations that accompanied the southern loss in the Civil War. The archdeaconry system halted the decline and initially promised to reverse it. White ambivalence about black membership, evident in such elements as the proposed Sewanee canon of 1883 and the gradual restriction of black participation in diocesan conventions, however, soon slowed that rate of increase.

Episcopalians still had not reached a common mind in 1916,

when they discussed legislation for the selection of black bishops. One group at the General Convention of that year favored revival of the Sewanee proposal, arguing that black jurisdictions could elect black bishops. A second coalition, which eventually prevailed, believed that a 1910 canon for suffragan bishops (assistant bishops without the right of succession) offered greater promise for promoting black leadership. In 1918, Henry B. Delany (1858–1928) of North Carolina and Edward T. Demby (1869–1957) of Arkansas became the first black Episcopal (suffragan) bishops to serve in the United States.[17]

It was during roughly the same period that the Episcopal Church assumed a leading role in the ministry to the deaf. While Bishop White and others had taken part in the founding of institutions for the deaf during the first half of the century, it was with the ordination of Thomas Gallaudet (1822–1902) in 1850 that the Episcopal Church began its effort to provide sign-language worship. Gallaudet, a teacher at the New York Institution for Deaf-Mutes and the son of a pioneering educator (Congregational clergyman Thomas Hopkins Gallaudet, founder in Hartford, Connecticut in 1817 of the first permanent American school for the deaf), began what was to become St. Anne's Church for Deaf-Mutes in New York City in 1852. In 1858, he began to travel, encouraging the formation of deaf congregations in Albany, Baltimore, Boston, Chicago, Washington, and a host of other cities.

Gallaudet, whose mother was deaf, became convinced that the deaf themselves should provide leadership for signing congregations. He recruited a number of hearing-impaired people to assist him. The first of these was Henry Winter Syle (d. 1890). As a teacher at the New York Institution for Deaf-Mutes, he was active in Gallaudet's congregation. When a new job took him to Philadelphia, he transferred his efforts to the Episcopal Congregation there, which was then meeting at St. Stephen's Church. Ordained two years later as the the first deaf clergyman in the Episcopal Church (deacon, 1876; priest, 1883), Syle nurtured the congregation at St. Stephen's to the point that it was able to move to its own facility (All Souls'

Church for the Deaf, 1888). By 1930 twenty-four other deaf men would enter Episcopal orders. The great majority of them (twenty-one of the twenty-four) would be graduates of the new college for the deaf (Gallaudet College, Washington, D.C.) established by Thomas Gallaudet's brother Edward Miner Gallaudet.[18]

Episcopalians expanded their ministry to other groups during the same period of time. In San Francisco, Deaconess Emma B. Drant opened the True Sunshine Mission for Chinese-Americans (1905) and Paul Murakami worked at a Japanese Mission (1916). In South Dakota, Missionary Bishop William Hobart Hare (1838–1909) continued the tradition of ministry among the Sioux begun by Bishop Whipple and Deacon Enmegahbowh of Minnesota. By the end of Hare's episcopate, one-half of the Native Americans in South Dakota were Episcopalians.[19] In Wyoming, Bishop Ethelbert Talbot (1848–1928) and others carried on a ministry among the Arapahoe and Shoshone on the Wind River Reservation.[20] In 1893, Eliza W. Thacara began the ministry of the Episcopal Church to the Navajo with a hospital in Ft. Defiance, Arizona. In Wisconsin, Cornelius Hill (d. 1907), the son of a chief, became the first Oneida priest. In 1905, Episcopalians began work at the Unitah and Ouray Reservation in Utah near the Colorado border. By 1908 the dioceses of Virginia, West Virginia, and Lexington had appointed archdeacons with special responsibilities for the residents of Appalachia.[21]

Employing this technique for expansion, Episcopalians doubled the number of their churches between 1880 and 1920 (from 4,151 to 8,365) and tripled the number of parishioners (from 345,433 to 1,075,820).[22] The pattern of congregational growth contrasted strongly with that followed in the church after 1920. In the 1880 to 1920 period the number of congregations increased more rapidly than the number of parishioners per congregation (102 percent growth in the number of parishes as opposed to a 55 percent increase in average congregational size). From 1920 to 1965 the number of parishes decreased by 10 percent (from 8,365 to 7,539), while the average number of communicants per congregation swelled by 127 percent (from 128.61 to 292.16).[23]

The Church Congress

Turn-of-the-century Episcopalians held together this impressive coalition of agencies and special ministries with a new vision of their church. The primary institutional manifestation of this vision was the Church Congress (1874–1934), a series of national conferences upon issues of social and religious interest. Edwin Harwood (1822–1902), Edward A. Washburn (1819–1881), and Phillips Brooks (1835–93) were among the organizers of the congress. Harwood and Washburn had both taught at Berkeley Divinity School before going on to serve parishes respectively in New Haven and New York. Harwood had attended a session of the English Church Congress (1861–1938) in 1864; Washburn had chaired a local discussion group in New York. Brooks had done something similar in Philadelphia and Boston. Together with others, they agreed upon a simple plan of operation: a "committee of arrangements" designated topics and recruited speakers. The speakers were lay and clerical, black and white, and (after 1911) both male and female. The meetings were open to the public of all denominations and were widely covered by the secular press. George Wildes (d. 1898) of Christ Church, New York, served as general secretary until the mid 1890s, collecting and publishing the results of each conference.[24]

Members of the committee of arrangements were careful to invite representatives of the major church parties to speak. James DeKoven, a leader of an Anglican catholicism that was maturing into an increasingly well-defined Anglo-Catholic party, spoke, for example, to the 1876 congress, as did Bishop Alfred Lee (1807–87) of Delaware, one of the older evangelical bishops. Attitudes on the steering committee and the committee of arrangements were, however, more focused. Phillips Brooks characterized the initial members of the steering committee by remarking that "all of us [were] broad churchmen" who would "see what could be done to keep or make the church liberal and free."[25] Members of the Church of England, particularly the contributors to *Essays and Reviews* (1860), had coined the phrase *broad church* at midcentury. In the American setting, the term was used by Phillips Brooks and others who combined the liturgical openness and commitment to social ministry of William Muhlenberg's evangelical catholicism with a willingness to entertain the intellectual challenges presented by such scholars as geologist Charles Lyell (1797–1875), naturalist Charles Darwin (1809–82), and psychoanalyst Sigmund Freud (1856–1939).

Planners of the Church Congress movement hoped that by providing a forum for discussion of important issues—one in which all points of view were represented and no vote or official action was ever taken—they could instill in their church a broad tolerance for diversity of thought. Alexander Vinton, who chaired the first of the Church Congresses, suggested that the gatherings could at the same time contribute to the unity of the church. They could do this in two ways. First, by emphasizing the unity that was implicit in "missionary work, . . . when men get together with the heart of Christ, and labor side by side and hand to hand to do his work."[26] In concrete terms, this meant that the regular invitations to those engaged in the various special ministries of the church provided a common point of contact. At the 1875 congress, for example, speakers included William Welsh (a Philadelphia layman who served as head the Congressional Board of Indian Commissioners and was also an important supporter of women's ministries), Thomas Gallaudet, Bishop Henry Whipple (active in the church's ministry to Native Americans), and Bishop Schereschewsky (Missionary Bishop to Shanghai). Topics, moreover, included "Ministrations of the Church to the Working Classes" and "Free Preaching."

Vinton hoped that the congresses could also provide a unifying element for the church in a second way. He believed the congresses could set a tone for the church at large, so that all Episcopalians would come to share the broad church belief in "a broader platform, upon which our distinctive views have each an accredited and equally valid position . . . [a] state where prejudices and passions shall go to sleep."[27] By the 1880s it was already evident that his hope was justified, at least in terms of the national leadership of the denomination. Increasingly, the Church Congress served as a "think tank" for the General Convention. Congress members were behind the major legislation passed at Convention: resolutions on industrial workers, canons regularizing the office of deaconess, revision of the *Book of Common Prayer*, and a statement on ecumenism. Church leaders who had not initially supported the congress movement joined its ranks and some congress organizers, such as Phillips Brooks, were elected to the episcopate.

It was in large measure because of the tone that biblical scholar R. Heber Newton (1840–1914) and others set at the congresses that the Episcopal Church avoided the divisions over biblical scholarship that marked some other American denominations. There was an occasional trial of a priest for heresy, such as that which led to the conviction of Thomas Howard MacQuery for the denial of the Virgin Birth (Ohio, 1891) or to the conviction of Algernon Sidney Crapsey for the denial of the Virgin Birth, the resurrection, and the Trinity (Western New York, 1906), but there were no wholesale inquisitions of seminary or college faculties. When such trials did take place elsewhere, some scholars, such as Presbyterian Old Testament scholar Charles A. Briggs (1841–1913), sought refuge in the Episcopal Church. Edward Lambe Parsons (1868–1960), later Bishop of California, was among Briggs's students at Union. Encountering difficulties of his own with a presbytery that suspected him of modernism, Parsons approached William Lawrence (1850–1941) about entering the Episcopal Church.[28]

Lawrence, who served as dean of the Episcopal Theological School in Cambridge, Massachusetts, before election as Bishop of Massachusetts, apparently had several such encounters. He reported another in his autobiography:

I recall now the anxious face of a Harvard student who came hurriedly into the Preacher's Room and said, "I was brought up at home a Christian boy; I came here to college and hoped to remain a follower of Christ: but I am no longer a Christian; my faith is gone." "What is the trouble?" I asked. "I cannot any longer believe that the world was created in six days, and a friend has told me that I cannot deny that and remain a Christian." Would you believe that that conversation took place in the late eighties—and I suppose may take place even now? With what dismay the boy looked at me as I answered, "If that is the case, I am not a Christian either"; and how his face lightened up as I told him of the spiritual purpose of the Scriptures and their essential truths.[29]

Lawrence agreed with Phillips Brooks, his predecessor as Bishop of Massachusetts and the Episcopal Church's best-known preacher at the century's end, who had argued that intellectual inquiry was quite different from heresy. Brooks believed the latter to be a willful breaking of the unity of the church but the former, an honest search for truth.[30]

Fig. 36. Phillips Brooks

This openness to inquiry often led Episcopalians to lines of thought that reinforced their perception that the church needed to be involved in social action. Edward Parsons, who after ordination and a curacy with William Reed Huntington founded the philosophy department at Stanford University, explained his commitment to social action as the result of a conversion to "philosophical socialism."

Rather suddenly as I worked over the New Testament, it came upon me that the whole structure was wrong, that competition as we knew it was utterly inconsistent with the Christian faith, and that since man's environment influences so deeply his life, it was the part of the church to get behind those movements which looked to shifting the basis of society rather than merely ameliorating its bitter conditions."[31]

For Parsons, it was the study of the Bible that led him to the conviction that sweeping social change was needed.

The American Church

If the Church Congress movement was the major institutional manifestation of turn-of-the-century Episcopal broad church attitudes, "American" theology was its major intellectual vehicle. Those who advocated this American theology shared certain basic premises: that only a national church could cope with the social and intellectual complexities of modern industrial America; that episcopacy was a logical form of leadership for such a church; and that, while such a national church did not yet exist, the Episcopal Church could play a leading role in its formation.

Episcopalians believed that their church could play a leading role in the formation of a national church for several reasons. It was a national denomination, not divided into geographical areas (as were the Baptists, Methodists, and Presbyterians) or ethnic segments (as were the Lutherans). Its traditional strength was in the cities, which were increasingly replacing the farming areas as the hub of American life. It recognized and attempted to address serious American social problems. With a representative form of government and a commitment to a traditional Christian faith, it already provided a model of what W.D.P. Bliss called, "democracy organized in Christ."[32] Lay members were, moreover, providing national leadership in the political realm. This was particularly evident to the deputies at the General Convention of 1880, whose members included an all time high of fifteen former, current, or future members of U. S. Congress.[33]

Among the authors who developed these themes were William Montgomery Brown (1855–1937), William Porcher DuBose (1836–1918), and William Reed Huntington. In his *Church for Americans* (1895), Brown explained that the Episcopal Church was more fit for leadership in a national church than was the Roman Catholic Church because it had a representative government and was not tied to any foreign power. The book, popular enough to go through eleven editions within five years, contributed to Brown's election as Bishop of Arkansas.

DuBose was a chaplain and professor in the school of theology at the new University of the South from 1871 until 1908. (Though chartered in 1858, the University of the South at Sewanee, Tennessee, did not begin full operation until after the Civil War. The preparatory department opened in 1868, and the college in 1870. The first dean of the theological school was appointed in 1878.) DuBose wrestled with the concreteness of Christian life. Divinity, he noted in a paper to the fifth Church Congress (1878), was always manifested "in and through" humanity. That led him to conclude, as he later explained in his *Turning Points* (1912) that the Episcopal Church's "claim to be a catholic Church must mean only this, and nothing more, that we desire and intend and believe ourselves to be within all the essential and necessary principles of the catholic faith, life, and worship, and of the one Church of Christ." This in turn, meant that Episcopalians "must be turning [their] face toward [the theory of the one Church of Christ] and moving . . . in the direction of it."[34]

Huntington combined intellectual interest in the national church idea (evident in such works as *The Church-Idea* of 1870 and *A National Church* of 1899) with specific legislative efforts at General Convention. In the 1880s, for example, he became a major proponent of liturgical flexibility, arguing that the Episcopal Church needed to revise its liturgy so as to make it useful for a broader segment of the American population. The *Book Annexed* (1883), a revision of

Fig. 37.
William Reed Huntington

189

the *Book of Common Prayer* proposed by a General Convention commission on which Huntington played a major role, would have provided prayers for industrial workers, short daily offices suitable for midday services, and a greater variety in worship. General Convention from 1886 to 1892 decided that the proposal was too radical, however, and adopted a less innovative *Book of Common Prayer* (1892).

Huntington was more successful with a second proposal. In 1886, he convinced the House of Bishops to adopt the *quadrilateral*, an outline of four basic elements that the Episcopal Church would expect in any national church it helped to create (the Holy Scriptures, the Nicene Creed, the sacraments of baptism and eucharist, and the historic episcopate adapted to local circumstances). Subsequent sessions of General Convention (1895, 1907, 1922, 1949, 1961, 1973, and 1982) endorsed the statement, which the Episcopal Church added to a historical documents section of the *Book of Common Prayer* 1979.[35]

At roughly the time in which Huntington was proposing the quadrilateral, W.H. Fremantle and Herbert Symonds (d. 1921) were suggesting national church themes to the Church of England and the Church of Canada.[36] When Anglican bishops from throughout the world gathered for the third Lambeth Conference (1888), therefore, they were well acquainted with the import of the proposal that Huntington had made. Before the session ended, they adopted Huntington's four principles with a much abbreviated introduction that stated only that they were the "basis on which approach may be by God's blessing made towards Home Reunion."[37] Conferences of 1920, 1930, 1948, and 1978 also endorsed the statement.

While the quadrilateral did not lead to immediate incorporation with other denominations, it did open one door that had been closed for two centuries. From the time that Thomas Bray's Society for the Propagation of the Gospel had popularized Anglican covenant theology in America, a significant portion of Episcopalians had refused to participate in ecumenical associations with Protestants who lacked the historic episcopate. For most Episcopalians, the quadrilateral offered a way around this roadblock. By designating apostolic succession at the outset as a necessary element in any reunited church, Episcopalians felt that they could both safeguard their tradition and engage in dialogue with others.

Charles Henry Brent (1862–1929), Missionary Bishop of the Philippines and later Bishop of Western New York, was a leader in opening this dialogue. After attending the 1910 Edinburgh World Conference on Missions with Women's Auxiliary leader Julia Emery, he persuaded the General Convention of 1910 to request an international meeting on Christianity and church order. Near the end his life, Brent presided over the first session of the World Conference on Faith and Order (Lausanne, Switzerland, 1927). Robert H. Gardiner, an active layman from Maine, did much of the preliminary work in organizing the gathering. The conference joined with other agencies to form the World Council of Churches in 1948.

While most Episcopalians welcomed this opening of dialogue with Protestants, some did not. This was particularly true of the Anglo-Catholic party, whose members had an agenda for Christian reunion somewhat different from that of the advocates of American theology. Rather than looking to a national Protestant church for which the Episcopal Church would provide only one of any number of liturgical traditions, they urged the Episcopal Church to embrace a Western liturgical tradition of which the Roman Catholic Church was the most consistent guardian. Thus, while broad church figures like William Reed Huntington campaigned for a modernization of the liturgy to meet the circumstances of modern life, anglo-catholics called for a continuing recovery of liturgical elements that had been abandoned at the Reformation. Francis J. Hall (1857–1932), the Western and General Seminary professor who was the leading Anglo-Catholic theologian at the turn of the century, wrote with pride that the reintroduction of auricular confession was "a recovery of sound doctrine and practice . . . bitterly but vainly opposed by evangelical Churchmen."[38] In Chicago and later at St. Ignatius' Church, New York City,

Arthur Ritche (1849–1921) introduced Benediction of the Blessed Sacrament in apparent contradiction to both the 1874 General Convention's prohibition of eucharistic adoration and the wishes of the bishops of Chicago and New York. Broad church New York bishop Henry Codman Potter eventually prevailed upon him to abandon the practice.[39]

When Anglo-Catholics envisioned reunion with other Christians, it was with the Orthodox and Roman Catholic churches that their hopes lay. They watched, therefore, with interest the ongoing Anglican-Roman Catholic dialogue, in which English layman Lord Halifax (Charles Wood, 1839–1934) of the English Church Union played a leading role, and were discouraged by the apparent rejection of those efforts by Popes Leo XIII and Pius XI. Leo's *Apostolicae Curae* (1896) declared Anglican orders invalid, and Pius's *Mortalium Animos* (1928) forbade repetition of Anglican-Roman Catholic conferences of the sort that Lord Halifax helped arrange at Malines, Belgium (1921–26).[40]

Anglo-Catholics feared that ecumenical discussions with Protestants would endanger the chance of the eventual reunion with Rome or Eastern Orthodoxy. When the General Convention of 1907 amended the canons to allow Episcopal clergy to invite Protestant guest preachers, the members of the Companions of the Holy Savior were particularly upset. The Companions were an Anglo-Catholic order, centered at Nashotah House, Wisconsin, and in the Philadelphia area, that advocated clerical celibacy, private confession, and an intense personal spiritual life. William McGarvey and a several other members of the Companions converted to the Roman Catholic Church.[41]

While Anglo-Catholics and broad church Episcopalians did not embrace the same goals of ecumenism, there were a number of points in which they did agree. One of these was the cathedral movement. While in Faribault, Minnesota, in the 1850s, James Lloyd Breck had begun to call for the establishment of a cathedral, an ecclesiastical institution that American Episcopalians abandoned at the time of the Revolution as

Fig. 38. President Theodore Roosevelt at the laying of the foundation stone of the Washington National Cathedral in 1907.

unsuited for their democratic nation. Breck and others of his generation saw the cathedral as an institution with which Episcopalians could ennoble the society of which they were a part. The example of Chicago's Cathedral of Saints Peter and Paul (1861) and Minnesota's Cathedral of Our Merciful Saviour was soon followed in other dioceses. In 1892, Episcopalians in the Diocese of New York, including financier J.P. Morgan, began the Cathedral of St. John the Divine, projected to be upon completion the largest in the world. The building plans were altered in 1910 to reflect a purer gothic design that was also to be used in the National Cathedral (begun in 1907) in Washington, D.C., and Grace Cathedral in San Francisco (begun in 1910). The Episcopal Church was a national church able to provide gracious and beautiful houses of worship for the American people.

Foreign Missions

By the end of the nineteenth century, the United States was well on the way to becoming a significant world power. America's victory in the Spanish-American War (1898) and its success with an open door policy in China gave American diplomats and business representatives access to large portions of the world that had once been closed to them. The growth of American power also opened new possibilities for American missionaries. In the case of the Episcopal Church, the number of communicants in foreign missionary districts and dioceses increased from

408 to 28,136 in the forty years between 1880 and 1920.[42]

Much of the expansion was in the Orient and the Pacific. Bishops Channing Moore Williams (Missionary Bishop to China and Japan, 1866–74) and Samuel Isaac Joseph Schereschewsky (Bishop of Shanghai, 1877–83) built on the work that Bishop William Jones Boone (1811–64) had begun in the Diocese of Shanghai. By the first decade of the twentieth century, Episcopalians had organized three Chinese missionary dioceses (Shanghai, 1844; Hankow, 1901; and Anking, 1910). Schereschewsky, a Lithuanian convert from Judaism with a considerable flair for language, translated the Bible and portions of the prayer book into the Mandarin and Wenli dialects. Williams (1829–1910) was also active in Japan, of which he became sole bishop in 1874. He founded Rikkyo (St. Paul's) University in Tokyo, formed two dioceses (Tokyo and Kyoto), and began the translation of the prayer book into Japanese.

After the American victory in the Spanish-American War, Charles Henry Brent (Bishop of the Philippines, 1901–18) led the way in the creation of an Episcopal mission; he was also a leader in a multinational campaign against the opium trade. At roughly the same time (1902), the American church took jurisdiction of the Missionary Diocese of Hawaii from the British. The work of the Church of England had begun there during the

Fig. 39.
Kamehameha IV

Fig. 40. Emma

reign of King Kamehameha IV (1852–63). Kamehameha welcomed Anglican missionaries to the island and personally translated portions of the *Book of Common Prayer* into Hawaiian. His queen, Emma Rooke (d. 1885), was the leading patroness of the church. Among the projects that she supported were Queen's Hospital (1860), St. Andrew's Priory (a school for girls), and St. Andrew's Cathedral.[43]

Turn-of-the-century Episcopalians were also moving beyond their initial effort in Latin American missions at Aspinwall, Panamá. A team of American missionaries from Virginia Seminary (James W. Morris, Lucien Lee Kinsolving, Ida Mason Dorsey and William Cabell Brown, John G. Meem, and Mary Packard) arrived in the state of Rio Grande do Sul, Brazil, for example, in 1890 and 1891, the year after that nation's successful revolution against Emperor Dom Pedro II (1889). Their initial work met with sufficient success to justify the visit of Bishop George W. Peterkin (1841–1916) of West Virginia in 1893. The bishop administered confirmation and ordained the first Brazilian Episcopalians to the diaconate (Vicente Brande, Antônio Machado Fraga, Américo Vespucio Cabral, and Boaventura Oliveira). In 1898 Kinsolving (1862–1929) became the first bishop of the Brazilian church. The Igreja Episcopal do Brasil (Episcopal Church of Brazil) had a particularly successful ministry to Japanese-Brazilians, many of whom came to the Brazil for plantation work at the turn of the century.[44]

Episcopalians who advocated American theology at home recognized the value of a national theology in these overseas missions. While they were not consistent in their efforts, they often relied upon local leadership and initiative. In 1874, the General Convention agreed to consecrate James Theodore Holly (d. 1911) as the Bishop of the Orthodox Apostolic Church of Haiti. The initial core of the church was a group of black American expatriates, who had left the United States in 1861. In 1898, the two American and four British dioceses in Japan joined to form the Nippon Seikokai (the Holy Catholic Church in Japan). In Mexico (1904) and Puerto Rico (1923), the Episcopal Church merged with local churches that had taken the name La Iglesia de Jesús (The Church of Jesus). Suffragan bishops Manuel Ferrando (consecrated for Puerto Rico in 1924) and Efraín Salinas y Velasco (consecrated for Mexico, 1931) were the Episcopal Church's first hispanic bishops. Pedro Duarte, a Cuban who had learned of the Episcopal Church while in exile in Flordia, founded the first Cuban congregation (La Iglesia de Fieles a Jesús in Mantanzas in 1883), and a Virgin Islander ordained by Bishop Holly of Haiti (1897) carried the ministry of the Episcopal Church to the Dominican Republic.[45]

As in the United States, the missionary work was often carried on by wives of clergy, female lay workers, and deaconesses. Mary Elizabeth Wood (1861–1931) was but one example. A librarian by training, she visited her brother Robert in Wuchang China in 1899. An Episcopal missionary, he convinced her to remain in China to work with the mission's school. She stayed on, not only teaching at the school but expanding it into a college. She built a fine library, opened it to the public, and established branch libraries. She eventually developed a library school at the college that would train five hundred Chinese in modern library techniques before 1949. An excellent fund raiser, Miss Wood was able to convince the U.S. Congress in 1924 to return a portion of the Boxer Rebellion indemnity money for cultural projects in China.[46]

The political events of the second decade of the twentieth century indicated how much the Episcopal Church had changed since the early nineteenth century. When America was again involved in a major European war, there was no longer any question about the patriotism of the denomination

Fig. 41. John Joseph Pershing

or its reticence to support American policy. On the contrary, the denomination heartily endorsed the American cause. Episcopalians pointed with pride to the confirmation of expeditionary force leader General John Joseph Pershing (1860–1948) shortly before departing for Europe.

The church was also active in providing chaplains. Faculty members at the Episcopal Theological School joined with others in theological schools in the Boston area to train clergy for the armed forces.[47] In Europe, General Pershing turned to Bishop Charles Henry Brent, on the continent in 1919 on assignment for the YMCA, for advice on the organization of military chaplains. Brent suggested, and Pershing agreed to, a permanent executive committee. Brent, a civilian at the time he made the proposal but commissioned a major soon after, served as chairperson of that executive board and therefore used the title "Chief of Chaplains of the American Expeditionary Force."[48]

The House of Bishops quieted the one vocal antiwar spokesperson among their number, Bishop Paul Jones (1880–1941) of Utah, who resigned his see in 1918. Bishop Jones's opposition to the war left him in a distinct minority, but he was not the only Episcopalian with reservations about the war. John Nevin Sayre (1884–1977), whose brother Francis married President Woodrow Wilson's daughter Jessie, was, for example, a founding member of the American branch of a pacifistic organization known as the Fellowship of Reconciliation (1915). Bishop Jones served as the organization's secretary and Sayre as its co-secretary and chairperson.[49]

NOTES

1. *The Living Church Annual, 1910* (Milwaukee, 1910), 48.

2. The 1919 canon provided for a six-year term. The Convention of 1936 made the term continue until a mandatory retirement age of sixty-eight. The Convention of 1967 limited the term to twelve years and age sixty-five. The Convention of 1985 retained the twelve-year term but increased the retirement age to seventy.

3. Charles Howard Hopkins, *The Rise of the Social Gospel in American Protestantism, 1865–1915* (New Haven: Yale University Press, 1940), p. 38, and Henry F. May, *Protestant Churches and Industrial America* (New York: Harper & Brothers, 1949), 182–83. Hopkins dated the Episcopal Church's involvement to the Church Congress of 1874; May, to the General Convention of 1886.

Frank Sugeno has suggested that the Episcopal Church's belief that it must minister to the needs of those outside of its bounds is the result of an "establishmentarian ideal" that runs throughout the history of the Anglican Church. See Sugeno's "The Establishmentarian Ideal and the Mission of the Episcopal Church," *Historical Magazine of the Protestant Episcopal Church* 53 (December 1984):285–292.

4. Phyllis Barr, "Trinity's Slum Tenements: The Real Story," *Trinity News* (Trinity parish newsletter, New York City) 30 (October 1983):14–15.

5. Sydney E. Ahlstrom, A *Religious History of the American People* (New Haven: Yale University Press, 1972), 515–16.

6. James Thayer Addison, *The Episcopal Church in the United States, 1789–1931* (New York: Charles Scribner's Sons, 1951), 282.

7. Mary Donovan, *A Different Call: Women's Ministries in the Episcopal Church, 1850–1920* (Harrisburg, PA: Morehouse, 1986), 67–68.

8. Ibid., 78, 128, 162.

9. Ibid., 81–85.

10. Ibid., 108–14.

11. *The Living Church Annual and Churchman's Alamanac, 1922* (Milwaukee: Morehouse, 1922), 202–6.

12. Donovan, *A Different Call,* 147.

13. *Living Church Annual, 1910,* 116–20.

14. George F. Bragg, *History of the Afro-American Group of the Episcopal Church* (Baltimore: Church Advocate Press, 1922), 150–61. Some southern whites, such as Bishop Wilmer of Alabama, opposed the Sewanee canon.

15. Esther Barnhart McBride, *Open Church: History of an Idea* (U.S.A.: n.p., 1983), 41.

16. John C. Cort, *Christian Socialism: An Informal History* (Maryknoll, New York: Orbis Books, 1988), 231–36, 261–65.

17. The 1910 canon did not allow suffragan bishops the right to vote in the House of Bishops. In 1925, the House of Deputies defeated an attempt of the bishops to extend voting rights to suffragans. It would not be until 1943 that the suffragan bishops would win the right to vote. See Edwin Augustine White and Jackson A. Dykeman, *Annotated Constitution and Canons for the Government of the Protestant Episcopal Church in the United States of America, Otherwise Known as the Episcopal Church,* 2 vols. (New York: Office of the General Convention, 1982), 1:57–62.

18. Otto Benjamin Berg, *A Missionary Chronicle: Being a History of the Ministry to the Deaf in the Episcopal Church, 1850–1980* (Hollywood, Md.: St. Mary's Press, 1984), xiii–xxviii.

19. Francis Prucha, *The Great Father,* 2 vols. (Lincoln: University of Nebraska Press, 1984), 1:263.

20. Ethelbert Talbot, *My People of the Plains* (New York: Harper & Brothers, 1906), 242. Talbot notes that President Grant gave individual denominations responsibilities for specific reservations. In 1872 the Episcopal Church was given the responsibility for Wind River and seven other reservations. William Welsh, the active Episcopal layman who served as the head of the Congressional Board of Indian Commissioners, may have lobbied for the substantial Episcopal role in Indian missions. Welsh's nephew, Herbert Welsh, formed the Indian Rights Association (1882) to campaign for better treatment for Native Americans.

21. Owanah Anderson, *Jamestown Commitment: The Episcopal Church and the American Indian* (Cincinnati: Forward Movement Publications, 1988), 36–37, 84; Sarah T. Moore, "Utah Church Revived," *Living Church* 198 (March 12, 1989):8; Walter Hughson, *The Church's Mission to the Mountaineers of the South* (Hartford, Conn.: Church Missions Publishing, 1908).

22. *The Episcopal Church Annual 1968* (New York: Morehouse-Barlow, 1968), 18–19.

23. Ibid.

24. Richard M. Spielmann, "The Episcopal Church Congress, 1874–1934," *Anglican and Episcopal Church History* 58 (March 1989), 50–80.

25. Ibid, 55.

26. *Authorized Report of the Proceedings of the First Congress of the Protestant Episcopal Church in the United States, Held in the City of New York, Oct. 6 and 7, 1874* (New York: T. Whittaker, 1875), 10.

27. Ibid.

28. Edward L. Parsons, "Autobiography of Edward L. Parsons" (Address to the Pacific Coast Theological Group, c. 1951), 2–5.

29. William Lawrence, *Fifty Years* (Boston: Houghton Mufflin, 1923), 42–3.

30. Phillips Brooks, *Essays and Addresses* (New York: E.P. Dutton, 1894), 7–19.

31. Parsons, "Autobiography," 6.

32. W.D.P. Bliss quoted in Cort, *Christian Socialism,* 233.

33. David L. Simpson, Jr., "A Data Base for Measuring the Participation Levels of Episcopalians in Elected Office and Including a List of the Lay Delegates to the General Convention of the Church from 1789 to 1895" (M.T.S. thesis, Protestant Episcopal Theological Seminary in Virginia, 1987), 13–14. Simpson found that the number of past, current, or future members of Congress at the General Convention varied between zero (1795, 1799, 1801, 1808, 1832, 1850) and fifteen (1880). While the pattern was somewhat inconsistent, in general it rose from a low at the turn of the century to a high in the 1880s (1880, fifteen; 1883, eleven; 1886, four; 1889, eleven) with a slight decrease in the two conventions surveyed in the 1890s (seven each). The size of both the General Convention and the Congress was, of course, growing throughout the century.

34. Jon Alexander, ed., *William Porcher DuBose: Selected Writings* (New York: Paulist Press, 1988), 23, 71.

35. J. Robert Wright, "Heritage and Vision: The Chicago Lambeth Quadrilateral," *Anglican Theological Review,* supplemental series no. 10 (March 1988): 8–46.

36. Paul T. Phillips, "The Concept of a National Church in Late Nineteenth-century England and America," *Journal of Religious History* (Sydney, Australia) 14 (June 1986):29–37.

37. *Book of Common Prayer* (New York: Seabury Press, 1979), 877.

38. Francis J. Hall, *The Sacraments,* vol. 9 of *Dogmatic Theology,* 10 vols. (New York: Longmans, Green, and Co., 1921), 219.

39. E. Clowes Chorley, *Men and Movements in the American Episcopal Church* (New York: Charles Scribner's Sons, 1946), 334–36.

40. Leo XII found Anglican orders invalid in part because of defective form. The Anglican ordinal did not name the person ordained to the priesthood as a "sacrificing priest." The English archbishops immediately responded with their *Answer to the Apostolic Letter of Pope Leo XIII on the English Ordinal* in which they pointed out that the earliest formularies used in the Church of Rome also lacked such language.

Following the breakdown of ecumenical talks in the 1920s, the Church of England signed the Bonn Agreement (1931), recognizing the Old Catholic Churches of Europe, a confederation of churches that separated from the See of Rome during the eighteenth and nineteenth centuries. The Episcopal Church ratified the Bonn agreement in 1934.

41. Edward Hawks, *William McGarvey and the Open Pulpit* (Philadelphia: Dolphin Press, 1935), 36–39, 147, 171.

42. *The Living Church Annual and Churchman's Almanac* (Milwaukee: Morehouse Publishing Co., 1921), 446–49; *The Episcopal Church Annual, 1968,* 18. The 1921 *Annual* listed 21,075 communicants in the missionary dioceses of China (three dioceses), Japan (two), Cuba, Haiti, Liberia, Mexico, Panamá, and Brazil; and 7,161 communicants in the American territories of the Philippines, Alaska, Hawaii, and Puerto Rico.

43. *Notable American Women, 1607–1950* ed. Edward T. James, s.v. "Emma Rooke" by Alfons L. Korn (Cambridge: Belknap Press of Harvard University Press, 1971).

44. James W. Morris, "The History of the Brazil Mission," in *History of the Theological Seminary in Virginia and Its Historical*

Background, ed. W.A.R. Goodwin, 2 vols. (Rochester, N.Y.: Du Bois Press, 1924), 2:371–86.

The English had founded English-speaking chaplaincies earlier in the century in Rio de Janeiro, Sao Paulo, Santos, and Pernambuco. The congregation in Rio, which may have been the oldest, dated back to at least 1819. Two American clergy—W. H. Cooper of Pennsylvania and Richard Holden (d. 1886) of Ohio—had also tried unsuccessfully at midcentury to found Episcopal missions in Brazil. A shipwreck prevented Cooper from reaching Brazil; Holder, who concentrated on translation of texts into Portuguese, moved on to Portugal (Custis Fletcher, "Beginnings of the Anglican Communion in Brazil" [unpublished paper, n.d.])

45. *Anglicanos: Boletín Internacional Misionero* 14 (Abril-Junio de 1987), 7; *Anglicanos* 16 (Octubre-Diciembre de 1987); and Justo L. González, *The Ministry of the Episcopal Church in the Metropolitan Area of New York and Environs* (New York: Trinity Parish, 1985), 14–15.

The *Iglesia de Jesús* of Mexico began soon after the promulgation of Benito Juarez's constitution of 1857. In 1860 three members of the church visited the United States and initiated discussions with the Episcopal Church. The church of the same name in Puerto Rico was formed in the early part of the twentieth century.

Cuba (1901) and Haiti (1913) later became missionary districts of the Episcopal Church.

46. *Notable American Women 1607–1950,* 6th printing (1982), 3 vols., s.v. "Mary Elizabeth Wood" by A Kaiming Chu.

47. John F. Piper, Jr., *The American Churches in World War I* (Athens, Ohio: Ohio University Press, 1985), 123.

48. Roy J. Honeywell, *Chaplains of the United States Army* (Washington: Office of the Chief of Chaplains, 1958), 199.

49. Nathaniel W. Pierce and Paul L. Ward, *The Voice of Conscience: The Episcopal Peace Fellowship* (Charleston, Mass.: Charles River Publishing for the Episcopal Peace Fellowship, 1989), 2–7.

8

The Twenties,
Depression, and War
(1920–45)

The years between the end of the First World War and the end of the Second were volatile ones for American Christians. Americans found Prohibition, the object toward which an alliance of church groups had been working for a century, unsatisfactory and unenforceable; that discovery led many, in turn, to question the wisdom of religious involvement in the setting of public policy. The trial of Tennessee school teacher John Thomas Scopes (1925) brought the apparent conflict of evolution and divine creation to the front page of American newspapers. The Methodist Church, which had been the nation's largest Protestant church in the last half of the nineteenth century, slowed its rate of growth, in part because of the appearance of new Pentecostal and holiness denominations. Northern Baptists, Northern Presbyterians, and Disciples of Christ divided into warring factions, as their leaders hurled charges of heresy at one another.

In broad terms, the conflict was a religious referendum on a complex of intellectual and social choices that resulted from the increasing secularization of American institutions. Fifty years earlier, American churches had played a leading role in medicine, education, and even entertainment. Churches and church groups formed hospitals in which nuns and deaconesses provided much of the ongoing care. Many colleges and universities were founded to provide a supply of educated clergy, and even when they began to take on wider programs of study, a significant percentage of professors and administrators were ordained people. Public schools in many areas were outgrowths of an earlier attempt to provide Sunday school instruction. Women's church groups were often the chief source of community entertainment and culture.

By the end of the nineteenth century, however, this situation was changing rapidly. Doctors, who employed sophisticated techniques, shaped an increasingly secular apparatus for the delivery of medical care. Colleges bypassed clergy with rounded educations and chose their faculty members from among those who had earned Ph.D. degrees in carefully delineated fields of study. Secular nurses and social workers replaced deaconesses and nuns in the halls of hospitals and charitable agencies. An entertainment industry based in Hollywood provided alternative forms of inexpensive entertainment.

Christians were faced, therefore, with the question of whether to accept the leadership and insights of these new secular institutions. One group of Christians, who often accepted the label *modernist,* said yes; they attempted to reconcile modern scholarship with their religious views. Many, like the twelve hundred Presbyterian signers of the Auburn Affirmation (1923), believed that biblical literalism was an obstacle to such a reconciliation.

The signers of the Auburn Affirmation objected to an earlier Presbyterian statement of faith (the Five Point Deliverance of 1910), which had affirmed biblical inerrancy and the literal truth of the Virgin Birth, substitutionary atonement, the resurrection of the body, and the miracles of Jesus. Others, like John Wallace Suter (1859–1942), an Episcopal liturgical scholar who would later become the custodian of the *Book of Common Prayer,* identified the "the once current belief in original sin" as objectionable to the modern mind.[1]

Modernists also hoped to incorporate advances in secular institutions into the life of the church. In the 1920s and early 1930s, for example, the Conference of Theological Seminaries and Colleges (formed in 1918 and renamed the American Association of Theological Schools in the United States and Canada in 1936) attempted to create academic standards for seminaries similar to those for secular institutions. Two other associations (the Council for the Clinical Training of Theological Students, 1930, and the New England Theological Schools Committee on Theological Training, 1933) sought to bring the insights of the medical profession to the practice of pastoral care.[2]

A second group of Christians, who took the name *fundamentalist* from a prewar collection of pamphlets on the basics of the Christian faith (*The Fundamentals*, 1910–14), equated the embrace of the new secular institutions with infidelity. They supported alternative educational institutions (Bible colleges), formed interdenominational alliances (the World's Christian Fundamentalist Association, 1918), pressed for doctrinal tests, and, when all else failed, formed new denominational structures (North American Christian Convention of the Disciples of Christ, 1927; General Association of Regular Baptists, 1931; and Orthodox Presbyterian Church, 1936).

In 1929, the fall of the stock market exacerbated this crisis of faith and reason. The financial resources of the church diminished. Annual giving for foreign missions in the Episcopal Church, for example, fell from $2.25 to $0.96 per capita in the decade following the crash.[3] In addition, both fundamentalist and modernist Christians found that their visions of the faith—grounded on an optimistic vision of American progress—did little to address the situation of Americans in the Depression. The experience with social ministry of the turn of the century did provide some models for those Episcopalians, such as President Franklin Roosevelt (1882–1945) and his secretary of labor Frances Perkins (the first female cabinet member), who began to address some of the worst ills of the Depression era. It would be the Second World War, however, that would gradually pull America out of the Depression. When economic recovery came, moreover, national resources were concentrated on the war effort. Any revival of the churches in America had to wait until the completion of the fighting.

Fig. 42. St. Francis Mission, North End, Boston in the 1920s

The Debate over the Creeds

While the leadership of the Episcopal Church, which had been nurtured by the Church Congress's broad church vision, was clearly in sympathy with the modernist option, it was not itself immune from the modernist-fundamentalist debate. Many of the propositions that fundamentalists were working hard to defend appeared in the liturgy that Episcopalians regularly recited. The speakers at the 1924 Church Congress on the topic "How shall the Church deal with fundamentalism," recognized as much. Although, for example, Bishop of Albany George Ashton Oldham (1877–1963) suggested that some fundamentalists "may be obsessed or may be suffering from some 'complex' which the psychologists alone can explain," he had to agree with the fundamentalist "tenet that there are certain underlying fundamentals in religion which in essence are permanent."[4] Bishop Arthur A.C. Hall (1847–1930) of Vermont suggested that the best repository of such permanent truths were the creeds, for they contained the "great truths" of the Bible.[5]

This conviction, which many shared, gave a particular character to the modernist-fundamentalist debate insofar as it took place in the Episcopal Church. Episcopal scholars with modernist leanings could talk about the value of psychology and modern medicine or question the literal reading of Old

Testament passages with relative impunity. When they began to question the literal truth of passages from the Apostles' and Nicene Creeds, however, trouble instantly followed.

Such trouble would come as a shock to some of the participants in the Church Congress. Many assumed, as did John Wallace Suter in a 1919 Church Congress address, that there was "readiness on the part of the whole church, in all its parties or schools of thought," for modernist revisions in doctrine.[6]

Events four years later showed that such a confidence was unfounded. In that year (1923), a venerable Bishop William Lawrence of Massachusetts published his autobiography. Titled *Fifty Years,* it was a frank discussion of his life and thought. Among his observations was the comment that there was "no essential connection between belief in the Virgin Birth and the Incarnation."[7] Lawrence argued that a Christian's belief that Jesus was fully man and fully God did not require that Christian to accept the virgin conception of Jesus as literal fact. Bishop Lawrence did not state that he himself disbelieved the Virgin Birth, but he did make it clear that many clergy held such a position.

It soon became evident that many of the laity were less than comfortable with such a modernist interpretation of an article of the creed. A group of Philadelphia laity, including U.S. Senator George Wharton Pepper (1867–1961), wrote a letter of protest to the General Convention. Bishop of New York William T. Manning (1866–1949), who was not among the leaders of the Church Congress, communicated with others about the issue and, when the House of Bishops convened in New York for the election of several missionary bishops later that year, set the tone for the committee that drafted a reply to the petition.

Manning's position on the issue might best be summarized with the title of a sermon that he delivered shortly before the meeting of the bishops: "Neither Fundamentalism Nor Modernism, but Belief in Jesus Christ the Son of God."[8] He believed that it was possible to avoid the polarization between modernism and fundamentalism that was troubling other denominations at the time.

Fig. 43. George Wharton Pepper (left) with Henry J. Heinz

In the pastoral letter it drafted, the committee on which Manning sat attempted to avoid that polarization by distinguishing *belief in,* which they defined as "entire surrender to," from the facts *that we believe.* The committee suggested that this *belief in* involved the embrace of "something deeper and higher, and more personal" than the mere facts *that we believe.* It was not, for example, "the fact of the Virgin Birth that [made] us believe in our Lord as God." Thus the statements of the facts *that we believe* in the "creeds . . . [gave] a point of departure for free thought and speculation on the meaning and consequences of the facts revealed by God. The Truth [was] never a barrier to thought. In belief, as in life, it [was] the Truth that [made] us free."[9]

The pastoral letter cautioned, however, that this free thought and speculation could not lead one directly to contradict the traditional statements *that we believe.* Thus it reminded Episcopalians that

a clergyman, whether Deacon, Priest, or Bishop, [was] required as a condition of receiving his ministerial commission, to promise conformity to the doctrine, discipline and worship of this Church. Among the offences for which he [was] liable to be presented for trial [was] the holding and teaching publicly or pri-

vately, and advisedly, doctrine contrary to that of this church. . . .
[Further,] to explain away the statement "conceived by the Holy
Ghost and born of the Virgin Mary," as if it referred to a birth in
the ordinary way, of two human parents, under perhaps excep-
tionally holy conditions, [was] plainly an abuse of language. . . .[10]

Content that they had found a way around the impasse between
modernists and fundamentalists, the members of the committee
completed their statement by noting that "objections to the
doctrine of the Virgin Birth, or to the bodily Resurrection of
our Lord Jesus Christ, [were] not only contrary to the Christian
tradition, but [had] been abundantly dealt with by the best
scholarship of the day."[11] The House of Bishops passed the
statement unanimously.

The House of Bishops apparently did not understand the
action as a rebuke of Bishop Lawrence, for it never presented
him for trial. Bishop Lawrence did, however, express regrets
about the role he had played in stirring the debate. He told the
participants in the 1924 Church Congress, which devoted a
major portion of its agenda to the fundamentalist-modernist
debate, that he had come to suspect that he was "perhaps too
little weighted with respect for tradition and overbalanced
in . . . anxiety to keep the Church alert to the thought of the
day." He feared that he had pressed "interpretations of certain
articles of the Creed with too little regard for the feelings of
those who are more conservative." He still believed that "the
conviction of truth as revealed in modern thought and Biblical
criticism" at times compelled the Christian to "act in order to
save what he believes is the life of the Christian faith" but suggested that any such effort must be made with "utmost rever-
ence and sympathy" and with skill, like that of "a surgeon."[12]

Not everyone involved in the debate took the irenic stance
of Manning or Lawrence. Some took more partisan positions
in the hope of forcing the House of Bishops to take a more
openly modernist stance. The Reverend Dickenson Sergeant
Miller (1868–1963), for example, resigned his position as professor of apologetics at General Seminary in protest against the

pastoral letter. He moved to a position at Smith College. Leighton Parks (1852–1938), rector of St. Bartholomew's, New York, whose *What is Modernism?* (1923) had commended the modernist movement, chose another vehicle for his protest—a sermon in which he exchanged his surplice and stole for an academic gown in order to emphasize the opposition between scholarship and the church hierarchy. Parks told his congregation that he agreed with Bishop Lawrence and felt that the Bible, not the House of Bishops, was the judge of heresy. Three members of the faculty of the Episcopal Theological School (ETS, later EDS with the 1974 merger with the Philadelphia Divinity School) joined the debate by suggesting that the opinions of pastoral letters were not canonically binding on the church.[13]

Miller and Parks voluntarily injected themselves into the theological debate; others did so under duress. In Texas, the Reverend Lee W. Heaton (1889–1973) of Fort Worth was criticized by a clergyman of another denomination for his stand on the Virgin Birth. His diocese lacked procedures for heresy trials. The adoption, therefore, of canons to cover such matters was seen by the clergy and laity in the diocese as a preliminary step in bringing him to trial. A cause célèbre, Heaton headed East in order to rally support from the East Coast seminaries and succeeded in lining up endorsements for his position from the faculties of General, the Philadelphia Divinity School (PDS), and ETS.[14] With such formidable support, Heaton was able to avoid trial. He felt it wise, however, to leave the diocese.

The debate in the church at large did not quiet with the departure of Heaton from Texas, however. A new figure, William Montgomery Brown (Bishop of Arkansas, 1898–1912), soon took center stage. Brown had been deeply committed to the social ministry of the church. After his retirement as Bishop of Arkansas he was attracted to the reports of the Russian Revolution of 1917. Gradually, he moved from the belief that a marriage of Christianity and communism offered hope for the church to the belief that communism had made the Christian faith outmoded. In his *Communism and*

Christianity (1920), he suggested that it was time to "banish the Gods from the skies and capitalists from the earth and make the world safe for Industrial Communism."[15] While most Episcopalians assigned his aberrant behavior to insanity and had little fear that others would follow his course, they were deeply disturbed by his explanation of why he remained within the church. He believed, he explained, in the creeds in a symbolic fashion. This was permissible because "there [is] no one in [the Episcopal] church or in any among the churches who believe all of the articles of the creed literally." When personal initiatives failed to quiet Brown, a court of bishops tried and deposed him (1924).[16]

The following year the full General Convention met for the first time since the publication of Bishop Lawrence's biography had triggered unrest. The session, whose work included adoption on first reading of a new *Book of Common Prayer,* went amazingly smoothly. One action soon aroused the ire of the critics of modernism, however. The convention's draft of the prayer book dropped the Thirty-nine Articles as a statement of faith. When the bishops and deputies gathered in 1928 to deliberate on the second reading of the book, they were greeted with a series of petitions—one contained 34,057 signatures—demanding a restoration of the Articles.[17] Both the House of Bishops and the House of Deputies bowed to the obvious and unanimously reversed their position.[18]

The Decline of the Church Congress Movement

One casualty in the war over doctrine was the Church Congress movement and the broad church coalition it represented. After the skirmishes in the midtwenties, participants on all sides began to lose confidence in the ability of the organization to bring consensus through open discussion. The death of general chairman and Bishop of Massachusetts Charles Lewis Slattery (1867–1930) and the election of Harold Adye Prichard (1882–1944) as his replacement only confirmed such suspicions. Prichard, an English-born New York clergyman, had made his own modernist sympathies clear the year before Slattery's death, when he had called the Apostles' Creed "a museum piece of revered antiquity" that the Episcopal Church should replace with a "Twentieth Century Creed as an effective means of bringing in the Kingdom of God." Such a creed, Prichard's remarks seemed to suggest, would dwell less on such "negative things" as Jesus' death and suffering and more on his "doing good."[19] By 1934, the Congress halted its regular meetings. The minutes of the final session were not even published.[20]

When the Congress began to falter, Episcopalians created new institutions and organizations to help them deal with the fundamentalist-modernist conflict. Three faculty members at ETS joined with other modernist Episcopalians to establish the Modern Churchman's Union. Shirley Carter Hughson (1867–1949), the superior of the Order of the Holy Cross (1918–21, 1930–36) played a leading role in a new Anglo-Catholic Congress (1923). Walter Russell Bowie, (1882–1969), rector of Grace Church, New York City (1923–39) and faculty member of Union Theological Seminary, New York (1939–50), played a major role in organizing a similar set of congresses for broad church Episcopalians with more evangelical leanings (1933).[21]

Many of those who had participated in the Church Congresses transferred their efforts to these new, less comprehensive bodies. Bowie had been a member of the executive committee of the Church Congresses since 1924. Harold Adye Prichard, who had chaired the final Church Congresses, assisted him. Frank Gavin of General Seminary and Father James O.S. Huntington, who had both participated in the Church Congress movement, worked with the new Anglo-Catholic Congresses.

Sensing that nineteenth-century party titles did not quite fit their own situation, church members scrambled for new party labels. Frank Gavin of General Seminary suggested *liberal catholicism* in his *Liberal Catholicism in the Modern World* (1934). Walter Russell Bowie and those who cooperated with him in the creation of a more evangelical church congress chose the name *liberal evangelical* for their gatherings. As the *liberal* titles indicated, both groups believed that they had more in common with the modernists than with the fundamentalists. Yet both also hoped to avoid what they regarded as a false opposition of faith and modern science. In order to do so, liberal catholics looked to tradition; liberal evangelicals, to a personal relationship with God. Thus, Frank Gavin voiced a common liberal catholic hope when he wrote that "whatever we have learned of truth, both from the tradition of the Church and from the adventures of human thought, is all of a piece, since man's knowledge of truth derives from Him who is all truth."[22] In the same year (1934), Bishop of California Edward Lambe Parsons (1868–1960) explained that liberal evangelicals "stress the unity of all truth and the revelation in scientific and historical discovery of the wider meanings of the Personality of God," in order to get behind "dogmas . . . to discover that they are but the clothing of a deep and essential personal relationship."[23]

There were, as always, other differences that separated these reconstituted church parties. The liberal evangelical leadership supported closer ecumenical relationships with Protestant denominations—in particular a dialogue with the Northern Presbyterians about possible merger initiated at the 1937 General Convention by a commission on unity that Parsons chaired—and the liberal catholics opposed it. An innovation in secular dress gave rise to another distinction. The liberal evangelical leaders joined Protestant clergy of other denominations in adopting the shirts with attached collars in their weekday dress; liberal catholics preserved the detachable starched collars of the Victorian era.[24]

The debate over modernism also had an effect on the church's theological seminaries. Faculty members, many of whom had themselves been vocal participants in the national discussion on the side of modernism, began to suspect that the laity did not share all their opinions. Fearing that they would lose their intellectual independence, several seminaries moved to new locations closer to major universities, where they hoped to preserve academic freedom. Dean William Palmer Ladd (1870–1941) engineered the moving of Berkeley Divinity School from Middletown to New Haven, Connecticut, and the environs of Yale University (1917). The Church Divinity School of the Pacific moved to Berkeley, California (1930), and Seabury Theological School left Minnesota to unite with Western Seminary near Northwestern University in Chicago (1933).

Reassessing the Social Ministry of the Church

By the 1920s, the commitment of turn-of-the-century Episcopalians to broader participation in the church was beginning to bear fruit. Black (suffragan) bishops sat in General Convention. The number of deaconesses continued to increase. Laywomen were more and more vocal about their desire to play a larger role in the decision making of the church. Women missionaries from the Diocese of Hankow (China) petitioned the General Convention of 1916, for example, for representation in their diocesan Council of Advice. Three years later, two working-class women violated the normal rules of order to address the Rochester session of the Church Congress on the subject of capitalism.[25]

Some of the white male leaders of the church began to have second thoughts about such developments. They were content to support female and minority leadership only so long as that leadership was exercised within separate parallel structures; they questioned the ability or propriety of female or minority leadership for the church as a whole. Not all agreed with them, yet those who questioned such leadership were sufficiently numerous that the church gradually retreated from its earlier commitment to democratization.

This retreat was particularly clear in the case of the movement for ethnic suffragan bishops. In 1918, the first two black suffragans had been elected in North Carolina and Arkansas. When Bishop William Alexander Guerry (1861–1928) called for the election of a black suffragan in South Carolina, however, a white opponent of the plan assassinated the bishop (1928).[26] The Diocese of North Carolina decided not to elect a replacement for Bishop Delany, who died in the same year.[27] Bishop Demby of Arkansas continued to serve as a suffragan for another eleven years, but with his retirement in 1939, the Episcopal Church was left without any active black bishops in the United States. Similarly, when Suffragan Bishop Manuel Ferrando of Puerto Rico died in 1934, the General Convention made no move to replace him. While a black suffragan bishop (Theophilus Momolu Firah Gardiner, suffragan 1921–41) did remain active in Liberia, the House of Bishops elected (1919, 1925, 1937) three successive white bishops to serve as diocesan. That situation would remain unchanged until the 1960s, when John Burgess of Massachusetts became the third black to serve as an American suffragan bishop (1962) and the first to serve as diocesan (1970). In the same decade, Romulado González Agueros (1906–66) and Francisco Reus Froylan (b. 1919) became the first Hispanics to serve as diocesan bishops in Cuba (1961) and Puerto Rico (1964).[28]

Even without additional black suffragans, however, black and white Episcopalians became increasingly isolated from one another. In the 1880s, black and white Episcopalians in the South had at least on some occasions worshiped with one another.[29] By the 1920s, however, black suffragans, archdeacons, and parish clergy ministered to black parishes whose primary representation was in black convocations. This segregation caused some black Episcopalians to ask why they should have any contact with whites at all. George Alexander McGuire (1866–1934), for example, led a small group of black Episcopalians to form the African Orthodox Church in 1921. McGuire was a West Indian who joined the Episcopal Church after coming to the United States. Ordained a deacon (1896) and priest (1897) by Bishop Boyd Vincent (1845–1935) of Southern Ohio, he served parishes and held administrative positions in rapid succession in Cincinnati, Philadelphia, Richmond, Little Rock (Archdeacon of the Colored

Convocation), Cambridge, and New York (field secretary of the Episcopal Church's American Church Institute for Negroes). After spending six years in Antigua (1913–19), McGuire returned to the United States as an active supporter of Marcus Garvey's (1887–1940) United Negro Improvement Association of the World. With Garvey's backing, McGuire organized the African Orthodox Church and served as its first bishop.[30]

Episcopal women suffered a similar setback. The 1920s had opened with an optimistic note. Though the 1919 General Convention rejected a resolution from the Diocese of Maine to grant full rights and privileges to women in the church, the Lambeth Conference of 1920 went on record as supporting admission of women "to those Councils of the Church in which laymen [were] admitted," and it defined the order of deaconesses as an "order of the Ministry which has the stamp of Apostolic approval."[31]

The General Conventions of 1922, 1925, and 1928 passed, however, without the Episcopal Church following the Lambeth recommendation on admission of women. The Conventions of 1925 and 1928 also rejected a deaconesses' request for inclusion of an office of ordination of deaconesses in the new *Book of Common Prayer* (1928). The Lambeth Conference of 1930 qualified its stance of ten years before by removing the phrase "the stamp of Apostolic approval" from the description of the female diaconate and by directing that deaconesses not be ordained in the joint services with male deacons or priests.[32] The General Convention of 1931, confused about the status of deaconesses, suspended the requirement that deaconesses who marry leave their orders. The following Convention reversed the policy, again requiring all those who exercised the female diaconate to be unmarried.[33]

Increasingly, younger women interested in church vocations turned to another avenue of service, that of professional church worker. The church workers, who were often, but not exclusively, engaged in Christian education, worked as employees of the church without taking the vows of either deaconesses or

Fig. 44. The setting apart of Deaconess Harriet Bedell (front row, right of Bishop Tuttle) in 1922, the year in which the greatest number of deaconesses served in the Episcopal Church

nuns. While the number of deaconesses began to decline after 1922, the number of such church workers grew rapidly. Existing educational institutions adapted to the change in interest, often dropping deaconess from their titles and increasing their focus on Christian education. In 1939, for example, the Church Training and Deaconess School of the Diocese of Pennsylvania affiliated with the Philadelphia Divinity School as the women's department and designated Katharine Arnett Grammer as the dean of women. In 1942, the Deaconess Training School of the Pacific in Berkeley began to advertise in church periodicals as St. Margaret's House. Three years later, Katharine Grammer moved from Philadelphia to serve as dean. Two new institutions opened as well: Windam House (New York City, 1928) and the Bishop Tuttle Training School (Raleigh, North Carolina, 1925).

During the Depression years, women were losing some of their authority in the church in another way. From the middle of the nineteenth century on, the ability of women to raise money had been one of the chief sources of their power. It was often, for example, the women's circles that footed the bill for the purchase of rectories and for improvements in church buildings. The social and community events that turn-of-the-century women had found to be the most valuable mechanisms for fund raising proved decreasingly effective during the Depression and the austere war years, however. Many people simply lacked the funds to contribute. Even where funds were not lacking, moreover, church events had to compete with movies (America's fifth largest industry with an annual gross income of $1.5 billion by 1926) and other elements of a growing entertainment industry.[34]

The social ministries in which women played such important roles also suffered. The more conservative mood and the dramatic loss of funds that followed the onset of the Depression meant that less money was available for the many special ministries that had characterized the Episcopal Church at the turn of the century. The number of deaf men entering the priesthood declined sharply, for example. There had been eleven ordained between 1922 and 1931, and only two between 1932 and 1941.[35] If clergy in what had been strong, self-supporting parishes were badly in need of funds, how could the special ministries of the church expect full support?

The combined receipts of the Episcopal parishes in 1927 were $44.7 million. By 1934, this sum had fallen to $30.6 million. One rural rector later recorded his frustration in an autobiography. Retelling what was not a unique experience, he explained that his salary was cut so deeply by the vestry that he and his wife were no longer able to survive on what the church provided:

> Soon afterward the vestry notified me of an impending cut in salary. This I refused to accept but countered by offering my resignation dated two years hence, when, by my age, I should qualify for pension. The vestry replied, I think quite truthfully, that they could no longer raise the pittance they gave. I said, quite as truthfully, that I could not live on the reduced salary. The discussion was conducted, of course, in the best Anglican manner but led to a complete impasse.
>
> The upshot was that [my wife] Susie went to live with our daughters while I took mission work near Richmond. There was

more money than I got at [Berryville], but no rectory. My very dear wife and I at last were parted— after forty years.[36]

Clergy, who had already lost ground in the economically volatile 1920s to the point that average Protestant clergy salaries in 1928 were lower than those of factory workers, often changed during the Depression from respected members of the community to the recipients of charity. Even by 1960, some clergy had not regained salaries on a level equivalent to those held by their predecessors in similar positions in the 1920s.[37]

World War II

Episcopalians embraced the cause of the American armies in the Second World War much as they had in the First. Laymen and laywomen, as well as clergy chaplains, went off to war, taking with them abbreviated prayer books (the *Prayer Book for Soldiers and Sailors,* 1941) and Episcopal service crosses.

Episcopalians were not, however, all supporters of the war effort. In October 1939, John Nevin Sayre, Mrs. Henry Hill (Katharine Pierce, d. 1967), and some five hundred others met at the Church of the Incarnation, New York City, to create the Episcopal Pacifistic Fellowship. Sayre had been active in the interdenominational Fellowship of Reconciliation. Hill was both a member of the church's National Council and the first woman to serve on a vestry in New York City. She was the Episcopal Pacifistic Fellowship's first secretary and an active member for almost thirty years.

The new organization, which would later change its name to the Episcopal Peace Fellowship, pressured the National Council to establish the list of conscientious objectors that the General Convention had authorized in 1934 and to appoint a Commission on Conscientious Objectors (1943) in order to provide advice and published materials on pacifism. During 1943 and 1944, the Pacifistic Fellowship membership stood at about eight hundred. The organization listed among its accomplishments the inclusion of six new peace hymns in the *Hymnal 1940,* such as "Lord Christ, when First Thou Cam'st to Earth," composed by fellowship supporter Walter Russell Bowie.[38]

One result of the war effort was a temporary elevation of women in the church to more positions of leadership. While the United States did not follow the lead of Bishop R.O. Hall of the Diocese of South China, who ordained Deaconess Florence Li Tim Oi (1907–92) a priest in 1944, women did rise to levels of leader-

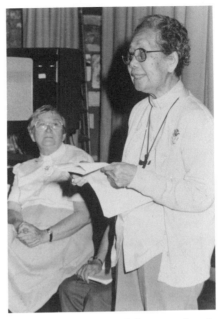

Fig. 45. 1988 photo of first two female priests, Li Tim Oi (1944) and Joyce Bennett (1970)

ship that they had not previously exercised. Mrs. Randolph Dyer, for example, attended the General Convention of 1946 as one of the deputies from Missouri.

These events would, however, be looked upon as departures from the norm. In 1949, the General Convention denied women voice and vote. Similarly, the Lambeth Conference of 1948 rejected a proposal from South China that would have validated Deaconess Li's ordination to the priesthood, warning that such an action "would be against [the Anglican] tradition and order and would gravely affect the internal and external relations of the Anglican Communion."[39] Her diocese inhibited her from exercising her priesthood.

Searching for New Beginnings

When the war ended and Americans were able to enjoy a measure of peace and prosperity, the seeds for a new growth were already in place. During the Depression, Episcopalians had out of necessity taken the time to search for new meaning in their faith. Two particular results of this search—the beginnings of a liturgical revival and the discovery of continental theology of crisis—would be important for the future.

The liturgical revival began at a number of theological seminaries across the church. Dean William Palmer Ladd of Berkeley Seminary visited Europe in the interwar years and returned with news of a liturgical movement among the Roman Catholics centered in the Maria Laach Monastery in Germany. Frank Gavin of Nashotah and General seminaries prepared an *Anglican Missal* and interested a widening group of colleagues and students in liturgical enrichment. Bishop of California Edward L. Parsons joined with Bayard Hale Jones (1887–1957) to produce the *American Prayer Book* in 1937, a commentary on the new *Book of Common Prayer* (1928).

English author Arthur Gabriel Hebert suggested one motive behind this new interest in liturgics. He wrote in *Liturgy and Society* (1935) that the shared meaning of liturgy offered an escape from the confusion of the modernist–fundamentalist debate.[40] A second English author, Dom Gregory Dix (1901–1952), prepared an exhaustive study of early eucharistic rites *(The Shape of the Liturgy,* 1945) whose major thesis—that the early celebrations were built around the four actions of taking, blessing, breaking, and giving of bread and wine—affected the revisions of the *Book of Common Prayer* in the decades that would follow.

One of the shared concerns of these liturgical scholars was an increased lay involvement in the liturgy. Liturgical innovators introduced new services that used dramatic action in an attempt to incorporate parishioners in the liturgical action. Many congregations initiated, for example, Palm Sunday processions and the midnight Christmas Eve services during these years. The *Book of Common Prayer* 1928 did not provide for such additions to the liturgy, but the General Convention of 1937 authorized a separate *Book of Offices* (first published in 1940) that provided a form for many such parish observances.

While some were advocating liturgical renewal, others were finding solace in the crisis theology that Reformed theologians Karl Barth (1886–1968), and Emil Brunner (1889–1966), had forged in the wake of World War I. Their modernist predecessors had confidently supported the German war effort as an advance of German culture. The German loss on the battlefields, however, led Barth and his colleagues to reject any simple equation of culture and faith. While not rejecting the fruit of a century of German biblical scholarship, they injected a new note of judgment—God was the one who called all human intellectual and social endeavors into question. Americans of the twenties, celebrating their victory in Europe, had little interest in such a message, but this theology of crisis found fertile ground in the United States of the Depression. Lutheran Paul Tillich (1886–1965) came from Germany to New York, where combining forces with Evangelical and Reformed Reinhold Niebuhr (1892–1971) he turned Union Seminary into a stronghold of what Americans came to call neo-orthodoxy. Walter Lowrie (1868–1959), the Episcopal rector of St. Paul's in Rome (1907–30) and translator of the works of Søren Kierkegaard (1813–55), was another scholar who carried continental crisis theology to America of the 1930s.

The outlines of the theology of crisis blurred in the American setting as Americans combined conflicting European trends. The goal of this new theology, however, was clear. American Christians wanted a theology that took the modern situation—with its failures as well at its successes—seriously, while still proclaiming the essence of an orthodox Christianity. The movement of the earlier modernism had been in many cases one-directional—scientific reason discarded that which was not modern in the Christian tradition. The proponents of this new orthodoxy, in contrast, were anxious to move in two directions. Scientific reason might question some traditional interpretations of Scripture, but the Christian's faith could question the goals and delusions of contemporary life.

Frederick Clifton Grant (1891–1974), a prolific Episcopal

theologian who had taught in sequence at Bexley Hall, Berkeley, and Seabury–Western, joined the faculty at Union Seminary in 1938. The following year he led an effort to revive the Church Congress movement as a vehicle for crisis theology. Only two of the Congresses (renamed the Triennial Church Congress in the modest expectation that they would meet less regularly than the previous body) were ever held, but they provided the first opportunity for many Episcopalians to hear directly about crisis theology from Grant's colleague Paul Tillich. Tillich touched Episcopalians in other ways as well. Albert T. Mollegen (1906–84) and Clifford L. Stanley (1902–94) of the Virginia Seminary faculty both spent periods of study with Tillich at Union in New York.

NOTES

1. John Wallace Suter, "The Essentials in Prayer Book Revision," in *The Church and Its American Opportunity: Papers by Various Writers Read at the Church Congress in 1919* (New York: Macmillan, 1919), 106.

2. Robert W. Lynn, "Why the Seminary? An Introduction to the Report of the Auburn History Project" (Paper presented to the faculty of the Candler School of Theology on September 15, 1978), 90, 95; E. Brooks Holifield, *A History of Pastoral Care in America: From Salvation to Self-Realization* (Nashville: Abingdon Press, 1983), 234.

3. David L. Holmes, "The Anglican Tradition and the Episcopal Church," in *Encyclopedia of American Religious Experiences,* ed. Charles Lippy and Peter Williams (New York: Scribner's, 1987), 411.

4. George Ashton Oldham, "How Shall the Church Deal with Fundamentalism," in *Honest Liberty in the Church: A Record of the Church Congress in the United States on Its Fiftieth Anniversary* (New York: Macmillan, 1924), 375.

5. Arthur A.C. Hall, "How Shall the Church Deal with Fundamentalism," in *Honest Liberty,* 398.

6. Suter, "Essentials," in *Church and Its American Opportunity,* 106.

7. William Lawrence, *Fifty Years* (Boston: Houghton Mifflin, 1923), 72.

8. *The Living Church* (October 6, 1923):730.

9. *Journal of the General Convention of the Protestant Episcopal Church in the United States . . . 1925* (printed for the convention, 1925), 470–71.

10. Ibid.

11. Ibid.

12. William Lawrence, "The Present Situation in the Church," in *Honest Liberty,* 406–7.

13. Hugh Martin Jansen, Jr, "Heresy Trials in the Protestant Episcopal Church, 1890–1930" (Ph.D. diss., Columbia University, 1965), 234, 238–39, 251–52.

14. Ibid., 259.

15. William Montgomery Brown, *Communism and Christianity* (Galion, Ohio: Bradford-Brown Educational Company, 1922), 3.

16. Jansen, "Heresy," 294–301.

17. *Journal of the General Convention 1928,* 197.

18. Ibid., 350, 357.

19. H. Adye Prichard, "To What Extent Are the Articles of the Christian Faith as Contained in the Apostles' Creed Subject to Change or Revision?," in *The Church and the Future: A Record of the Church Congress in the United States on its Fifty-Fifth Anniversary* (New York: Edwin S. Gorham, 1919), 79–81.

20. Richard M. Spielmann, "The Episcopal Church Congress, 1874–1934," *Anglican and Episcopal Church History* 58 (March 1989):78.

21. Ibid. An English Churchman's Union (1898; renamed Modern Churchman's Union, 1928) and Anglo–Church Congress (1920) provided the inspiration for the American bodies of the same name.

22. Frank Gavin, *Belief,* vol. 1 of *Liberal Catholicism and the Modern World* (Milwaukee: Morehouse Publishing, 1934), vi.

23. Edward Lambe Parsons, *The Liberal Evangelical Message in Our Church Today,* Liberal Evangelical Pamphlets no. 2 (Cambridge, Mass.: Cosmos Press, 1934), 2.

24. Bishop William Scarlett of Missouri (1883–1973) was one of the leaders in the adoption of the tie as a standard of clerical dress for liberal evangelicals. The 1953 *Stowe's Clerical Directory,* the first to include photographs of all Episcopal clergy, showed six dioceses (Missouri, Bethlehem, Georgia, Eastern Oregon, New Mexico and Southwest Texas, and Southern Ohio) in which a third to a fifth of the clergy appeared in soft collars and ties and five other dioceses (Northern Michigan, East Carolina, Virginia, Southern Virginia, and Idaho) with at least ten of the clergy in the same fashion. In some cases, however, clergy appear in liturgical vestments. See *Stowe's Clerical Directory of the Protestant Episcopal Church in the United States of America, 1953* (New York: Church Hymnal Corporation, 1953), P1–P84.

25. *Journal of the General Convention, 1916,* 41, 74; Spielmann, "Episcopal Church Congress," p. 76. The General Convention

rejected the petition from the female missionaries in the Diocese of Hankow.

The normal procedure at the Church Congress, which the two working-class women violated, was to address questions only in writing.

26. J. Kenneth Morris, *Elizabeth Evelyn Wright 1872–1906, Founder of Voorhees College* (Sewanee: University of the South, 1983), 242. Following the attack, the assassin, the Rev. James Herbert Woodward, committed suicide.

27. Lawrence Foushee London and Sarah McCulloh Lemmon, eds., *The Episcopal Church in North Carolina, 1701–1959* (Raleigh: Episcopal Diocese of North Carolina, 1987), 348.

28. The major exception to the Episcopal retreat from native bishops in Latin America was Mexico. As a result of that nation's revolution, national law forbade foreign clergy from serving native congregations. Suffragan Bishop Efraín Salinas y Velasco was elected diocesan bishop in 1934. José Saucedo succeeded him in 1957.

29. C. Vann Woodward, *The Strange Career of Jim Crow,* 3d rev. ed. (New York: Oxford University Press, 1974), 42–43. Woodward quoted Charles Dudly Warner about integration in an Episcopal Church and in a community festival in New Orleans at the time of the International Exposition of 1885. In his book *Lee: the Last Years* (Boston: Houghton Mifflin, 1981), Charles Bracelen Flood reported a similar story about Virginia in the 1860s. A black man came forward to receive communion at St. Paul's Church, Richmond, in the spring of 1865. Lee joined him at the communion rail (p. 66).

Woodward warned, however, that modern readers were not to interpret such information as indicative of a golden age of race relations. The 1880s and 1890s were marked by racial violence.

30. Donald S. Armentrout, *Episcopal Splinter Groups: A Study of Groups Which Have Left the Episcopal Church, 1873–1985* (Sewanee, Tennessee: School of Theology of the University of the South, 1985), 2–7.

31. V. Nelle Bellamy, "Participation of Women in the Public Life of the Church from Lambeth Conference, 1867–1978," *Historical Magazine of the Protestant Episcopal Church* 51 (March 1982): 89–90.

32. Ibid., 91.

33. William Wilson Manross, *A History of the American Episcopal Church* (New York: Morehouse-Barlow, 1935), 353.

34. See, for example, Joan R. Gundersen, *"Before the World Confessed": All Saints Parish, Northfield, and the Community, 1858–1985* (Northfield, Minn.: Northfield Historical Society, 1987), 99 and 153. Gundersen notes that turn-of-the-century women's organizations at All Saints controlled a budget larger than that disbursed by the parish vestry. By the 1950s, that was no longer the case.

The figures on the movie industry are from John Gregory Dunne, "Goldwynism," *New York Review* (18 May 1989):29.

35. Otto Benjamin Berg, *A Missionary Chronicle: Being a History of the Ministry to the Deaf in the Episcopal Church (1850–1980)* (Hollywood, Md.: St. Mary's Press, 1984), 121, 262. Berg noted, however, that even with declines the Episcopal Church remained, together with the Lutheran churches, as a leader in the ministry to the deaf.

36. Louis Tucker, *Clerical Errors* (New York: Harper & Brothers, 1943), 346.

37. Holifield, *A History of Pastoral Care,* 217; Raymond Albright, *A History of the Protestant Episcopal Church* (New York: Macmillan, 1964), 345. The average Protestant salary in 1928 was $1,407.

38. Nathaniel W. Pierce and Paul L. Ward, *The Voice of Conscience: A Loud and Unusual Noise? The Episcopal Peace Fellowship 1939–1989* (Charlestown, Mass.: Charles River Printing for the Episcopal Peace Fellowship, 1989), 7–10.

Walter Russell Bowie attended the organizing conference in 1939 and served as a counsellor for the fellowship.

39. Bellamy, "Lambeth Conference," 93.

40. Urban Holmes, "Education for Liturgy," in *Worship Points the Way: a Celebration of the Life and Work of Massey Hamilton Shepherd, Jr.,* ed. Malcolm C. Burson (New York: Seabury Press, 1981), 118.

9
The Church Triumphant
(1945–65)

When the soldiers returned home from the war, America entered an unprecedented period of growth and expansion. The army had taken many young men from their communities and shown them a wider world. Equipped with this experience and with the "G.I. Bill," which subsidized their education, the returning soldiers married and flocked to the newly growing suburbs, where they and their wives produced a record number of children. Churches followed the new families to the suburbs. Denominations expanded at an astounding rate, and the percentage of Americans who claimed church affiliation reached an all-time high.

Table 5. Ratio of Church
Members and Communicants
of the Episcopal Church to the Population of the United States Since 1830

Year	Population	Church Members (Baptized Persons)		Communicants	
		Number	Ratio	Number	Ratio
1830...	12,866,020	....	....	30,939	1–416
1840...	17,069,453	....	....	55,477	1–308
1850...	23,191,876	....	....	98,655	1–235
1860...	31,443,321	....	....	150,591	1–209
1870...	38,558,371	....	....	231,591	1–166
1880...	50,155,783	....	....	341,155	1–147
1890...	62,947,714	....	....	531,525	1–118
1900...	75,994,575	....	....	742,569	1–102
1910...	91,972,266	....	....	930,037	1–99
1920...	105,710,620	....	....	1,073,832	1–98
1930...	122,775,046	1,886,972	1–65	1,261,167	1–97
1940...	131,669,275	2,073,546	1–64	1,437,820	1–92
1950...	150,697,361	2,478,813	1–61	1,640,101	1–92
1960...	179,323,195	3,269,325	1–55	2,095,573	1–86

Source: *The Episcopal Church Annual, 1966*

These were good years for the Episcopal Church from a statistical point of view. The ratio-of-communicants charts that had been carried in copies of the *Church Annual* since the turn of the century showed record gains. In 1960, one out of every eighty-six Americans was a member of the Episcopal Church.[1] Signs bearing the Episcopal Church's seal (adopted by the General Convention of 1940) and announcing that "the Episcopal Church Welcomes You" became regular fixtures in the expanding suburbs.

Fig. 46.
The Episcopal Church Welcomes You

Theology

The neo-orthodoxy of which members of the seminary communities took increasing notice in the 1930s provided a theological framework for this new surge of church growth. Post–World War II American Christians found that neo-orthodoxy addressed many of the questions that preoccupied them. Francis Lincoln and other Washington, D.C., area laypersons, for example, began to meet weekly in 1946 in order to discuss the Christian faith in the context of the modern world. Attendance increased so rapidly that participants quickly outgrew both the house in which they were meeting and the informal discussion format. In 1947, they moved to the library of the National Cathedral and asked Virginia Seminary professors Albert T. Mollegen and Clifford Stanley to lecture.[2] Organizers continued the series, which they titled "Christianity and Modern Man," until the 1960s. In addition to Mollegen and Stanley, the lecturers would eventually include Lutheran theologian Paul Tillich; St. Paul's (Los Angeles) Cathedral dean and later Bishop of Southern Ohio John Krumm (1913–95); and Virginia Seminary theologian and Harvard University preacher Charles P. Price (b. 1920).

The hunger for an exposition of the Christian faith was not a local Washington area phenomenon. From New York, for example, Dean James Pike (1913–69) of the Cathedral of St. John the Divine, a former chairperson of the department of religion at Columbia University, broadcast a religious television program that was carried on a major network for six years.

The national church attempted to fill the need for serious explanation of the faith for adults. From 1949 to 1955, the Episcopal Church's new publishing house, Seabury Press, published a six-volume Church's Teaching Series intended to provide the interested adult a grounding in the Christian faith and the Episcopal tradition. Robert C. Dentan (1907–95), a professor of Old Testament at General Seminary, produced an initial volume on Holy Scriptures. Powel Mills Dawley (1907–85), his colleague at General and a professor of ecclesiastical history, wrote volumes on the history of Christianity and the working of the Episcopal Church. Dean Pike collaborated with W. Norman Pittenger (b. 1905), who was then an apologetics professor at General, to produce a volume on the faith of the church. Massey H. Shepherd, Jr. (1913–90), an Episcopal Theological School and Church Divinity School of the Pacific faculty member, wrote a volume on the worship of the church; and Stephen Bayne, Jr. (1908–74), then Bishop of Olympia and later the Anglican Communion's executive officer, wrote the volume on Christian living. Together the six volumes were an impressive presentation of the Christian faith, one that, in keeping with the neo-orthodox goals of the day, combined a sophistication in dealing with the modern world with a constructive effort to put the Christian faith in clear language.

In the same years, Randolph Crump Miller (b. 1910) and members of the Episcopal Church's education board prepared the Seabury Series to replace the 1915 Christian Nurture Sunday school materials. Miller, a professor of religious edu-

cation first at CDSP and later at Yale Divinity School, explained the theory and method of the new curriculum in his
1956 *Education for Christian Living*. The church school teacher was to use a variety of techniques to bring biblical material
to life for the students:

> The recounting of Bible events is for the purpose of letting God
> speak to the one who reads or hears.
>
> Sometimes this can be accomplished by telling the Bible story
> and then by recounting a modern tale of the peer group that has
> exactly the same plot. Such obvious examples as the lost sheep or
> the lost coin or the widow's mite can be adapted to the modern
> conditions of almost any age group. Characters who are already
> established and whom the children recognize as their favorites
> may have experiences that parallel those of people in the Bible,
> and thus relevance of the Bible for the contemporary scene is
> made vivid.
>
> Bible paraphrases are essential with small children and are ef-
> fective with almost any age group. The telling of a familiar story
> with a different vocabulary and with an interpretation that brings
> out its deeper meaning will often send the listeners to the Bible
> for more information.[3]

The series paid less attention to social action than did the earlier Christian Nurture material and focused more on the complexities of modern life. Miller hoped that the retelling of
stories in contemporary settings could provide children with
the same grounding in faith that the Church's Teaching Series
was providing for their parents. The father who asked his sons
to labor in the vineyard of Matthew 21 became the father who
wanted his car washed, and Lent became the church's "spring
training."

While any educational materials have their weaknesses, the
Church's Teaching Series and the Seabury Series had obvious
strengths, providing a growing church an identity as a denomination both engaged in the problems of modern life and concerned with the proclamation of the gospel.

The neo-orthodox theologians to whom Episcopalians
turned agreed that modern culture was to be taken seriously

but were never blind to the sinfulness inherent in all of human life. Evangelical and Reformed theologian Reinhold Niebuhr had warned in *Moral Man and Immoral Society* (1932), for example, that "no society will ever be so just that some method of escape from its cruelties and injustices will not be sought by the pure heart." The cross, he wrote, was "not triumphant in the world and the society. Society, in fact, conspired the cross. Both the state and the church were involved in it, and probably will be to the end."[4]

Such theology gave the Episcopalians who embraced it in the post–World War II years a tool with which they could examine contemporary social ills. Some Episcopalians were willing to make such a critique. Reinhold Niebuhr's good friend Bishop William Scarlett (1833–1973) of Missouri, for example, edited a volume entitled *Christianity Takes a Stand* (1946) with essays critical of segregation (by Walter Russell Bowie) and the wartime internment of Japanese Americans (by Edward L. Parsons). Most in the church were not, however, anxious to pursue such a line of thought. Filled with a postwar optimism about the prospects of American society, they were more willing to listen to a neo-orthodox analysis of the errors of their enemies than they were to look closely at the ills of their own nation. As the House of Deputies indicated in 1946 by refusing without debate to sponsor publication of Scarlett's book, not all thought that it was time for Christianity to take a stand.[5]

Patterns in postwar seminary education reinforced this muting of the critical elements of neo-orthodoxy. Seminaries were at the time adding clinical pastoral education (a hospital-based summer internship that had been introduced in the thirties by the Council for the Clinical Training of Theological Students and the New England Theological Schools Committee on Clinical Training) and expanding the number of courses in psychology in their curricula. What seminarians learned from clinical pastoral education and from the reading of psychologists, of whom Carl Rogers (b. 1902) was perhaps the most influential, was more in accordance with the modernism of the 1920s than with neo-orthodoxy. They left seminary convinced that good pastoral care involved listening, caring, and enabling parishioners to reach their own decisions but that it rarely involved criticism or unsolicited advice. Reinhold Niebuhr's brother, H. Richard Niebuhr of Yale, warned in a 1955 survey of theological education of the impact this emphasis on pastoral care had on the theological curriculum as a whole, but few heeded his warning.[6]

Institutional Change

The major motif of the 1950s was growth. In New York, the church began to seriously overflow the offices on Fourth Avenue that it had occupied since 1894. Branch offices were opened in other parts of the city, in Connecticut, and in Chicago. Presiding Bishop (1958–64) Arthur Lichtenburger asked General Convention for a new office complex. In 1960, the national offices moved into a new building at 815 Second Avenue with three times the space of the previous headquarters.

Such a growing denomination could no longer be led by a part-time presiding bishop. In 1944, Henry St. George Tucker (1874–1959), presiding bishop from 1938 to 1946, resigned his position as Bishop of Virginia. The General Convention adopted legislation requiring subsequent presiding bishops to resign their dioceses within six months of election.[7] In 1964, the General Convention, recognizing the increasing work load of the president of the House of Deputies, created the position of vice president for the body.[8] In 1958, similar concerns led the Anglican Communion to create the new position of executive officer, of which Bishop of Olympia Stephen F. Bayne, Jr., became the first.

Seminaries grew rapidly in the 1950s. The Joint Commission on Theological Education of the General Convention reported in 1952 that the number of seminary students had risen from 508 in 1947–48 to 1,043 in 1950–51.[9] Individual seminaries expanded their facilities and their faculties to make room for their expanding classes. In addition, Presiding Bishop (1947–58) Henry Knox Sherill and then Bishop of Texas John

Elbridge Hines (1910–97) led the way in providing for a new theological seminary in Austin, Texas. In 1952, Gray M. Blandy (1910–90) became the first dean of the school, which took the name the Episcopal Theological Seminary of the Southwest (ETS-SW).

The church of the post–World War II years was also more willing to join in ecumenical organizations than had the church at the turn of the century. The Episcopal Church, which had refused to join in the Federal Council of Churches (1908) and rejected a proposed merger with the Presbyterians (1946), joined both the World Council of Churches (formed in 1948) and the National Council of Churches (formed in 1950). The decision to join in such bodies reflected the greater confidence of a growing church, a recognition of the interrelated nature of modern life that had been brought by World War II, and a belief that the Faith and Order movement in which Episcopalians had been active was dealing with such issues as apostolic succession in a serious way. The Faith and Order movement was one of the organizations involved in the creation of the World Council.

Patterns of Church Life

The institutional patterns of the church in these years reflected the predominant American social patterns. Typically, an all-male leadership presided over a governmental organization, while adult females participated in a series of parallel organizations and children of both sexes participated in activities planned for their age groupings.

The General Conventions of the 1950s repeatedly reaffirmed their principle of male leadership; no women were to be allowed voice or vote. While there were exceptions, most dioceses and parishes also limited vestry and diocesan convention participation to males.

Women's auxiliaries and guilds did not have the financial clout that similar organizations had had before the Depression. Pre-Depression women's groups, at least in some parts of the country, had budgets that were equal in size to those under control of the vestries.[10] The Depression and a continued movement away from church-sponsored activities, however, cut into the income that could be produced by women's bazaars and other traditional fund-raising activities. By the 1950s, even the most ambitious women's groups raised budgets that represented only a small percentage of the general parish funds.

Women's leadership patterns in the church were changing in another way. From 1922 on the number of women entering the office of deaconesses had begun to fall. The 1930 *Living Church Annual* listed 222 (active) deaconesses. By the 1950 *Annual,* the number had dropped to 164 (active and retired); by 1960, to 86 (active and retired).[11] The decline was due in part to the elimination of the very jobs that deaconesses had filled. Secular nurses replaced deaconesses in the halls of hospitals, and the small congregations in which many deaconesses had served were rapidly disappearing. The widespread availability of the automobile made it possible to consolidate small rural and urban congregations and to build large new congregations in the suburbs. Thus, the number of baptized members increased (from 1,939,453 in 1930 to 3,615,643 in 1965) at a time when the number of congregations was declining (from 8,253 parishes and missions in 1930 to 7,539 in 1965).[12] The larger congregations that resulted rarely relied upon deaconesses, calling instead on one or more male clergy.

If the deaconess movement had passed its prime, however, the female professional church worker movement that had begun in the 1920s was entering its golden age.[13] Women with solid training in theological education learned that they had needed skills that equipped them to work in the larger congregations of the 1950s. They soon discovered that parish rectors, who were overwhelmed by the rapidly increasing number of children produced by post-World War II parents, were eager to hire women as salaried directors of Christian education.

A variety of programs, most of which were closely linked to theological seminaries, provided training for women interested in professional church work. Students at Windham House in New York (which began to grant a degree in religious education in a joint program with Columbia University and Union Seminary in 1946) and at the renamed St. Margaret's House in Berkeley took some of their classes from the faculty of General Seminary and the Church Divinity School of the Pacific. Bishop Payne Divinity School in Petersburg, Virginia, accepted female students in a special Christian education program from 1945 to 1950, and the Philadelphia Divinity School continued it program for female students until 1952.

In 1949, Windham House sponsored a conference that led to the formation of the Association of Professional Women Church Workers. In 1958, the association submitted a memorial to General Convention that led to a Joint Commission on the Status and Training of Professional Women Church Workers and eventually to the 1964 adoption of a canon titled "Of Professional Women Church Workers."[14]

The first females to teach in Episcopal seminaries were teachers of Christian education. Adelaide Teague Case (the Episcopal Theological School professor of Christian education beginning in 1941), Katharine Arnett Grammer (resident tutor in Christian education at the Philadelphia Divinity School, 1943; Dean of St. Margaret's House, 1945), Martha Pray (Bishop Payne Divinity School, instructor in Christian education, 1945–49), and Marian T. Kelleran (Virginia Seminary, adjunct professor 1949–62, and professor of Christian education 1963–72) joined the faculties of their respective institutions in the 1940s. Female students, who initially focused their studies on Christian education, appeared on seminary campuses about the same time. Clara O. Loveland, a graduate of Berkeley Divinity School in 1939, may have been the first woman to receive a Bachelor of Divinity degree from an Episcopal seminary. In 1947, the three graduates (Lillian Clarke, Iris King, and Matilda Syrette) completed the two-year program in Christian education for black women at Bishop Payne Divinity School, which was cosponsored by the Women's Auxiliary to the Board of Missions.[15] Eight years later, Jane Buchanan completed her studies at the Church Divinity School of the Pacific. An increasing number followed, including Muriel James and Marianne H. Micks (1923–97) in the class of 1957 at the Church Divinity School of the Pacific.[16] The Episcopal Theological School and Virginia Seminary enrolled their first women in the following year.[17]

At the same time that female professionals were moving from leadership in isolated missions to roles within larger male-led parishes and seminaries, representatives from the Women's Auxiliary to the Board of Missions were able to affect the organization of the National Council (General Convention's executive body that would change its name in 1964 to the Executive Council). A 1919 reorganization of the body had allowed for female membership on the Board of Missions, one of the five departments of the National Council. As a result of a request from the Women's Auxiliary, in 1958 the Council incorporated the Auxiliary's efforts in Christian education and Christian social relations with the Council's departments devoted to the same subjects, thus opening up three of the five departments to female participation. Finance and publicity remained for the time as male preserves. The Council also upgraded the status of the Women's Auxiliary to that of General Division for Women's Work. The 1958 Triennial Meeting of the Women of the Church applauded the changes and recommended that diocesan women's groups adopt the name Episcopal Church Women in the place of the "Women's Auxiliary" title that had implied subordinate status.[18]

Foreign Missions

The focus of foreign mission activities shifted in the 1950s. The victory of Mao Tse-tung in 1949 closed the Chinese mission field just at the time when the first generation of post–World War II seminary graduates was completing its education. Many, who had been abroad during the war, were anxious to return with the gospel now that the fighting had ended. At Virginia Seminary, for example, one-quarter of the class of 1950 enlisted in foreign mission work.[19]

While many of these new graduates went to Japan or the Philippines, others served in the Western Hemisphere. The election of William Gordon, Jr. (b. 1918), as Bishop of Alaska even before he reached the canonical age of thirty caught the imagination of many who volunteered for service in what was then an American territory. Others headed to Latin America, where the Episcopal Church was gradually taking over responsibilities for mission from the Church of England.

In Brazil, where the Episcopal Church had a firm foundation, Episcopalians divided into three dioceses in 1949. Work in Central America was slower, however. It was not until 1957 that the Episcopal Church formed the Missionary Diocese of Central America. After the bishops at the 1958 Lambeth Conference called Latin America a neglected continent, Episcopalians expanded their work to Colombia and Ecuador and subdivided the Diocese of Central America into five national dioceses (1968). In 1964, the Episcopal Church created Province IX so that Latin American dioceses could work toward greater autonomy.

Liturgy

For the first time in its long history, the Episcopal Church had as many priests as congregations in 1956.[20] This rise in the number of clergy combined with the increased speed of automobile transportation to make it possible for parishes to develop their liturgical life in a way that the smaller scattered missions of earlier in the century could not have done. The liturgical rhythm of small congregations with shared clergy often depended more upon the weather and the priest's schedule than upon the church year.

The swelling baby boom generation that followed the Second World War may have also contributed to greater liturgical flexibility. Children became so numerous that many congregations felt the need to separate them from adults on Sunday morning. Separate children's chapels and double sessions of Sunday school provided education and piety for younger children. Older children participated in worship with their parents until the sermon, at which time they left for classes of their own. Their exodus created congregations composed entirely of adults, who were more willing and more interested in the subtleties of the church year than were the intergenerational congregations of the 1930s. Parishes were able to dramatize the church year and focus on the centrality of the eucharist in a way in which they had not previously been able.

In 1946, Massey Shepherd, then an Episcopal Theological School history professor but later a professor of liturgics at the Church Divinity School of the Pacific, joined with a number of parish clergy to create the Associated Parishes. The organization, which scheduled conferences and published liturgical materials, was one of the most effective organizations for carrying the 1930s seminary liturgical movement to a parish level. Its *The Parish Eucharist* (1951) advocated the weekly celebration of the eucharist. *Holy Week Offices* (1958) supplemented the devotions available in the *Book of Offices* that had been approved by the 1937 General Convention. The Associated Parishes' volume added, for example, a form for the Way of the Cross and Tenebrae, and a Good Friday Office. *Before the Holy Table* (1956), also from Associated Parishes, explained the rationale for a change in celebrants' posture:

> It is commonly claimed in favor of celebrations of the Eucharist, in which ministers face the people, that the corporate participation of the congregation in the rite is thereby enhanced. The people are enabled to see, and not merely to imagine, all the necessary, no less than symbolic, ceremonies that are associated with the breaking of the Bread. The rite is clearly visualized in its essential character as the holy Supper of the Lord, the festal banquet of the Church, which is our earnest of the Messianic Feast in the Kingdom of God.[21]

The celebrant who faced the congregation made the parallel between Christ's Last Supper and the parish eucharist more vivid.

The adoption of this posture at the eucharist in most cases required a redesign of the chancel, for in 1950 most Episcopal church buildings had altars affixed to the wall. Canon Edward West (1909–90) of the Cathedral of St. John the Divine in New York City, an early advocate of celebration facing the people, was one of the first to see the multiple possibilities resulting from such a redesign. He favored broader, more open chancels in which dramatic processions and eucharistic celebrations with multiple clergy were possible.

Canon West's only authority over liturgy outside of his cathedral stemmed from the persuasiveness of personal argument and the example of the liturgy at St. John the Divine. The Associated Parishes was only a voluntary organization within the church. Yet West and the Associated Parishes were both extremely influential. West's ideas were incorporated in many of the new church buildings of the 1950s. A number of the Associated Parish's liturgical suggestions would, moreover, eventually appear in the *Book of Common Prayer* 1979.

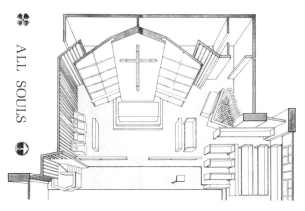

Fig. 47. Chancel design of All Souls Church, Berkeley, California c. 1955

In 1949, the General Convention authorized the Standing Liturgical Commission to produce a series of prayer book studies. *Prayer Book Studies IV* (1953) proposed a revision of the eucharistic rite. In it, the liturgical commission suggested three basic changes that the General Convention would later incorporate in the *Book of Common Prayer* 1979: (1) moving

the breaking of the bread from the middle of the prayer of consecration to immediately after the Lord's Prayer; (2) reintro-
ducing the verbal exchange of the peace, which had been
absent from Anglican prayer books since 1552; and (3) relo-
cating the Gloria in Excelsis at the introduction of the rite,
where it had been in the 1549 *Book of Common Prayer.*

In 1953, the House of Bishops authorized "special use on a
particular occasion" of the form proposed by the commission.[22]
While this permission was extended to any liturgical form prepared by the commission, it would be the eucharistic rite, later
published as a separate booklet with the bishops' resolution,
that would be most frequently used. Because the resolution
forbade use at "regular public worship," most members of the
Episcopal Church never attended a *Prayer Book Studies IV* eucharistic service, but a number of church leaders did share in
such celebrations.

Desegregation

Paradoxically, the years immediately following the Second
World War were both the most segregated years in American
history and the years in which the president and the Supreme
Court undercut the legal grounds for segregation.

While segregation was enforced by law in the South, much
of the pre–World War II North and West did not have rigid
racial bars. The black population was small, and the historical
advocacy of black rights from the previous century still left
something of a legacy. The war, however, began to change this
situation. During wartime, industrial employers attracted
blacks and other minorities from an underemployed South.
When the war ended, black soldiers with greater experience
outside the South often chose not to return to their native states.

Whites responded to the shift in population by fleeing from
the center cities to the new suburbs. Guarded by housing prac-
tices that effectively barred minorities, whites in the North and
in some urban areas of the West began to live lives as segregated
as any in the South.

In 1948, President Harry Truman ended the segregation of the armed forces and civil service. In 1954, the Supreme Court ruled in *Brown v. the Board of Education* that school segregation was illegal. The newly invigorated American segregation patterns would remain in place, however, until after the 1964 Civil Rights Act provided legislation to enforce the Supreme Court decision.

The Episcopal Church began to dismantle its institutional segregation policies in the late 1940s. The General Convention had never adopted a national segregation policy. With the exception of the Conventions of 1889 and 1892, however, no dioceses sent black deputies to the Convention. The pattern began to change in the 1940s, with at least some black deputies attending each convention.[23] At the same time, individual dioceses began to abandon their systems of indirect representation that had limited black participation in diocesan conventions. Southern Virginia, for example, eliminated its colored convocation in 1948; South Carolina did so in 1954. Relationships began to change at the same time in dioceses with Native American populations. In 1947, the Diocese of South Dakota dropped a racial system that distinguished white from Indian church members and adopted a geographical pattern that recognized the special status of the Niobrara Deanery in which most Indian parishioners lived.

Such changes, however, did little to affect the composition of local congregations. In most cases, neighboring black and white congregations would not attempt to merge until the 1960s and 1970s. In addition, some white congregations located within increasingly black inner city areas closed their doors, sold their property, and followed their white parishioners to the suburbs.

After 1950, Episcopalians began to replace the segregated pattern

Fig. 48. John Walker

243

of theological education that had existed in the South. In 1951, John Walker (1927–89), later Bishop of Washington, entered the Virginia Theological Seminary. Walker, who had strong support from Bishop Richard S. Emrich (1910–97) of Michigan, was the first black student at the school. Two years later, Bishop Payne Divinity School, the institution for the preparation of black men for the ministry that had been located in Petersburg, Virginia, officially merged with Virginia Seminary. The Episcopal Theological Seminary of the Southwest in Austin adopted a pro-integration policy from its founding in 1951, but the School of Theology of the University of the South moved more slowly. In the spring of 1953, the board of trustees at Sewanee accepted the resignation of six full-time professors and the transfer of thirty-five of the fifty-six returning students in protest of its admissions policy. Soon after, the trustees reversed their position. In the fall of 1953, the first black student entered the graduate school at Sewanee, and in the following year, Merrick William Collier of Savannah became the first black student in the seminary.[24]

NOTES

1. *The Episcopal Church Annual 1962* (New York: Morehouse-Barlow, 1962), 12.

2. A.T. Mollegen, "Classical Christianity" in *Christianity and Modern Man* (Washington, D.C.: Ward and Paul mimeograph, 1947), 1.

3. Randolph Crump Miller, *Education for Christian Living* (Englewood Cliffs, N.J.: Prentice-Hall, 1956), 193.

4. Reinhold Niebuhr, *Moral Man and Immoral Society* (New York: Charles Scribner's Sons, 1960), 81–82.

5. Nathaniel W. Pierce and Paul L. Ward, *The Voice of Conscience: A Loud and Unusual Noise? The Episcopal Peace Fellowship, 1939–1989* (Charlestown, Mass.: Charles River Publishing for the Episcopal Peace Fellowship, 1989), 15.

6. E. Brooks Holifield, *A History of Pastoral Care in America: from Salvation to Self-Realization* (Nashville: Abingdon Press, 1983), 234, 259, 269–76; Charles P. Price, "The Episcopal Church in the 1950s, 60s, and 70s" (Lecture delivered at Virginia Seminary, December 6, 1989).

7. While General Conventions since 1943 have been consistent in requiring that the presiding bishop resign diocesan responsibility, they have made changes in the term of office for the presiding officer. At the time of Tucker's resignation in 1944, the presiding bishop served until retirement at sixty-eight. The General Convention of 1967 limited the term to twelve years and lowered the retirement age to sixty-five. The General Convention of 1985 retained the twelve-year term but increased the age of retirement to seventy.

8. Edwin Augustine White and Jackson A. Dykman, *Annotated Constitution and Canons for the Government of the Protestant Episcopal Church in the United States of America, Otherwise known as The Episcopal Church,* 2 vols. (New York: Office of the General Convention, 1982), 1:169.

9. *Journal of the General Convention of the Protestant Episcopal Church in the United States . . . 1952* (printed for the Convention, 1952), 642.

10. Joan R. Gundersen, "The Local Parish as a Female Institution: The Experience of All Saints Episcopal Church in Frontier Minnesota," *Church History* 55 (September 1986):307–22.

11. *The Living Church Annual* (Milwaukee: Morehouse Publishing, 1929), 180–83; *The Living Church Annual* (New York: Morehouse-Gorham, 1939), 131–33; *The Episcopal Church Annual* (New York: Morehouse-Barlow, 1960), 133–34.

12. *The Episcopal Church Annual 1983,* (Wilton, Conn.: Morehouse-Barlow, 1983), 18–19.

13. Heather Ann Huyck, "To Celebrate a Whole Priesthood: the History of Women's Ordination in the Episcopal Church" (Ph.D. diss., University of Minnesota, 1981), 9–10.

14. White and Dykman, *Annotated Constitution and Canons,* 959.

15. Odell Greenleaf Harris, *Bishop Payne Divinity School, Petersburg, Virginia, 1878–1949: A History of the Seminary to Prepare Black Men for the Ministry of the Protestant Episcopal Church* (Alexandria, Va: Protestant Episcopal Theological Seminary, 1980), 17.

16. Marianne Micks, "Forty Years in the Wilderness," *The Witness* 70 (July-August 1987):7.

17. Heather Huyck, "Indelible Change: Woman Priests in the Episcopal Church," *Historical Magazine of the Protestant Episcopal Church* 51 (December 1982):386. In dating the first admission of women at Virginia at 1961, Huyck overlooked Marian Smollegan, who attended Virginia during the 1958–59 academic year.

18. Margaret Marston Sherman, *True to their Heritage* (New York: National Council of the Episcopal Church, 1964), 1–4.

19. Robert W. Prichard, "Virginia Seminary Since World War II," *Virginia Seminary Journal* 37 (June 1985):34.

20. *The Episcopal Church Annual 1960,* 20.

21. Massey H. Shepherd, Jr., et al., *Before the Table: A Guide to the Celebration of the Holy Eucharist, Facing the People, According to the Book of Common Prayer* (Greenwich, Conn.: Seabury Press, 1956), 5.

22. The Standing Liturgical Commission of the Protestant Episcopal Church in the United States of America, *Prayer Book Studies XVII: The Liturgy of the Lord's Supper, A Revision of Prayer Book Studies IV* (New York: Church Pension Fund, 1966), 4.

23. J. Carleton Hayden, "The Black Ministry of the Episcopal Church: An Historical Overview," in *Black Clergy in the Episcopal*

Church: Recruitment, Training, and Deployment, ed. Franklin Turner and Adair T. Lummis (New York: Office for Black Ministries of the Episcopal Church, n.d.), 19.

24. Donald Smith Armentrout, *The Quest for the Informed Priest: A History of the School of Theology* (Sewanee: School of Theology of the University of the South, 1979), 307–12.

10
Growing Pains
(1965–80)

In terms of baptized membership, the fifteen years between 1965 and 1980 were the most devastating for the Episcopal Church since the American Revolution. The optimistic growth charts that had adorned the *Church Annuals* and had appeared as appendices in the Church's Teaching Series volumes suddenly disappeared. After almost two centuries of sustained growth, the church began to decline in percentage of the population and in absolute numbers. From a high of 3.64 million in 1966, baptized membership fell to 3.04 million in 1980.[1] The Methodists, Presbyterians, Congregationalists, Disciples of Christ, and Lutherans all lost members during the same years.

Two elements combined to produce this statistical decline: a drop in the American birthrate and a theological reorientation that alienated existing members. After remaining at above 4 million a year since 1954, the annual number of American births dipped to 3.76 million in 1965. By 1973 it reached a low of 3.13 million. The annual number of baptisms (in 1966 under 90,000 for the first time since 1951) and church school attendance (in 1967, under 900,000 for the first time in a decade) in the Episcopal Church fell with the declining birthrate.[2]

The theological reorientation was both necessary and painful. The obvious success in the suburbs of the 1950s had narrowed the perspectives of many Christians. They began to see new buildings and growing Sunday schools of white middle-class children as the sole goal of the church. When the birthrate dropped and black and other ethnic groups that had been excluded from the new suburban center of American life began to demand more equitable treatment, such Christians were forced to reexamine their premises. Some responded to the challenge in positive ways; they attempted to make the liturgy more accessible to the laity, removed limitations on the participation of women in the church, called for a greater responsibility to minorities, and adjusted the pastoral ministry of the church for the problems of a new decade. Others, troubled by a rate of change that they believed to be either too rapid or too slow, left the Episcopal Church.

This was a period of unusual fluidity in church membership. Those who wished to make the church more open to others outside the denomination were successful, so that by 1978 an estimated 48 percent of adult Episcopalians had been raised in other traditions.[3] Yet it was precisely this effort that alienated many existing church members, who left the denomination in almost equal numbers. Attendance figures showed modest increases (up 19 percent between 1974 and 1979), but total membership figures fell, reflecting a loss in those marginal members for whom change was the most difficult.[4] This loss in membership figures, emphasized by critics of the church, along with such symbolic events as the decisions in the dioceses of Washington and New York to halt construction on their

Fig. 49. John Elbridge Hines, twenty-second presiding bishop

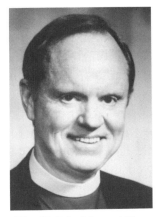

Fig. 50. John Maury Allin, twenty-third presiding bishop

gothic cathedrals, combined to create for many the perception of a depression in the life of the church.

Presiding bishops John Hines (1965-74) and John Allin (1974-85) led the church during these stormy years. Hines was a prophet, who called the church to active responsibility for the poor and the outcast. Allin was a reconciler, who helped to calm some of the more conservative church members. They were two quite different men, yet they presented a striking image of the Episcopal Church in the late 1960s and early 1970s: a church with both prophets who challenged comfortable assumptions and pastors with compassion for those church members who were confused and troubled by a turbulent age.

Liturgical Change

For many Episcopalians the most visible sign of the redirection of the church was the revision of the *Book of Common Prayer.* Members of the Standing Liturgical Commission believed that revision was made necessary both by new strides in liturgical scholarship and by the "increasing awareness of the profound relationship that exists between the worship of the Church and its mission in all kinds of societies and cultures of our contemporary world."[5] The 1928 prayer book was familiar and comfortable, and, perhaps for that very reason, it often did little to point Christians toward active ministry in the world.

The 1964 General Convention revised article ten of the church's constitution to provide for "trial use throughout the Church." The experimentation with *Prayer Book Studies IV* in the 1950s had been confined to a few carefully regulated occasions; this new provision in the constitution allowed the General Convention to authorize regular Sunday parish use. Subsequent Conventions approved three products of the Standing Liturgical Commission for such trial use: *The Liturgy of the Lord's Supper* of 1967, *Services for Trial Use* (the "Green Book") of 1970, and *Authorized Services* (the "Zebra Book") of 1973.

All of these revisions incorporated the three liturgical changes that had been proposed in *Prayer Book Studies IV*

(1953): they separated the breaking of the bread from the eucharistic prayer, restored the exchange of the peace, and moved the *Gloria in excelsis* to the entrance rite. Bishop W.R. Chilton Powell (1911–94), Charles Mortimer Guilbert (1908–98), Massey H. Shepherd, Jr., and other members of the Standing Liturgical Commission went beyond the 1953 proposal, however, seeking to make the prayer book more participatory and accessible. They wrestled, for example, with the question of Elizabethan language. While there was an undeniable beauty to the thee's and thou's of the 1928 liturgy, they were difficult for some Americans to understand. In *The Liturgy of the Lord's Supper,* the liturgical commission attempted to deal with the problem by compromising between traditional and contemporary speech; the book referred to God as "thou" but to individual people as "you." In *Services for Trial Use* and *Authorized Services,* the commission carried the compromise further, preparing two alternatives for the eucharist and the daily office, one in Elizabethan language and one in contemporary speech.

Commission members also attempted to create alternatives to the 1928 "Prayer for the Whole State of Christ's Church" that were more inclusive. The 1967 trial liturgy's prayer of intercession included petitions for industrial workers, teachers, parents, and farmers. It also provided for a congregational refrain ("Hear us, good Lord."). *Services for Trial Use* and *Authorized Services* expanded liturgical possibilities further by offering seven different forms of intercession, some of which allowed members of the congregation to add their own petitions verbally.

Services for Trial Use and *Authorized Services* also included a major revision in the baptismal office that had first been suggested by Bonnell Spencer and other members of a subcommittee of the Standing Liturgical Commission that prepared *Prayer Book Studies XVIII* in 1968. The service moved the traditional prayer for the sevenfold gifts of the Spirit from the confirmation office, where it had been in all previous prayer books, to the baptismal office, where it had been in the third century.[6] The revision of the office made it clear that baptism, rather than confirmation constituted full initiation into the church.

Yet other changes stemmed from the fact that few if any congregations were following Thomas Cranmer's original pattern of Morning Prayer, Litany, and at least the initial portion of the eucharist on Sunday mornings.[7] Both Morning and Evening Prayer and the eucharist were expanded in order to compensate for their separate use. A sermon and offering, which had never been a part of the daily office because they followed in Holy Communion, were added to Morning and Evening Prayer. Similarly, an Old Testament lesson and psalm (part of the daily office) were added to the eucharist. Other allowances were also made for the sake of brevity. In the case of a celebration of the eucharist following the daily office, baptism, confirmation, marriage, or a funeral, the rubrics directed, for example, beginning the eucharist at the offertory.

While the long process of revision broke up many familiar patterns of worship, it did have one desired effect. It put newcomers on an equal footing with seasoned communicants, making the denomination more attractive to those from outside the tradition. The liturgical instruction that clergy and lay teachers had to provide for long-time members opened the church to others and contributed to a new awareness of the need for Christian education for adults.

Some members of the church, however, were not enthusiastic about the revisions. One group that shared this sentiment gathered in Sewanee, Tennessee in 1971 to form the Society for the Preservation of the Book of Common Prayer. The society, which later shortened its name to the Prayer Book Society, criticized not only the loss of a beautiful Elizabethan language of worship but also what it saw as a theological shift away from the traditional standards of the Christian faith. While 1928 prayer book loyalists did not halt the process of revision, they did have an effect on the liturgical proposals that followed *Services for Trial Use.* The Standing Liturgical Commission's *Authorized Services* and the *Draft Proposed Book of Common Prayer* that it presented to the General Convention of 1976 restored more of the character of the 1928 prayer book. In *Authorized Services,* for example, the liturgical commission reintroduced a separate confirmation rite that had been absent from *Services for Trial Use. Authorized Services'* first eucharistic service also included the 1928 eucharistic prayer without change. *The Draft Proposed Book of Common Prayer* separated the Morning and Evening Prayer offices, which had been combined in *Services for Trial Use* and *Authorized Services,* replaced a rubric in the eucharist that had made confession optional with one allowing only occasional omission, and introduced an Order for Burial that permitted the use of the 1928 office, when "for pastoral considerations neither of the [1979] burial rites . . . is deemed appropriate." The General Convention of 1976 accepted the *Draft Proposed Book of Common Prayer* with minor revisions, such as amending the Order for Marriage to make it possible to use the 1928 rite without alteration. When the 1979 Convention adopted it on second reading, it became the new standard for the church.

A revision of the hymnal followed a similar, though somewhat more compact procedure. The Church Hymnal Corporation produced six hymnal supplements and the one volume *Lift Every Voice and Sing* (a collection of black American spirituals) to allow congregations to use texts and tunes that were under consideration for the new hymnal. Like the members on the Standing Liturgical Commission, Alec Wyton (b. 1921) and others on the Standing Commission on Church Music sought to produce a work that would "reflect and speak to people of many races and cultures" and clarify "language . . . so obscure or so changed in contemporary usage as to have a different meaning."[8] The General Convention of 1982 approved the *Hymnal 1982.*

In addition to revising the prayer book and hymnal, the General Convention took other actions that strongly shaped congregational worship. Prior to 1961, most lay readers had served only in the absence of the priest. In that year, however, the General Convention revised the canon on lay readers in order to encourage use of lay readers as assistants at services in which the priest presided. In 1967, the General Convention expanded this assisting role by authorizing a limited number of lay people to assist with the chalice at the distribution of communion.[9] The Convention also gave the laity new input into the selection of clergy. In 1970 it adopted a new canon creating *commissions on ministry,* bodies designed to advise bishops in the choice of ordinands. The same convention created a Board for Clergy Deployment, which advocated broader congregational participation in the calling of clergy, and a General Board of Examining Chaplains, which administered a standard national exam to seminary seniors (the General Ordination Examination, 1972).

The bishops who participated in the Lambeth Conference of 1968 came to a new understanding of the nature of the initiatory rites of the church. Baptism, they reasoned, was full membership in the church and, therefore, the rubric in the 1928 and earlier prayer books that limited reception of Holy Communion to those prepared for confirmation was illogical. The decisions of Lambeth Conferences were not binding on member churches, but the discussion did lead General Convention to authorize the reception of communion for baptized adult visitors "where the discipline of their own church permits" (1967) and for unconfirmed children (1969).[10]

The General Conventions from 1964 to 1976 gradually removed bars to female participation in the church. In 1964, the General Convention gave deaconesses the same right to marry as male deacons. In 1965 Presiding Bishop John Hines appointed Bishop George Barrett (b. 1908) of Rochester to head a Committee to Study the Proper Place of Women in the Ministry of the Church. The committee returned to the House of Bishops in October 1966, suggesting in a report, drafted by Elizabeth Bussing (b. 1901), a committee member who was an active laywomen from the Diocese of California, that the bishops seriously consider the ordination of women to the priesthood. The 1967 Convention allowed women to serve as lay readers and amended (on the first of two required readings) the constitution in order to permit women to serve as General Convention deputies and dissolved the separate General Division of Women's Work. With a growing number of female students at the traditional seminaries, the two remaining theological schools for women closed their doors (St. Margaret's House, 1966; Windham House, 1967). The Episcopal Church Women halted the triennial meetings that had up to that time met concurrently with the General Convention. Some dioceses, such as West Texas and Iowa, also dissolved their diocesan women's structures.

In the spring of 1970, forty-five Episcopal women, whose number included Jeanette Piccard (1895-1981) and Pauli Murray (1910-85), gathered at Graymoor Monastery in New York to discuss the ministry of women. Deaconess Frances Zielinski (b. 1930) and other representatives of the group attended the General Convention later in that year. With the help of Henry Rightor (1910-88), a professor of pastoral theology at Virginia Seminary and a leading member of the General Convention's Joint Commission on Ordained and Licensed Ministries, they lobbied successfully for the elimination of distinctions in pension benefits, educational requirements, and ordination rites that separated the male deacons and female deaconesses.[11] The 1970 Convention also approved on second reading the constitutional change that allowed women to be seated as delegates.

A second gathering of women at Virginia Seminary in October 1971 brought together an impressive coalition of female church leaders. Sixty women, including older women who had been professional church workers, members of the Episcopal Church Women (as the Women's Auxiliary had been renamed), deaconesses, and young women enrolled in seminary, met together to map out a strategy. They noted with favor Elizabeth Bussing's "Report of the Bishops Committee to Study the Proper Place of Women in the Ministry of the Church," the work of the Joint Commission on ordained and Licensed Ministries on which Henry Rightor served, and a 1968 statement on the women from the Lambeth Conference. They organized a continuing group that they named the Episcopal Women's Caucus. Fifty-four of those who attended, angered by an unexpected statement against women's ordination made in the House of Bishops by C. Kilmer Myers (1914-81) of California and convinced that the time for committee work was past, addressed a letter to Presiding Bishop Hines in which they called "not for study, but for action." The caucus and the two sister organizations that developed from it (Women's Ordination Now and the National Coalition for the Ordination of Women to the Priesthood and Episcopacy) returned to General Conventions in 1973 and 1976 to ask that the priesthood and the episcopate be opened to women.[12] The resolution failed in the House of Deputies in 1973. Three years later, however, similar legislation would pass in both houses.

The process was too slow moving for some in the church. On July 29, 1974, in Philadelphia, retired bishops Daniel Corrigan (1900–94), Robert Dewitt (b. 1916), and Edward Welles (1907–91) ordained eleven female deacons—Merrill Bittner (b. 1946), Alla Bozarth-Campbell (b. 1947), Alison Cheek (b. 1927), Marie Moorefield Fleischer (b. 1944), Carter Heyward (b. 1945), Emily Hewitt (b. 1944), Suzanne Hiatt (b. 1936), Jeanette Piccard, Betty Bone Schiess (b. 1923), Katrina Welles Swanson (b. 1935), and Nancy Hatch Wittig (b. 1945)—without approval of their diocesan bishops or standing committees. Bishop George Barrett, then retired, ordained four other women—Eleanor Lee McGee (b. 1943), Alison Palmer (b. 1931), Elizabeth Rosenberg (b. 1945), and Diane Tickell (b. 1918)—in Washington, D.C., on September 7 of the following year under similar circumstances. These ordinations were undoubtedly a contributing factor in the decision of the bishops and deputies at the 1976 General Convention to alter the church canons to allow ordination of women to the priesthood and episcopate, but they also added to the dissatisfaction of more conservative church members.

Theological Probing

Episcopalians of the fifties and early sixties had often combined the insights of neo-orthodoxy with nondirective styles of pastoral care in such a way as to blunt criticism of the status quo. By the midsixties, many, discovering as Evangelical and Reformed theologian Reinhold Niebuhr had predicted in *Moral Man and Immoral Society* (1932) that "the new and just society has been built, and . . . it is not just,"[13] adopted more confrontational pastoral styles and became openly critical of the social order. For them, the orthodox Christian faith provided a perspective from which to engage in a critical dialogue with the apparently prosperous suburban American of the 1960s.

Some of those raised with neo-orthodoxy began, however, to ask whether such a dialogue went far enough. They feared that certain elements of the Christian tradition made it more difficult for Christians to recognize sin in their own society. The willingness of Paul and other New Testament authors to accept slavery and the inequality of men and women and the general other-worldly focus of the Bible might, for example, have led to a passivity that made it difficult for twentieth-century Christians to combat injustice.

In 1965, Paul M. van Buren (1924–98) became one of the more visible advocates of this position. His *Secular Meaning of the Gospel,* published in that year, argued that it was time to reject traditional ways of thinking about God. An Episcopal priest who had been a member of the faculty of the Episcopal Theological Seminary of the Southwest (1957-64) before moving to Temple University, he soon found himself the center of a swirl of controversy. The national press identified him as a "death of God" theologian.

In the same year, James Pike, the former New York cathedral dean who had become the Bishop of California in 1958, published his *Time for Christian Candor* in which he referred to the doctrine of the Trinity as "excess luggage." The bishop, who seemed to enjoy the national attention that attended such pronouncements, became for some a prophet who spoke to the troubled and alienated. Others saw him as a nuisance who questioned theological truth, a symbol of all that was wrong in the Episcopal Church of the later sixties. His personal life—alcoholism, two divorces, and publicized attempts to contact his deceased son through a spiritualist—only added to the controversy.

The House of Bishops' theological committee, of which Stephen F. Bayne, Jr., of Olympia was a leading voice, issued a report critical of Pike at the 1965 meeting of the House of Bishops at Glacier Park, Montana. When Pike did little to moderate his theological language following that meeting, others took a more decisive step. Henry Louttit (1903-84) of South Florida and eleven other bishops formed a "Committee of Bishops to Defend the Faith" and prepared a presentment (the bringing of charges that can lead to an ecclesiastical trial) against Pike in 1966. The bishops listed five charges (incorrect teaching about: the Trinity; the Holy Spirit; the centrality of Christ for salvation; the Incarnation and Atonement; and the elements of the Chicago-Lambeth quadrilateral) and cited passages from *Time for Christian Candor* to support their claims. The bishops eventually dropped the presentment in exchange for a resolution of censure that was prepared by an ad hoc committee (of which Bayne was again a leading member) and adopted at a session of the House of Bishops meeting in Wheeling, West Virginia in September 1966. The resolution, adopted by a margin of 103 to 36, characterized Pike's writings as "too often marred by caricatures of treasured symbols and at the worst, by cheap vulgarizations of great expressions of the faith."[14] Pike retired in that same year but continued to write, producing, for example, *If This Be Heresy* in 1967. He lived an increasingly eccentric personal life that ended with his death from exposure and thirst in the Holy Land in 1969.

Theological seminaries, perceived by many traditional supporters of theological education as the source of this theological probing, suffered hard times in the 1970s. Three were forced to make major changes in order to survive. In 1968 Bexley Hall Divinity School left Gambier, Ohio and Kenyon College and relocated in Rochester, New York as part of the Colgate-Rochester/Crozier/Bexley Hall consortium of theological schools. In 1971, Berkeley Divinity School in New Haven entered into an agreement with Yale University Divinity School, which involved selling Berkeley real estate and the creation of an Episcopal community within the Yale Divinity School. In 1974, Philadelphia Divinity School closed its doors and merged with the Episcopal Theological School in Cambridge, Massachusetts, to become the Episcopal Divinity School.

Social Ethics

Episcopalians of the late sixties and seventies dropped the accommodating styles of the pastoral care that they had learned in the fifties in order to take a harder look at questions of social ethics. As attorney William Stringfellow (1928-85) recognized, any serious dealing with such issues as civil rights necessarily involved Christians in the political process. Stringfellow suggested in his *Dissenter in a Great Society* (1966) that this was not bad. Indeed, for him any Christians who did not act politically were "under the peril of dishonoring—and even, at times, disowning—the estate of reconciliation with all men vouchsafed to them in Baptism."[15] Christians could not remain aloof of the political questions of segregation or war and peace and still be true to their calling.

Thomas Lee Hayes, who became the executive director of the Episcopal Peace Fellowship in 1966, and Herschel Halburt, the person in the church's national office designated as registrar for conscientious objectors, certainly did not want the church to remain aloof. They led the way in Episcopal opposition to the war in Vietnam. The two clerics toured the country in order to visit draft-age youths. Hayes encouraged young people to register with Halbert as objectors, and Halbert referred those who did so back to Hayes and the Peace Fellowship for advice and support. The two cooperated on a pamphlet entitled "Choosing Your Draft Classification," which the church began to distribute in the spring of 1966.[16]

Many disagreed with this line of action, however. So many protested that the Executive Council (as the old National Council had been renamed) stopped further distribution and prepared a new pamphlet that noted that "the majority of Episcopal young men choose active duty." Yet the Episcopal Peace Fellowship began to grow, from four hundred (1966) to 1250 (in 1969 when Robert Haskell and Nathaniel Pierce took over from Hayes as co-chairpersons) to 2500 (in 1971), and the number registered as conscientious objectors grew to be what the *Living Church* identified as a larger percentage of membership than in any other non-peace church. The enlarged fellowship sponsored both ongoing draft counseling and a series of symbolic protests, including demonstrations at the Pentagon and a prayer service at the Cathedral of St. John the Divine for those killed in the war, both held in 1969.[17]

With feelings running high within the church both in favor of and against the war, the General Convention of 1967 adopted a resolution declaring that "differences are painfully evident without our Church," and noting that on such a difficult issue, "the truth is known only to God."[18]

Episcopalians were also divided on matters of race. Prior to 1965, the most visible Episcopal advocates for desegregation in national life were members of the Episcopal Society for Cultural and Racial Unity (ESCRU). Members of the organization, which had been organized in 1958, staged a prayer pilgrimage prior to the 1961 General Convention and supported the second Selma-to-Montgomery march that was organized in March 1965 by Martin Luther King, Jr. An Episcopal Theological School student who was a member of the organization (Jonathan Myrick Daniels, 1939-65) was shot and killed on August 20, 1965, because of his organizing for civil rights in Hayneville, Alabama.[19]

John Hines, who became presiding bishop in 1965, came to believe, particularly after the onset of the urban rioting that began in Los Angeles in 1965, that this symbolic activity by a voluntary agency within the church was not enough. A tour of the poorest sections of Bedford-Stuyvesant with social worker Leon Modeste convinced Hines to propose a sweeping new program to the General Convention that met in September 1967. The convention agreed with Hines's proposal and adopted a special $9 million fund (the General Convention Special Program, GCSP) to deal with social inequities that were not being addressed within the existing church channels.

Hines turned to Modeste to administer the fund. Modeste, an Episcopal layman who had grown up in Brooklyn slums, was convinced that the fund would only be effective if the minority groups to whom grants were made were free to make their own decisions. He recruited minority staff members and began to make grants, most of which went to organizations outside of the Episcopal Church. This created some tension, especially when Modeste and his staff made grants to organizations other Episcopalians perceived as violent or hostile. Grants to Malcolm X University in Durham, to the Black Awareness Coordinating Committee in Denmark, South Carolina, and to the Alianza Federal de los Mercedes in New Mexico over the explicit objections of bishops Thomas Fraser (b. 1915) of North Carolina, Gray Temple (b. 1914) of South Carolina, John Pinckney (b. 1905) of Upper South Carolina, and Charles Kinsolving III (b. 1904) of New Mexico resulted in unfavorable publicity for the program.[20] By 1969, some Episcopalians were already calling for the termination of GCSP.

When the General Convention met in special session in August of that year at South Bend, Indiana, the GCSP became a major topic of discussion. The debate about the fund was heated, and emotions ran high. At one point in the session, Mohammed Kenyatta of the Black Economic Development Conference grabbed the microphone from a lay deputy in order to demand $200,000 in "reparations" from the Episcopal Church for past offenses against black Americans.[21] The bishops and deputies ultimately approved both a grant to the Black Economic Development Conference and the continuation of the GCSP. The stormy debate and the action that followed it, increased rather than quieted, anxiety in the church at large about the program, however.

Vine Deloria, Jr., an active Native American layman who resigned from a GCSP committee following South Bend, summed up the weakness of the program when he wrote the following:

The Episcopal Church had embraced the shades of Rudyard Kipling and the styles of imperialistic England for too long to make a sudden, sophisticated, and substantial move into America of the sixties. When it did move the Episcopal Church chose the most tangible but the least sophisticated weapon in its institutional arsenal. Money. Unless the church moves substantially into the support of theological education of considerable content, it will probably remain vulnerable to the ebb and flow of popular social issues and become a pale version of a private foundation.[22]

No single program could make rapid amends for a three hundred and fifty year history of American racism. GCSP moved too quickly, with too little popular support, and in the end had too few positive results. The General Convention discontinued it in 1973.

Despite the failure of the GCSP, Episcopalians did not abandon the cause of racial equality. Other organizations, such as the Union of Black Episcopalians (1968), carried on the struggle. Episcopalians were, moreover, able to set their own house in order in some important ways. A number of dioceses made concerted efforts to merge nearby black and white congregations. The Diocese of Massachusetts, which in 1962 had elected John Burgess as the first black suffragan bishop chosen for the United States since 1918, elected Burgess coadjutor in 1969. The following year Bishop Burgess became the first black diocesan bishop to serve an American diocese. In 1976, the Diocese of Washington followed suit, electing Suffragan Bishop John Walker, who had been the first black student at Virginia Seminary, as coadjutor. In 1971, Harold Stephen Jones (b. 1909, Santee Sioux) of South Dakota became the first Native American to be elected a

Fig. 51. Harold S. Jones and the one-room house in which he and his wife once lived

263

suffragan bishop. Nine years later, William C. Wantland (b. 1934, Seminole) became the Diocesan Bishop of Eau Claire. During the same years, the General Convention began to turn to indigenous bishops for overseas missionary dioceses. Native bishops served for the first time in the Philippines (1959), Cuba (1961), Puerto Rico (1964), Liberia (1969), Haiti (1971), the Dominican Republic (1972), Panamá (1972), Costa Rica (1978), Colombia (1979), and El Salvador (1992).[23]

Controversies over GCSP and parish integration did little to fill the collection plates of Episcopal congregations. By 1970, almost half of Episcopal dioceses were unable or unwilling to meet their quotas to the national church budget.[24] With less funds contributed to the church, less was available for such programs as overseas missions. The number of foreign missionaries and the percentage of the church budget devoted to such efforts declined consistently over the 1970s. The number of appointed missionaries, for example, fell from a high of about two hundred in the 1962-66 period to seventy-one in 1977.[25] This decrease in financial support coincided with the Fidel Castro's suppression of what had been a relatively healthy Cuban church and with the 1977 arrest and imprisonment of two members of national church Hispanic affairs staff (Maria Cueto and Raisa Nemiken, who were charged with supporting the Puerto Rican terrorist group FALN) to produce for many a perception of decline in foreign missions that paralleled a decline at home.

Conservative Movements and Charismatic Renewal

The innovative theologians and advocates of social reform of the late 1960s jarred the Episcopal Church out of its suburban isolation. They were not as successful, however, in constructing a new theological consensus. Many Episcopalians agreed upon a program—the liberation of the oppressed—but could agree upon no single strategy or object of liberation to replace the suburban expansion to which the church had devoted itself in the 1950s. Different interest groups within the church competed for attention for their favorite projects. The result, complained political scientist Paul Seabury of the University of California at Berkeley in a 1978 *Harper's* magazine article, was a church whose slogan might well be "trendier than thou."[26]

Some members of the Episcopal Church who were uncomfortable with the activist tilt and the apparent lack of a theological center to the denomination formed organizations intended to nudge the church back on a less innovative track. Of these organizations, some, such as the Society for the Preservation of the *Book of Common Prayer* and the Evangelical and Catholic Mission (formed in 1976 by bishops Stanley Atkins and Charles Gaskell) remained within the church.[27] Other more disgruntled Episcopalians felt that they could not do the same. A "Congress of Concerned Churchmen" met in St. Louis in the year following the General Convention's approval of the ordination of women and its acceptance on first reading of a new liturgy. Some of those who attended the meeting met again in January 1978 in Denver to inaugurate a new church body. Retired bishop Albert Chambers (1906–93) of Springfield and Philippine Independent Catholic bishop Francisco Pagtakhan joined in an irregular consecration—one that lacked the traditional three bishops—of candidates for the new "Anglican Church in North America." Despite the name the traditionalists chose, the Archbishop of Canterbury and other Anglican leaders continued to recognize the Episcopal Church as the only American member of the Anglican Communion. Moreover, the participants in the new church soon discovered that they themselves were unable to agree on essentials. By 1982, this continuing church movement included twenty-three bishops in nine different denominations.[28]

While some Episcopalians looked to traditionalist liturgical groups for an alternative to rapid change, others looked to another theological tradition. In 1960, two marginal parishioners of a California parish attended a neighborhood prayer meeting led by a Pentecostal. Anxious to have what he apparently had—a joyous faith—they went with him to his Pentecostal church, where the pastor prayed that they would receive the Holy Spirit and the gift of speaking in tongues.[29] They not only spoke in tongues but within several months were able to lead neighboring parish priest Dennis Bennett (1917–91) to have the same experience.[30] Bennett and his wife Rita described the events in a popular book titled *Nine O'Clock in the Morning* (1970).

Other Episcopalians reported similar stories. In 1964, W. Graham Pulkingham (1926–93), rector of a failing inner-city Church of the Redeemer in Houston, Texas, visited Assembly of God clergyman David Wilkerson, who had an active urban ministry in New York City. Wilkerson laid hands on Pulkingham, who began to speak in tongues. Returning to Texas, Pulkingham was able both to reproduce similar experiences in his parishioners and to revitalize his parish.[31] Charles Irish (b. 1929), who learned of glossalalia through Pentecostal friends of his children, built St. Luke's, Bath, Ohio into a major center for Pentecostal Episcopalians. Everett "Terry" Fullam (b. 1930), the organist at St. Mark's, Riverside, Rhode Island, who would later become the rector of St. Paul's, Darien, Connecticut, first spoke in tongues at a conference led by Dennis Bennett.[32]

The growing number of Episcopalians who had the experience of glossolalia were joined by Christians from the Lutheran, Roman Catholic, and Methodist traditions. They designated themselves as *charismatics* to differentiate themselves from the older Pentecostal denominations such as the Assembly of God. These charismatic Christians found in the exercise of spiritual gifts an assurance of God's personal presence in a decade in which many of their coreligionists preferred to speak of faith in social rather than personal terms. Yet the normative expectation that those who received the Spirit would speak in tongues ran counter to the traditions of the churches of which many of the new charismatics were members. Those who lacked charismatic experiences sensed that Pentecostal theology left them among the damned and often questioned the orthodoxy of the charismatics. Some charismatics moved from the Episcopal Church to the Assembly of God or other traditional Pentecostal denominations, but most remained, carving out a place within the life of the church. They created a supportive network through such organizations as the Episcopal Renewal Ministries (Episcopal Charismatic Fellowship) and gathered in a series of conferences, such as the First National Conference on Renewal held at St. Philip's Cathedral in Atlanta in October 1974.

By 1973, liturgical traditionalists and charismatics had begun to nudge the Episcopal Church away from radical theological probing and social empowerment. In that year, Presiding Bishop John Hines submitted an early resignation and was replaced by a more conservative Bishop John Allin (1921–98). The same Convention that elected Allin as Hines's replacement discontinued funding for the GCSP of which Allin had been a critic.

It was in the House of Bishops that Allin's more conservative leadership style was most evident. In 1977, he told a special session of the house that met at Port St. Lucie, Florida, that he himself had personal reservations about the ordination of women. The bishops responded by adopting a "conscience clause" designed to appease the opponents of the ordination of women:

> No Bishop, Priest, or Lay Person should be coerced or penalized in any manner, nor suffer any canonical disabilities as a result of his or her conscientious objection to or support of the 65th General Convention's actions with regard to the ordination of women to the priesthood or episcopate.[33]

Since it was adopted only by the bishops and not by the House of Deputies, the statement lacked any canonical authority. Bishops, however, preside at ecclesiastical trials for other bishops and pronounce sentences on deacons and priests. In practical terms, therefore, the bishops' agreement guaranteed that no person would be punished for opposition to the ordination of women.

The adoption of the conscience clause and the ending of the General Convention Special Program combined with the departure of some of the more adamant liturgical conservatives to quiet tensions within the church. After the 1976 General Convention, Episcopalians embarked upon the "Venture in Mission" (VIM) program, an attempt to recapture both the spirit and the financial means for domestic and foreign mission. There was relative peace in the church, though one troubling issue remained on the horizon.

The General Convention
Compromise on Homosexuality

John Allin and his fellow bishops addressed a second issue at the 1977 Port St. Lucie meeting. In 1973, the General Convention had rewritten the church's 1946 canon on remarriage. The earlier canon allowed remarriage in the church only when one of nine impediments (consanguinity, insanity, bigamy, fraud, etc.) existed in the first marriage. The new canon, which focused on the health of the relationship that a person intended to enter rather than upon previous marriage, gave the parish priest greater pastoral freedom in dealing with divorced people. Some within the church perceived this decision as a first step in a broader revision of traditional standards for personal morality. For example, the members of Integrity, a support group for gay and lesbian Episcopalians formed by Louie Crew in October 1994, called for recognition of homosexual relationships as acceptable lifestyles for Christians.

Early in the year in which the bishops met at Port St. Lucie, Bishop Paul Moore, Jr., of New York (b. 1919) ordained Integrity co-president Ellen Barrett (b. 1946) to the priesthood. The majority of the bishops at St. Lucie disagreed, supporting a resolution that declared that it was "clear from Scripture that heterosexual marriage [was]... affirmed and that... homosexual activity [was] condemned," and that it was the "mind of this House that... no Bishop of the Church shall confer Holy Orders in violation of these principles."[34]

By the 1970s many Episcopalians made a distinction between homosexual orientation and homosexual activity.

Some believed that the distinction provided the church with an intermediate path between full acceptance of homosexual behavior advocated by Integrity and condemnation of gay and lesbian persons. The church, they reasoned, might accept candidates for ordination who were homosexual in orientation but remained celibate, just as it had come to accept some "recovering alcoholics," who recognized their weakness for alcohol and yet refrained from its use. The bishops at Port St. Lucie declined to take this course, saying only that "it was not clear from Scripture just what morality attaches to homosexual orientation."[35]

Those at the General Convention of 1979, however, thought otherwise. The bishops and deputies at the convention coupled a restatement of the inappropriateness of sexual relations outside of heterosexual marriage with the affirmation that "there should be no barrier to ordination of qualified persons of... homosexual orientation whose behavior the Church considers wholesome."[36]

The resolution passed in the House of Bishops by a vote of 99 to 34.[37] Later in the same day, however, some of the dissenting bishops signed a statement indicating that they would not "accept [the] recommendations or implement them" in their dioceses. John M. Krumm of Southern Ohio introduced the resolution, and twenty others signed it. The signers included Paul Moore of New York and future presiding bishop Edmond Lee Browning (b. 1929) of Hawaii.[38]

Despite the action of the dissenting bishops, the resolution would bring relative peace in the church over the issue of homosexuality for a decade. The statement was a somewhat elastic standard. Some bishops and commissions on ministry accepted the resolution and began to consider celibate persons who were open about their homosexual orientation as appropriate candidates for ordination. Other bishops complied with the letter but not the spirit of the resolution by either routinely regarding those of admitted homosexual orientation as lacking other qualities necessary for ordination or by refraining from inquiring too closely into candidates' ability to remain celibate.

Some ordinands of homosexual orientation entered the ordained ministry with the full intention of remaining celibate, but found it increasing difficult to keep that resolve as American society became more and more tolerant of homosexual activity.

NOTES

1. *The Episcopal Church Annual 1984* (Wilton, Conn.: Morehouse-Barlow, 1984), 19.

2. David E. Sumner, "The Children Shall Lead Us: The Relationship Between the U.S. Birthrate and Episcopal Church Membership," *Historical Magazine of the Protestant Episcopal Church* 54 (September 1954): 253–60.

3. "Report of the Committee on the State of the Church," *The Blue Book: Reports of the Committees, Commissions, Boards, and Agencies of the General Convention of the Episcopal Church* (produced for the General Convention by Seabury Professions Services, 1982), 320.

4. *The Episcopalian* 150 (September 1985): 9.

5. The Standing Liturgical Commission of the Protestant Episcopal Church in the United States of America, *Prayer Book Studies XVII: The Liturgy of the Lord's Supper* (New York: Church Pension Fund, 1966), 13.

6. The members of the Standing Liturgical Commission, who would have preferred to replace any separate confirmation with a Form of Commitment to Christian Service that priests could use in the parish with adults, did not include a separate confirmation rite in *Services for Trial Use*. The General Convention of 1973 did not agree, however, and as a result the commission added a separate confirmation office in *Authorized Services*. The prayer for the sevenfold gifts of the spirit—once the heart of the confirmation service—remained in the baptismal office in this and in subsequent revisions, however, creating some confusion about the church's understanding of confirmation. For a discussion of the continuing debate see Charles P. Price, "Rites of Initiation," *The Occasional Papers of the Standing Liturgical Commission*, collection no. 1 (New York: Church Hymnal Corporation, 1987), 24–37.

7. While rubrics and church canons at the time of the reformation directed Anglicans to read Morning Prayer, the Litany, and the beginning of the Holy Communion service each Sunday, they directed the priest not to complete the eucharist if parishioners did not receive communion (a very common practice in the late Middle Ages). The prayer book provided, therefore, several exhortations that the priest was to read at the midpoint of the eucharist, which instructed the people about the importance of the eucharist and identified the

next occasion on which it was to be celebrated. The people were then dismissed. Episcopalians preserved this pattern at least in theory through the 1928 prayer book.

8. Standing Commission on Church Music, *Hymnal Studies Two: Introducing the Hymnal 1982* (New York: Church Hymnal Corporation, 1982), 11–13.

9. In 1985, the General Convention further expanded the role of laypersons in the distribution of the eucharist by authorizing "lay eucharistic ministers" who could in some circumstances bring communion in both kinds to the sick.

10. *Journal of the General Convention of the Protestant Episcopal Church in the United States of America . . . 1967* (New York: printed for the Convention, 1967), 47, 570–73.

11. Pauli Murray, *Song in a Weary Throat: An American Pilgrimage* (New York: Harper & Row, 1987), 418. Heather Ann Huyck, "To Celebrate a Whole Priesthood: The History of Women's Ordination in the Episcopal Church" (Ph. D. diss.: University of Minnesota, 1981), 44.

12. Huyck, "Priesthood," 58–63.

13. Reinhold Niebuhr, *Moral Man and Immoral Society* (New York: Charles Scribner's Sons, 1960), 82.

14. William Stringfellow and Anthony Towne, *The Death and Life of Bishop Pike* (Garden City, N. Y.: Doubleday, 1976), 342–53, 437–43.

15. William Stringfellow, *Dissenter in a Great Society: A Christian View of America in Crisis* (New York: Holt, Rinehard and Winston, 1966), 156. In 1967, the General Convention altered the canons to make the trial of a bishop more difficult by increasing the number of bishops required to bring a presentment against a fellow bishop to ten.

16. Nathaniel W. Pierce and Paul L. Ward, *The Voice of Conscience: A Loud and Unusual Noise? The Episcopal Peace Fellowship, 1939–1989* (Charlestown, Mass.: Charles River Publishing, 1989), 30–32.

17. Pierce and Ward, *Voice*, 32–42.

18. Pierce and Ward, *Voice*, 35–36.

19. David Sumner, *The Episcopal Church's History, 1945–1985* (Harrisburg, PA: Morehouse, 1987), 38–43.

20. Sumner, *History*, 50–51.

21. Sumner, *History*, 52.

22. Vine Deloria, Jr., "GCSP: The Demons At Work," *Historical*

Magazine of the Protestant Episcopal Church 48 (March 1979): 90.

23. Bishop Francisco Reus Froylan was the first Puerto Rican to serve as Bishop of Puerto Rico. The earlier suffragan bishop, Manuel Ferrando, was Spanish. Similarly Bishop Luc Garnier was the first Haitian native to be consecrated; Bishop Holly had been a black American expatriate.

24. Sumner, *History,* 50.

25. Neil Lebhar and Martyn Minns, "Why Did the Yankees Go Home? A Study of Episcopal Missions: 1953–1977," *Historical Magazine of the Protestant Episcopal Church* 48 (March 1979): 27–43.

26. Paul Seabury, "Trendier Than Thou," *Harper's* (October 1978): 39.

27. Donald S. Armentrout, *Episcopal Splinter Groups: A Study of Groups Which Have Left the Episcopal Church, 1873–1985* (Sewanee, Tenn.: School of Theology of the University of the South, 1985), 31, 41–42.

28. "The Continuing Church Today," *Christian Challenge* 21 (December 1982): 8–16.

29. Glossolalia, or speaking in tongues, is a form of prayer in which the normal syllables and sounds of speech are rearranged in an ecstatic utterance that has no apparent logical meaning. Biblical authors, Christians over the centuries, and some non-Christian groups have attested to the phenomenon. It was not, however, until the early part of twentieth century that Christian groups, such as the Assemblies of God, made the experience a normative expectation for church members.

30. Dennis J. Bennett, *Nine O'Clock in the Morning* (Plainfield, N. J.: Logos International, 1970), 8–20.

31. Graham Pulkingham, *Gathered for Power* (New York: Morehouse-Barlow, 1972), 75.

32. Bob Slosser, *Miracle in Darien* (Plainfield, N. J.: Logos International, 1979), 45–55.

33. *Journal of the General Convention of the Protestant Episcopal Church in the United States of America... 1979* (New York: produced for the General Convention by Seabury Professional Services, 1979), B–195.

34. *Journal of the General Convention of the Protestant Episcopal Church in the United States of America... 1979*, B–191, B–192.

35. *Journal of the General Convention of the Protestant Episcopal Church in the United States of America... 1979*, B–190–B–191.

36. *Journal of the General Convention of the Protestant Episcopal Church in the United States of America... 1979*, B–96.

37. *Journal of the General Convention of the Protestant Episcopal Church in the United States of America... 1979*, B–97.

38. *Journal of the General Convention of the Protestant Episcopal Church in the United States of America... 1979*, B–110–B–112.

11
Peaks and Valleys
(1980–1999)

Fig. 52. A television advertisement produced by the Episcopal
Media Center in the late 1990s captured something of the mixed
experience of the Episcopal Church in the 1980s and 1990s.

The 1980s and 1990s were a period of contrasts. The breakup
of the Soviet Union into a series of independent republics
(1990–91) left the U.S. as the undisputed world power, but a
rise of regional and ethnic violence (the Gulf War of 1991, the
Bosnian War of 1992–95, the Rwandan genocide of 1994) and
a rise in acts of terrorism (the bombing of Pan American flight
103 over Lockerby, Scotland, in 1988; the Oklahoma City
bombing of 1995) denied Americans any sense of increased
security. The American economy performed well and the stock
market climbed to unprecedented heights during the 1980s and
1990s, bringing prosperity to a broad segment of the U.S. population. Yet at the same time, cuts in government social programs for the poor, abandonment of a previous government
policy of institutionalizing the mentally ill, and a persistent
national problem with substance abuse combined to put large

numbers of poor and homeless people on the streets for the first time since the Great Depression of the 1930s.

Another source of contrasts was a significant shift in national moral behavior. The percentage of marriages ending in divorce approached 50 percent, non-marital cohabitation and out-of-wedlock births became common, and gay men and lesbians became open about their behavior. Some decried a loss of what they called "family values" and yearned for a return to the moral ethos of earlier in the century. Others took the reverse position, suggesting that traditional morality was itself a problem. The national discussion about Acquired Immune Deficiency Syndrome (AIDS), a deadly sexually transmitted disease first identified in 1981, was a case in point. Some Americans cited the disease, which was initially seen in greatest numbers among gay men, as an example of the dangers of the abandonment of traditional morality. They called the young to remain celibate outside of heterosexual marriage. Others blamed the high death rate from the disease on those who disapproved of gay and lesbian behavior. They believed that such persons (whose attitudes they identified with the newly coined terms "heterosexism" and "homophobia") obstructed health education and denied funds for medical research necessary to conquer the disease.[1]

Author James Davison Hunter (b. 1955) identified the debate over sexuality as a part of what he called "culture wars," which, he believed, divided Americans into competing camps.[2] Such culture wars marked American political life in the 1980s (the election of Ronald Reagan and George Bush with strong support from evangelical supporters of family values) and 1990s (charges of sexual misconduct at the confirmation hearing for Supreme Court Justice Clarence Thomas in 1991; President Bill Clinton's establishment of a "don't ask, don't tell" policy toward homosexuality in the military in 1992; Clinton's impeachment in December 1998 and trial in January 1999 for lying about sex with a female White House intern).

American Christians were deeply divided by the culture wars. Some denominations took clear stands on one side of the debate or the other. The United Church of Christ was, for example, generally supportive of the aspirations of gay and lesbian persons and was one of the first denominations to accept those who were open about their behavior into the ordained ministry. The Southern Baptist Church, on the other hand, was generally supportive of the campaign for family values. Other denominations, like the Episcopal Church, were themselves deeply divided, with a significant percentage of members on either side of the cultural divide. Following a period of relative tranquility in the early 1980s, Episcopalians entered a period of sustained debate that would last throughout the 1990s.

The years from 1965 to 1980 had also been turbulent for the Episcopal Church, but there was a significant difference in the 1990s. Episcopalians of the late 1960s and 1970s had, despite their differences, come to consensus on a series of major issues. They had decided to ordain women to the priesthood and episcopate, they had revised the prayer book, they had discontinued the General Convention Special Program, and they had adopted a compromise over homosexuality. There would, in contrast, be few significant changes made in the 1980s and 1990s. To be sure, individuals and groups within the church declared their ideas and goals, but the denomination as a whole was too divided to reach consensus. Instead, the years were marked by a prolonged stalemate. There would be some indications of a changed mood in the church, however, as the century came to a close.

The Early 1980s

There was relative calm in the church in the early 1980s. The post-1965 statistical decline appeared to halt during the first half of the decade with the number of baptized members stabilizing at around 2.7 million. In 1986, however, the adoption of a new method of reporting membership strength contributed to a further numerical loss.[3] Three other measures of church adherence told a more optimistic story. The denomination continued to attract new members. In 1982 the General Convention's Committee on the State of the Church estimated that the percentage of Episcopalians raised outside the denomination had risen from 48 to 58 percent between 1978 and 1981.[4] Church attendance increased slightly—by about 3 percent between 1980 and 1988.[5] In addition, the Gallup's *Religion in America* survey indicated that in 1984 the Episcopal Church had regained the percentage of the general population that it had attracted in 1965. The survey, which measured denominational preference rather than actual participation, showed that the Lutheran Church had also regained its previous percentage. Presbyterian and Methodist churches were still, however, attracting declining percentages of the national population.[6]

One rather dramatic sign of revival in the church of the 1980s was the reversal of the building freeze of the 1970s. In that decade, the dioceses of New York and Washington had halted the construction of their gothic cathedrals. In 1979, the Diocese of New York resumed work on the Cathedral of St. John the Divine. In the following year, the Diocese of

Fig. 53. The Washington National Cathedral, 1907–1990

Washington followed suit, resuming work on the Washington National Cathedral (the Cathedral Church of St. Peter and St. Paul). The completed building was consecrated and dedicated on September 29, 1990, eighty-three years to the day after construction was begun. Construction resumed again on a parish level as well, with Episcopalians founding over two hundred new congregations between 1979 and 1984.[7]

Another dramatic sign was the seriousness with which Episcopalians took stewardship. The Diocese of Alabama, the General Convention of 1982, and a host of individuals and agencies in the church went on record as accepting tithing as the norm for Christian giving. The Episcopal Church's giving per confirmed person climbed, and by 1987 the church's stewardship office noted that "for the third year in a row the Episcopal Church [led] North American Christianity in per-unit giving."[8]

Changing Perspectives on Renewal

Charismatic Episcopalians of the 1960s and 1970s had often adopted the defensive stance of a persecuted minority. Some outside of the movement regarded charismatic Episcopalians as psychologically or theologically immature; those charismatics who accepted the Pentecostal link between glossolalia and salvation questioned the faith of those without charismatic gifts. By 1980, however, it was evident that the charismatic revival was more than a passing phenomenon. As those with and without experiences of glossolalia lived together in the church, they gained a growing respect for one another. Those with experiences of glossolalia modified their position, seeing tongues as a possible, but no longer a necessary, element of the Christian faith.

Those outside of the charismatic community responded with formulations that recognized the place of the spiritual gifts in the life of the church. Virginia Seminary's Charles P. Price and the Episcopal Divinity School's Eugene V. N. Goetchius (b. 1921) argued in *The Gifts of God*, for example, that Episcopalians of the 1970s had erred in making too broad a distinction between ordinary and extraordinary gifts from God:

279

> We do not intend to imply that there is any sharp division between [the extraordinary gifts Paul calls charismata] and the more familiar gifts we call talents, abilities, skills, aptitudes, and faculties; all of these are also given by God, and all are available, valuable, and indispensable for "the work of ministry, for the building up the body of Christ..." (Ephesians 4:12).[9]

The authors went on to suggest that God gave charismata to all Christians, for faith and salvation were themselves charismatic gifts. They were "the basic equipment needed by every Christian for every form of ministry."[10]

Such a reformulation opened up the possibility of a broader consensus within the church, on what Episcopalians termed *renewal.* Charismatic Christians called the church to be renewed by a deeper relationship to Scripture and an increased understanding of the work of the Spirit. Those initially opposed to the movement recognized their commitment to pursuing God's justice in the world as an element of God's renewal of the world.

With this growing consensus on renewal and a resolution of some of the major issues that the General Convention had faced in the 1970s, Episcopalians found that they were able to devote more of their attention to congregational life. In 1982 Presiding Bishop John Allin suggested to the New Orleans General Convention that it was time to follow the 1976 Venture in Mission program with the "Next Step in Mission." He delineated five aspects of mission, which he linked in the acronym SWEEP: service, worship, evangelism, education, and pastoral care. The Convention endorsed Allin's proposal, which called each congregation to refocus attention on the five areas. Allin's letter to Episcopal congregations explained the program:

> Some of our congregations are doing more than others in the five functions which define Christian mission. None, however, should follow the temptation of believing that "we are doing all we can" or that "nothing needs to be changed."
>
> Needs and opportunities are before us in every place. It is through our congregations—through our renewed congregating—that needs will be met and God's work will be done![11]

Renewed congregations would carry on God's work in the world.

Those congregations that went through the process of self-evaluation often discovered that their parishioners shared an interest in adult Christian education. Episcopalians of the 1950s had concentrated their educational efforts on the products of the baby boom. Emptying Sunday school classes, a new interest in Scripture sparked by the renewal movement, and the need to acclimate parishioners to a revised liturgy combined to produce a new appreciation among Episcopalians for Christian education of adults.

A variety of groups and individuals provided adult education materials. In the early 1970s the Diocese of Colorado had introduced *Living the Good News*, a lectionary-based church school series designed for use with all ages. In 1979 Seabury Press released a new *Church's Teaching Series* for adults. Morehouse-Barlow published collections of essays under the title the *Anglican Study Series* (1983–85); it also took over publication of *Living the Good News*. In 1997 James E. Griffiss (b. 1928), a former Nashotah House professor of systematic theology, began to edit a *New Church's Teaching Series* for Cowley Press. In 1997 the Church Hymnal Corporation changed its name to Church Publishing, in recognition of its expanding list of publications.

Not all of the increasingly popular educational materials were designed for use with Sunday morning adult classes or for confirmation preparation. The School of Theology of the University of the South's Education for Ministry program (EFM), for example, provided adults with trained mentors and an intensive four-year curriculum. The Cursillo Movement (first Episcopal weekend, 1970; first national gathering, 1975) and Marriage Encounter, both initially products of the Roman Catholic Church, employed weekend retreats in order to teach about the Christian faith and about Christian marriage. The Shalem Institute in Washington, D.C. (1979), provided training for those interested in spiritual direction. Trinity Church, New York's Trinity Institute, which began to offer conferences on current intellectual issues in the life of the church in 1970, had by the 1980s expanded its program in order to offer courses on the West Coast as well. Trinity School for the Ministry, a new Episcopal seminary in Ambridge, Pennsylvania (founded in 1975, accredited in 1985), sought to provide a theological education with a particular emphasis on renewal and evangelism. A number of American parishes also held Alpha Courses, a program developed at Holy Trinity, Brompton in London by vicar Charles Marnham and popularized beginning in 1993 by his successor Nicky Gumbel.

The interest in education was not limited to adults. *Living the Good News* included lessons for all ages. Virginia Seminary created the Center for the Ministry of Teaching (1985) in order to equip clergy and others for the education of children. The center's director, Christian education professor Locke E. Bowman (b. 1927), initiated a monthly newspaper (*The Episcopal Teacher*), a master's degree program in Christian education (1990), and a new Sunday school curriculum (*Episcopal Children's Curriculum*) to support and encourage those who served in Sunday schools.

The Episcopal Church's new appreciation for Christian education and its increasing consensus on charismatic renewal offered a measure of hope not only to members of the denomination but also to some outside of it. Denominational lines continued to be fluid as they had been in the 1970s, but certain differences were evident. Those who entered the Episcopal Church from other denominations in the 1970s came most often from mainline Protestant denominations, particularly from the Methodist and Presbyterian traditions. While former Methodists and Presbyterians continued to represent a significant percentage of converts to the Episcopal Church in the 1980s (26 and 14.5 percent respectively in a 1982 report to the General Convention), an increasing number of former Roman Catholics (19.3 percent) and Baptists (16.9 percent) found a home in the Episcopal Church as well.[12]

Roman Catholics, oriented in a liturgical tradition that bore increasing similarity to that of the Episcopal Church, often came to the Episcopal Church because of its understanding of authority, pastoral care, and the ministry of the laity. Author, social reformer, and leading Roman Catholic layman John Cogley (1916–76) cited such motives for his conversion to the Episcopal Church (1973) in his book *A Canterbury Tale: Experiences and Reflections, 1916–1976* (1976). Cogley, who entered the ordination process and was ordained to the diaconate in the Episcopal Church, died shortly after the completion of the book. Many others, however, would follow in his footsteps.

In contrast to Roman Catholics, Baptists and those of other evangelical backgrounds were often attracted by a liturgical and historical tradition that could provide a context for personal faith. Southern Baptist pastor John Claypool (b. 1930) of the Second Baptist Church of Lubbock, Texas, who became an Episcopal priest in 1986, spoke of the sense of mystery that he had found in Episcopal worship.[13] In a book suggestively titled *Evangelicals on the Canterbury Trail* (1985), Robert E. Webber told the story of six evangelical converts with similar experiences.

Some Pentecostals were also attracted to the Episcopal Church's balance of tradition and renewal. In a highly publicized service in Valdosta, Georgia, in 1990, former Pentecostal clergyman Stan White (b. 1962) led his independent congregation into the Episcopal Church. More than two hundred parishioners were confirmed by Bishop Harry Shipps (b. 1926) of Georgia.[14]

Presiding Bishop Edmond Lee Browning

In 1985 the General Convention elected Bishop of Hawaii Edmond Lee Browning to succeed John Allin as presiding bishop of the Episcopal Church. Browning had spent much of his adult life outside of the continental U.S. In contrast to Allin, who had focused his attention inward, seeking to bridge divisions and reconcile differences within the church, Browning understood his vision in a global context. As he explained in a letter to the *Episcopalian* in March 1987, "Increasingly... I see my role as Presiding Bishop not so much as Chief Executive of one branch of the Anglican Communion but as one who must, at least in part, be a channel for the aspiration, hopes, strengths, and dreams of our brothers and sisters [outside of the U.S.]."[15]

Fig. 54. The celebration of the eucharist at Edmond Browning's Service of Institution in January 1986 brought together *(left to right):* John Allin, twenty-third presiding bishop; Browning; John Walker, Bishop of Washington; John Wantanabe, Primate of Japan; and Desmond Tutu, Primate of the Church of the Province of Southern Africa.

Bishop Browning traveled widely and spoke out on international issues. He played an active role in the campaign to convince American businesses to divest in South Africa as a means to pressure the minority white government to abandon its policy of racial apartheid. In 1989 he sent a team of bishops to El Salvador to investigate the government arrest of a group of clergy and church workers. Browning visited the State Department and scheduled a meeting at the Episcopal Church Center in New York between President Alfredo Christiani of El Salvador and a group of ecumenical church leaders. Most of the church workers were released soon afterward.[16]

Browning expressed his support for the rights of Palestinians in public and also in private meetings with Yasser Arafat. He visited both Baghdad and Washington on the eve of the Gulf War. The presiding bishop joined with others in a January 15, 1991 peace vigil outside the White House, while

President George Bush, who was an Episcopalian, was making the decision to begin bombing in Iraq.[17]

Bishop Browning reorganized the Presiding Bishop's Fund for World Relief to accord with his vision of the role of the Episcopal Church in the world. Since its inception, the fund had been a conduit for emergency disaster aid. Browning and Furman Stough (b. 1928), the former bishop of Alabama who assumed oversight of the Fund in 1988, reshaped the fund along the lines of the United Thank Offering. The reorganized fund supported seed projects and developmental programs, rather than responding exclusively to crises.

Some were critical of Browning's international policy.[18] More serious criticism was leveled at his domestic policy, however. The presiding bishop had a vision of a church in which "diversity is our strength."[19] He dreamed of a church in which "there will be no outcasts. The hopes and convictions of all will be respected and honored."[20] The vision proved difficult to sustain.

Part of the problem was geographical and demographic. During Browning's tenure, the relatively favorable signs of the early 1980s were replaced by less promising ones. The Gallup poll of 1984 turned out to be a one-year anomaly; the percentage of the population claiming affiliation with the Episcopal Church fell back to 2 percent the following year and remained there for the rest of the century. The number of baptized members in the church declined an additional 6.7 percent in the decade from 1986 to 1996, but that national figure masked important regional differences. An analysis of membership data from 1988 to 1991 commissioned by the Office of Evangelism revealed that Province IV (the dioceses in Alabama, Florida, Kentucky, Louisiana, Mississippi, North Carolina, South Carolina, and Tennessee) was the only one in which the church was "strong and stable."[21] A comparison of membership figures from 1986 to 1996 revealed much the same thing.

Table 6. Baptized Membership (1986–1996)

Province	1986 Baptized Membership	1996 Baptized Membership	Percent Change
I	284,093	262,561	-7.6%
II	354,621	305,845	-13.6%
III	396,760	374,956	-5.5%
IV	472,910	499,621	5.6%
V	282,684	236,616	-16.3%
VI	131,193	121,596	-7.3%
VII	270,613	260,226	-3.9%
VIII	311,633	304,633	-2.2%
Total Domestic	2,504,507	2,366,054	-6.7%

Source: 1986 and 1996 parochial reports as compiled in *The Episcopal Church Annual* of 1988 and 1998.

Province IV's growth of 5.6 percent contrasted with a 16.3 percent decline in Province V (the dioceses in Illinois, Indiana, Michigan, Ohio, Wisconsin, and eastern Missouri) and a 13.6 percent decline in Province II (the dioceses in New York and New Jersey). This geographical imbalance contributed to very different perceptions about the Episcopal Church. Those in Province IV agreed with the first recommendation of the Office of Evangelism's report on church membership: "Keep doing what you are doing in the areas of membership growth."[22] They saw little reason to question the renewal theology that had taken shape by the early 1980s. Many in Provinces II and V, in contrast, believed that the Episcopal Church was in deep crisis and searched for new ideas and approaches with which they might reverse population declines.

Nowhere was the contrast in perceptions more clear than in the area of sexual ethics. The debate over homosexuality was a complicated one. The vast majority of Episcopalians did agree: (1) that those in same-sex relationships were welcome in the church and entitled to receive its ministry; (2) that fidelity within heterosexual, monogamous marriage and chastity outside of it was the church's traditional standard for behavior; (3) that not all persons were successful in applying that standard to their lives.

Moderate advocates of the ordination of gays and lesbians argued that the church's understanding of exclusive, life-long sexual relationships should be expanded to include faithful same-sex couples. While recognizing that biblical authors regarded homosexual behavior as sinful, they argued that late twentieth-century gay and lesbian persons had established a new paradigm of faithful, egalitarian relating that was unknown to biblical authors. They argued that the church's support of those who lived according to that new paradigm would strengthen, rather than undermine, faithful heterosexual relationships.

Other advocates of the ordination of gays and lesbians took more radical positions, understanding the acceptance of same-sex relationships as part of a reversal of the church's traditional sexual ethics. In the late 1980s advocates of this more radical position became increasingly vocal. Bishop John S. Spong (b. 1931) of Newark wrote *Living in Sin?* (1988), suggesting that the church should bless same-sex unions, premarital sexual relationships for young people, and cohabitation by unmarried elderly persons affected by Social Security regulations.[23] L. William Countryman (b. 1941) of the Church Divinity School of the Pacific suggested in *Dirt, Greed, and Sex* (1988) that early Christians had framed a sexual ethic "in terms of purity and property systems that no longer prevail among us." In its place, he offered an ethic that he believed was constructed from six "generative" biblical principles and corresponded to the circumstances of the contemporary world. His new formulation found no prohibition in the gospel against homosexual acts, polygamy, or bestiality.[24] Carter Heyward of the Episcopal Divinity School argued in *Touching Our Strength* (1989) that monogamy "would seem to have little to commend it," and counseled her readers to maintain multiple sexual friendships.[25]

On December 16, 1989 Bishop John S. Spong of Newark ordained practicing homosexual Robert Williams (1955–1992) to the priesthood in a highly publicized service. Williams, a former student of Carter Heyward who was mentioned positively in *Touching Our Strength*, had a same-sex partner but did not believe in exclusive relationships. He later made his position quite clear in an article in *Witness* magazine. He described himself as a "an angry gay activist; a sexual radical" who when in his twenties "spent at least twice as much time in gay bars as [he] did in the Episcopal churches." Neither he nor his partner expected sexual exclusivity of the other. Indeed, Williams described himself as still active in the gay bar scene after entering into his relationship and as "more, not less radical." He regarded gays in exclusive relationships as "Uncle Toms." He criticized them for not visiting gay bars and for allowing heterosexual authority figures to dictate behavior to them.[26]

Both Williams and Kim Byham (the president of Integrity) agreed that Williams was quite open about his opinions. The Bishop and the Standing Committee of the Diocese of Newark seemed unaware of his attitudes, however, until Williams spoke at a forum sponsored by the Task Force on Gay and Lesbian Concerns of the Diocese of Michigan on January 13, 1990. Williams noted in the presence of the press that monogamy and celibacy were "unnatural"—a "crazy" ideal that no one held in practice.[27]

Bishop Spong demanded an apology. Williams refused. The bishop contacted Oasis (the diocesan outreach ministry to gay and lesbian people for which Williams worked) and convinced the board of directors to ask for Williams's resignation. After consulting Carter Heyward, Williams reluctantly agreed.[28] He angrily denounced the bishop as a "racist, sexist, homophobe."[29] Soon afterward he resigned his orders in the Episcopal Church. He later died of AIDS.

For some, Bishop Browning's vision of a church with no outcasts offered little in the way of resources in the difficult task of discerning between appropriate and inappropriate types of sexual behavior and between acceptance within the church and elevation to positions of leadership. On February 20, 1990 Browning reluctantly agreed with the nine bishops who made up his Council of Advice and "disassociated" himself from Spong's ordination of Williams. He also presided, in

September of 1990, at a meeting of the House of Bishops which voted by a narrow margin to support the Council of Advice's statement. Increasingly, however, Browning sided with the supporters of gay and lesbian ordination. According to Brian J. Grieves, who edited a collection of Browning's public statements, Browning had on a number of occasions early in his term "set aside his personal views and declined to be an advocate for one side or the other." This policy changed. "Toward the end of his tenure, Browning began to advocate more openly for gays and lesbians."[30] He participated in the annual meeting of Integrity in 1992 and joined with a group of advocates of the ordination of practicing gay and lesbian persons in a celebration in 1996.[31] In 1991 Seattle priest Linda Strohmier (b. 1945) expressed a willingness to perform a same-sex marriage despite the explicit prohibition of her bishop.[32] After the conflict became public, Browning appointed Strohmier to the national church's staff as evangelism officer.

Opponents of Williams's ordination regarded the action of the House of Bishops in September 1990 as a reaffirmation of the 1979 compromise. Advocates regarded it as a rejection of a particular candidate, rather than a rejection of all persons in same-sex unions. The leadership of the diocese of Newark made its position on the subject clear by ordaining gay candidate Barry Stopfel (b. 1947) to the diaconate. After conferring with Bishop Browning, Bishop Spong had delayed the ordination until after the House of Bishops meeting. According to Stopfel's same-sex partner, Spong's position changed after the bishops met. Bishop Spong wrote to Stopfel that he would "no longer prevent" his ordination from taking place. He himself would not preside but he would "not forbid another bishop who [was] willing to stand beside [Stopfel and Spong] in this fight, from proceeding immediately..."[33] Spong's assistant bishop, Walter Righter (b. 1923), ordained Stopfel to the diaconate on September 30, 1990.

In the spring of 1991, the church's Standing Commission on Human Affairs, chaired by Bishop George N. Hunt, III (b. 1931) of Rhode Island, released a report designed to bring the questions of ordination and marriage of practicing homosexuals before the 1991 General Convention. The report recommended "that the Standing Liturgical Commission study the theological and liturgical issues involved in affirming and blessing... covenants of gay and lesbian persons and begin the process of developing liturgical forms for them" and that "the church be open to ordaining gay men and lesbians otherwise qualified who display the same integrity in their sexual relationships which we ask of our heterosexual ordinands." The committee report included a resolution affirming the right of individual dioceses to make such determinations. Bishop Hunt believed that the adoption of the resolution would "negate the 1979 [General Convention] resolution" on sexuality.[34]

The 1991 General Convention became a battleground with tempers flaring so greatly in the House of Bishops that Bishop Browning later commented that he was "not sure that we could hold together as a church."[35] Neither side of the debate was able to gain a legislative majority, however, with a resolution by Bishops William Frey (b. 1930) and John Howe (b. 1942) against clergy sex outside of marriage failing in the House of Bishops by eighty-five to ninety-one and the proposal by Bishop Hunt not even reaching the floor for debate.[36]

Episcopalians sought to quiet tempers in two ways. The House of Bishops met the following year in what would become a regular non-legislative retreat at the Kanuga Conference Center in North Carolina. Jon Shuler (b. 1945) served as executive director of the *Shaping Our Future* symposium, which met in Saint Louis in August 1993 to consider ways in which the structure of the Episcopal Church might be altered to lessen conflict and refocus on mission. Over 1,000 attended.[37] A number of innovative ideas were discussed, but after two General Conventions (1994, 1997) the only major change was a consolidation of a number of the General Convention's interim bodies. The Liturgical Commission and the Commission on Church Music, for example, were consolidated into a Commission on Liturgy and Music.[38]

Tempers were less heated at the conventions of 1994 and 1997, but the church moved no closer to resolution of the debate over sexuality. The bishops adopted a traditional state-ment of the church's position on sexuality in 1994, but a minority *Koinonia* (Greek for "fellowship") statement circu-lated by John S. Spong attracted significant support. The 1997 convention approved a resolution on insurance rights for same-sex partners, but rejected a similar resolution on pension rights. The convention also established a committee to study the Kuala Lumpur Statement, a traditional statement on sexuality adopted in February 1997 by bishops from developing nations.

Increasingly, the church divided into two camps. The divi-sion mirrored the culture wars in the society at large. A set of overlapping orthodox organizations favored engagement with Scripture and classical Christian doctrine, and generally had serious reservations about ordination and marital blessings for those in same-sex unions. Among the organizations forming this coalition were Episcopalians United (which began in 1989 to publish *United Voice* as an alternative to the national church's newspaper *Episcopal Life*), the Irenaeus Fellowship (a group of bishops who began to meet together at the 1988 General Convention), AWAKE (the Association of Concerned Episcopalians to Inform and Awaken Our Church, based in Alabama, which circulated a *Catalogue of Concerns* about Bishop Browning's leadership in 1995), the American Anglican Council (an umbrella organization formed by a group of Episcopalians who first met in the Briarwood Conference Center north of Dallas, Texas, in December of 1995), the Ekklesia Society (a group that began in about 1996 to coordi-nate contacts with other parts of the Anglican Communion), the Emerging Church Network (an organization dedicated to evangelism, which held its first conference in a Dallas suburb in 1996), and First Promise (a group initiated at Pawley's Island, South Carolina, in September 1997 whose members make an affirmation of loyalty to traditional doctrine).

A countervailing progressive group called for a reformula-tion of doctrine to meet the changed circumstances of the mod-ern world and was generally supportive of the ordination and blessing of those in same-sex unions. This coalition included

Integrity, Christianity for the Third Millennium, Inc. (organized in 1993 by clergy and laity in the Diocese of Newark with Bishop Spong serving as an early chairman of its board of trustees), Millennium[3] (a project of a group of bishops who began a newspaper in 1996 to promote their ideas; Bishop Otis Charles, who in September 1993 became the first bishop to declare that he was gay, served as coeditor), the National Consultation of Episcopalians on Same-Sex Unions (a body considering same-sex marriage rites, which first met in 1993), the Center for Progressive Christianity (1995), and Beyond Inclusion (an organization that sponsored conferences at All Saints Church in Pasadena, California, in 1997 and at St. Bartholomew's in New York City in 1999).

With both coalitions frustrated by their inability to gain legislative majorities, individuals sought other means to influence church policy, including judicial remedies. In 1993 Professor Deirdre J. Good used a complaint to New York City's Commission on Human Rights to overturn the General Seminary's policy of not providing housing for same-sex partners of faculty and students.[39] The seminary adopted a new policy allowing same-sex couples to lives in campus housing so long as they had explicit consent of their bishops. In 1994 and 1995 members of the orthodox bloc tried to use the church courts to halt the ordination of practicing gay and lesbian persons. They brought charges against Bishops R. Stuart Wood, Jr. (b. 1934) of Michigan and Allen Bartlett, Jr. (b. 1929) of Pennsylvania. The committees of inquiry appointed by Bishop Browning dismissed the charges, however.[40] Charges against Assistant Bishop Walter Righter of Newark, who had ordained Barry Stopfel, took longer to resolve. After a long judicial process, a church court dismissed all charges against Bishop Righter. In its May 15, 1996 decision the court suggested it was not offering "an opinion on whether a bishop and diocese should or should not ordain persons living in same gender sexual relationships. Rather [the court decided] the narrow issue of whether or not under Title IV [of the church canons] a bishop is restrained from ordaining persons living in committed same gender sexual relationships."[41] The Court argued that the church was too divided, the matter of homosexuality too far removed from what it termed "core doctrine," and the resolutions of General Convention insufficiently clear about penalties to take action against Bishop Righter. In 1996 Bishop William Wantland founded a corporation that took the official, though uncopyrighted, name of the Episcopal Church (The Protestant Episcopal Church in the United States of America); two years later Bishops John S. Spong of Newark and Joe M. Doss (b. 1943) of New Jersey sued Wantland and the corporation for trademark infringement.[42]

The debate over homosexuality effectively derailed an initiative for evangelism adopted by the 1988 General Convention. In that year the Convention responded to a resolution from the 1988 Lambeth Conference and to a series of mission imperatives from the presiding bishop and Executive Council and designated the 1990s as a decade of evangelism. A badly divided church mustered little zeal for evangelism. The Standing Commission on Evangelism reported to the 1997 General Convention that "our potential for evangelistic outreach continues to be limited by two entirely avoidable counter-productive influences. First, there exists a tendency to focus on internal differences and discord when speaking about our church to others. Second, precious little has been done to raise the level of positive visibility of the Episcopal Church on a national level."[43]

Some of the causes of discord were unrelated to the sexuality debate. In 1986, for example, Browning sought to demonstrate his support for the leadership of women by appointing Ellen Cooke both as Treasurer of General Convention and Senior Executive for Administration and Finance. The double position enabled Mrs. Cooke effectively to avoid oversight. She resigned in January of 1995 in order to accompany her husband who had been elected rector of a parish in another state. After her departure it became evident that she had embezzled large sums of money from the church. An audit later revealed that $2.2 million was missing.[44] Cooke eventually went to jail and her husband resigned his orders.

The Electronic Church

The continuing discord did have one positive result. It provided incentive for Episcopalians to adopt new electronic means of communications. Bishop Browning and the President of the House of Deputies scheduled a satellite telecast on June 24, 1995 in order to answer questions about Ellen Cooke. Pamela Darling designed a page for the General Convention, which went on line in September of 1996.[45] A number of individuals and organizations established web pages as well. Thomas Bushnell, BSG, was among the first with his "unofficial Episcopal Church Home Page" (January 1995). Louie Crew, the Rutgers University professor who was the founder of Integrity, established his own web site in February of 1996.[46] His complicated site provided analysis of bishops' voting records and of episcopal elections; it became a valuable source of information for progressive groups. Many orthodox groups, such as Episcopalians United, linked their sites to the web site that the South American Missionary Society, led by director Thomas Prichard (b.1952), had established in August 1995. Both the orthodox and progressive coalitions disseminated information by e-mail and through the World Wide Web during the 1997 General Convention. By the end of the century most church organizations and dioceses, as well as many parishes, had their own home pages and electronic mail.

The Changing Character
of Church Leadership

The heated debate over sexuality distracted attention from changes of other sorts that were taking place in the church. Analysis of 1980 surveys found Episcopalians to be the most progressive of twenty-three religious groups on questions of racial justice. The denomination ranked fourth among eighteen predominantly white denominations in the percentage of black membership (5 percent).[47] The composition of the church's leadership was also proof that the denomination was quite different

Table 7. African American Bishops in the Domestic and Overseas Dioceses of the Protestant Episcopal Church

Name	(Birth–death)	Consecrated	Diocese
James Theodore Holly	(1829–1911)	1874	Haiti
Samuel David Ferguson	(1842–1916)	1885	Liberia
Edward Thomas Demby	(1869–1957)	1918	Arkansas (suffragan)
Henry Beard Delany (Delaney)	(1858–1928)	1918	North Carolina (suffragan)
Theophilus Momolu Firah Gardiner	(1870–1941)	1921	Liberia (suffragan)
Bravid Washington Harris	(1896–1965)	1945	Liberia
Dillard Houston Brown	(1912–1969)	1961	Liberia
John Melville Burgess	(1909–)	1962	Massachusetts (suffragan 1962–70; diocesan 1970–76)
Cedric Earl Mills	(1903–1992)	1963	Virgin Islands (1963–72); Los Angeles (Ass. Bp., 1972–84)
Richard Beamon Martin	(1913–)	1967	Long Island (suffragan)
George Daniel Browne	(1933–1993)	1970	Liberia
Luc Anatole Jacques Garnier	(1928–1999)	1971	Haiti
John Thomas Walker	(1925–1989)	1971	Washington (suffragan 1971–77; diocesan 1977–89)
Lemuel Barnett Shirley	(1916–)	1972	Panamá
Telesforo Alexander Isaac	(1929–	1972	Dominican Republic
Quintin Ebenezer Primo, Jr.	(1913–1998)	1972	Chicago (suffragan)
Harold Louis Wright	(1929–1978)	1974	New York (suffragan)
Henry Irving Mayson	(1925–1995)	1976	Michigan (suffragan)
Walter Decoster Dennis	(1932–)	1979	New York (suffragan)
Henry Boyd Hucles, III	(1923–1989)	1981	Long Island (suffragan)
Clarence Nicholas Coleridge	(1930–)	1981	Connecticut (suffragan 1981–93; diocesan 1993–99)
James Hamilton Ottley	(1936–)	1984	Panamá

Sturdie Wyman Downs	(1947–)	1985	Nicaragua
Arthur Benjamin Williams, Jr.	(1935–)	1986	Ohio (suffragan)
Egbert Don Taylor	(1937–)	1987	Virgin Islands
Orris George Walker, Jr.	(1942–)	1988	Long Island
Herbert Thompson, Jr.	(1933–)	1988	Southern Ohio
Franklin Delton Turner	(1933–)	1988	Pennsylvania (suffragan)
Barbara Clementine Harris	(1930–)	1989	Massachusetts (suffragan)
Chester Lovelle Talton	(1941–)	1991	Los Angeles (suffragan)
Victor Alfonso Scantlebury	(1945–)	1991	Panamá (suffragan)
Jean-Zaché Duracin	(1947–)	1993	Haiti
Clarence Wallace Hayes	(1928–)	1995	Panamá
Theodore Athelbert Daniels	(1944–)	1997	Virgin Islands

Source: J. Carleton Hayden, "From Holly to Turner: Black Bishops in the American Succession," *Linkage* (a newsletter of the Office of Black Ministries of the Episcopal Church), no. 10 (December 1988):4–6; *The Episcopal Church Annual*, 1988–1998.

from the white suburban church of the 1950s. At the time of his election in 1974, Presiding Bishop John Allin had agreed to a series of requests made by the Union of Black Episcopalians. He would establish an Office for Black Ministries, appoint African Americans to his senior staff, and select African American bishops and clergy to important General Convention committees.[48] Allin kept his promises. The prominent positions gave African Americans a higher visibility in the church and contributed to the escalating rate at which African Americans were elected to the episcopate. Franklin Tuner, Allin's first staff officer in the Office for Black Ministries, for example, was elected Suffragan Bishop of Pennsylvania in 1988. In the fifty years prior to 1974, only six African Americans had been elected as bishops in domestic dioceses, and only one of them (John Burgess of Massachusetts) as diocesan bishop. Between 1974 and 1990 domestic dioceses elected ten African Americans. They chose three of the new bishops and one suffragan elected before 1974 as diocesan bishops. African American bishops John Walker and Herbert Thompson, Jr. (b. 1933) were runners-up in the elections for presiding bishop in 1985 and 1997.[49] Lay persons also assumed important leadership roles.

Sociologist Charles Radford Lawrence II (1915–86) served as the first black president of the House of Deputies (1976–85).

The situation changed markedly during the later years of Bishop Browning. By 1995 Browning had reduced the percentage of African Americans working on his appointed staff to one quarter of what it had been in 1985. Former staff member Harold T. Lewis attributed the decline to two causes: Browning's service outside of the continental United States and his advocacy of other issues.[50] The rate of election of African Americans fell even more rapidly, with only one African American elected by a domestic diocese between 1990 and the end of 1998.

A careful analysis of clergy career patterns revealed that women ordained in 1970 (the year the General Convention eliminated the difference between the diaconate for men and women) advanced in their careers more rapidly than succeeding generations of female ordinands, though still at a slower pace than their male counterparts. A 1991 report revealed, for example, that males ordained in 1980 were receiving salaries that averaged 20 percent above those of women ordained in the same year.[51]

The apparent gap between male and female advancement may have led some women to reassess the elimination of

Fig. 55. Barbara Harris and David Johnson,
Bishop of Massachusetts

women's organizations that began in the late 1960s. In 1980 Joanna Gillespie, Betsy Rodenmayer (1909–85), and other Episcopal women met in New York to found the Episcopal Women's History Project, dedicated to raising the consciousness "about the historic place of women in the church." In 1985, following a resurgence of interest in diocesan gatherings, the Episcopal Church Women resumed national triennial meetings.

Soon afterward, however, women did begin to move into significant national leadership positions. In 1985, laywoman Pamela Pauly Chinnis (b. 1925) of the Diocese of Washington became the first female vice-president of the House of Deputies. In 1995, she became the first woman to serve as president of that body. Barbara Harris (b. 1930) was elected in 1988 and consecrated in 1989 as Suffragan Bishop of the Diocese of Massachusetts. She became the first female bishop in the Anglican Church.[52] By the end of 1997, eight women had been consecrated to the Episcopate.

Table 8. Women Bishops in the United States

	Birth Date	Consecrated	Diocese
Barbara Clementine Harris	1930	1989	Massachusetts (suffragan)
Jane Holmes Dixon	1937	1992	Washington (suffragan)
Mary Adelia R. McLeod	1938	1993	Vermont
Catherine A. Roskam	1943	1996	New York (suffragan)
Geralyn Wolf	1947	1996	Rhode Island
Carolyn Tanner Irish	1940	1996	Utah
Catherine M. Waynick	1948	1997	Indianapolis
Chilton Knudsen	1946	1997	Maine

Opposition to ordained female leadership gradually declined. The Anglican churches in Australia (1992), England (1993), and Scotland (1993) agreed to ordain women to the priesthood. Support declined for the Evangelical and Catholic Mission of the Episcopal Synod of America, which had been formed in Fort Worth, Texas in June 1989 by advocates of a male-only priesthood.[53] By 1997 only four of the one hundred domestic dioceses did not ordain women to the priesthood. In 1997 the General Convention adopted legislation that effectively repealed the House of Bishop's conscience clause of 1979, which had allowed bishops to decline to ordain women for theological reasons. The decision had two practical effects. It put pressure on the four dioceses that still declined to ordain women (Quincy, Fort Worth, San Joaquin, and Eau Claire), making it possible to present their bishops for trial. It also complicated relationships in the Anglican Communion, for Anglicans had agreed in international gatherings that opposition to ordination of women was a permissible theological option.[54]

Immigration to the United States, accelerated by political instability in Central America and Southeast Asia, also had an effect on the demographic profile of the Episcopal Church. The Marxist policy of Fidel Castro devastated the Episcopal Church in Cuba, but the Cuban Episcopalians who fled to the United States in the 1960s were by the 1970s providing leadership for the creation of Hispanic congregations in the United States and Central America. Joined by Hispanics of other nationalities, they created a new awareness about America's largest linguistic minority. The 1985 Gallup Religion in America survey indicated that 3 percent of American Episcopalians were of Hispanic background, the second highest percentage for the Protestant denominations surveyed.[55] Three years later a survey of theological students showed that the percentage of Hispanic people preparing for the ministry in the Episcopal Church (4 percent) was second only to that of the Roman Catholic Church (5 percent).[56] A bilingual St. Augustine College in Chicago (which joined the Association of Episcopal Colleges in 1988), the Episcopal Theological Seminary of the Southwest's Hispanic Center (1974), and the Instituto Pastoral Hispano of Stamford, Connecticut (1977–85) and New York City (1986–94) helped prepare clergy for this expanding Hispanic ministry. Forward Movement Publications began to include selections in Spanish in its catalogue (1988). In 1991 *Episcopal Life* (the new name given the *Episcopalian* in 1990) added a *Resumen de Noticias*, a summary of news items in Spanish.

Episcopalians were active in other ethnic ministries. In the twenty years after the creation of the Episcopal Asiamerica Ministry Office of the national church in 1973, the number of Asian and Pacific parishes and missions in the United States increased from under twelve to more than one hundred.[57] Other Episcopalians worked with renewed interest among Native Americans. In 1985, a gathering of Episcopalians interested in and involved in Native American ministry designated Seabury-Western Seminary in Chicago as the center for theological education. By 1989, the number of ordained Native Americans was triple what it had been just fifteen years before.[58] The General Convention's creation of the Navajoland Area Mission (1979) of Arizona, New Mexico, and Utah also indicated a willingness to try new approaches to Native American ministry. In 1990, Steven Tsosie Plummer (b. 1944), who had been the first Navajo priest (1976), was consecrated as bishop of the new diocese. In the following year Steven Charleston (Choctaw, b. 1949) was consecrated as Bishop of Alaska, a diocese in which one half of the communicants were American Indians or Eskimo.

Liturgical Change

The change in the character of the church also had liturgical manifestations. While the 1979 *Book of Common Prayer* and the *Hymnal 1982* remained the standards of the church, the General Conventions of the 1980s and 1990s made adjustments, adding, for example, women and minority persons to the list of predominantly white male figures on the church calendar.

In 1993 Church Hymnal issued an expanded *Lift Every Voice and Sing II* with music in the African-American tradition. It was followed in 1997 by *Wonder, Love, and Praise*, which contained inclusive language, multi-language texts, music composed since 1982, and some additional service music. The Episcopal Church joined with the Presbyterian Church (U.S.A.) and the United Church of Christ to produce a Spanish language *El Himnario* (dedicated at the 1997 General Convention, published 1998). The General Convention of 1997 approved plans for an additional supplement (tentatively titled *Voices Found*) featuring texts and tunes by women.

The Episcopal Church's Standing Liturgical Commission devoted its November 1981 meeting to the question of inclusive language. The commission decided to establish a subcommittee to investigate the issue further. Much of the leadership for the investigation was provided by the Episcopal Divinity School; four of five members of the subcommittee were associated with the school. The committee issued a report titled "The Power and Promise of Language in the Church: Inclusive Language Guidelines for the Church," which was later published in the first collection of the *Occasional Papers of the Standing Liturgical Commission*. The report initiated a broader discussion in the church about the use of gender language for the first person of the Trinity. As the introduction to the first inclusive text produced by the Standing Liturgical Commission explained:

> On the whole, the language of Rite II which refers to the people is genuinely inclusive. The real challenge was in connection with the language about God. In that regard, the language of Rite II continues the inherited masculine images which have been the conventional references to God throughout the history of the BCP.[59]

The General Convention of 1985 authorized experimentation with "inclusive language liturgies for the regular services for the Church" and approved *Litugical Texts for Evaluation* for use in selected evaluation centers.[60] Successive conventions approved additional materials. The 1988 convention granted permission for trial use of *Supplemental Liturgical Texts* in a broader number of sites. The General Conventions of 1991 and 1997 approved use of *Supplemental Liturgical Materials* and *Enriching Our Worship*.

Sexual Misconduct

In October of 1984 a priest from the Diocese of Minnesota paid a hospital call on a troubled woman. In the course of the visit, the woman revealed to the priest that she had been the victim of sexual misconduct by an Episcopal bishop. The priest, Margo Maris (b. 1942), began to search for ways in which to respond pastorally to the woman. In previous generations, those who had been sexually abused by the clergy had often kept silent out of a sense of shame; those in authority had often sought to shield the church from embarrassment, allowing offenders to resign quietly or to move to other areas. Margo Maris and a small group of like-minded clergy and laity, most of whom were women, envisioned an alternative in which the church put the pastoral needs of the victim before the church's desire for privacy. She worked with the Minnesota Council of Churches and with an ecumenical team of attorneys to develop models for dealing with such situations. Fellow cleric Susan Moss (b. 1950) worked with a committee of the same Council to influence the state legislature, which in the mid-1980s adopted new laws making clergy sexual abuse both a felony and a matter that could be subject for recovery in civil suits.[61]

Others began similar initiatives elsewhere. Coincidentally, both Marie M. Fortune of Seattle of the United Church of Christ and Chilton Knudsen (b. 1946) of the Episcopal Diocese of Chicago had encounters with victims of sexual abuse in the fall of 1984. Fortune would become among the best-known writers on the subject of clergy sexual misconduct.[62]

The process that Maris and her allies developed involved the appointment of a victim's advocate and full disclosure of any proven abuse. Maris found that many clergy, when confronted about misconduct in a church context, would admit their sins and submit to discipline. She believed that such a process accorded with the provisions for church discipline in Matthew 18. It also enabled victims to begin to trust the church again and to reclaim lost self-esteem. A legal process, in contrast, encouraged offenders to deny their actions and left victims with cash settlements as the only way to prove that they had indeed been wronged. Other states followed the Minnesota legislature in making clergy abuse a felony and the subject of civil suit, and courts and juries throughout the country proved willing to grant huge awards to victims. By one estimate, the Roman Catholic Church was directed to pay $800 million to victims of abuse between 1980 and 1998.[63] Awards against the Episcopal Church were smaller, but significant. By the end of 1992 the church had a potential liability of $7.2 million in claims. The number of new cases against the church was, moreover, rapidly growing. No claim had been filed against the Church Insurance Company prior to 1982. In the next few years, one to two cases were filed a year. By 1990 the number of cases filed annually had risen to twenty, and by 1992 it had risen to forty.[64]

Over time other dioceses imitated Minnesota's pastoral model, often only after learning first-hand of the costs involved in leaving such matters to the secular legal system. By the early 1990s, however, the church as a whole appeared ready to act. Margo Maris successfully lobbied the General Convention of 1991 to appoint a Committee on Sexual Exploitation. The committee, of which Maris served as cochair, encouraged a church-wide discussion, drafted educational material (*Respecting the Dignity of Every Human Being*), and convinced the General Convention of 1994 to establish a toll-free telephone number for the reporting of sexual abuse. The 1994 convention also thoroughly revised the canons concerning discipline: (1) making the complaint of a single alleged victim (or that person's family member) sufficient to initiate a judicial process against a priest or deacon; (2) providing for the possibility of the appointment of a victim's advocate; and (3) establishing clearer guidelines for a cleric who voluntarily submitted to the discipline of the church.[65]

The Church Insurance Company was the primary insurer for most of the Episcopal dioceses directed to make restitution to former victims. Under Alexander Stewart (b. 1926), the former Bishop of Western Massachusetts who became the Vice President of the Church Pension Fund in 1988, the Church Insurance Company made training in the avoidance of sexual abuse for all clergy and lay professionals a precondition of continued liability coverage. Those with experience with the Minnesota process joined the Church Pension Group staff, including Sally Johnson, the former chancellor for the Diocese of Minnesota, and David Ryder, who had become acquainted with the Minnesota model while chancellor of the Diocese of Southern Ohio. By 1994 training for clergy and lay leaders had become a standard expectation in most Episcopal dioceses.

The policy of openness proved painful. Some rather prominent figures in the church were involved in misconduct. Among those charged during the 1990s with misconduct were a popular charismatic leader, a seminary dean, and three bishops. While a majority of those charged were white males accused of misconduct with adult females, they did not have a monopoly on misconduct. African Americans and a Native American were also charged with misconduct, and the accused included male and female, lay and ordained. Some abuse involved same-sex parishioners and minors. Painful as such charges may have been, they represented a step in the direction of honesty.[66]

The Church in the World

A number of factors combined to make the 1980s and 1990s a period in which American Episcopalians were particularly aware that their predominantly white American church body was only a tiny element within Christ's Church. One contributing factor was a change taking place within the Anglican Communion itself. Anglican missionaries, particularly in the nineteenth century, had established churches in Africa, Asia, and Latin America. Though a growing percentage of parishioners were native to these Third World missionary dioceses, prior to 1960 many priests and virtually all of the bishops were from Britain, North America, Australia, or New Zealand. The post–World War II independence movement made this arrangement increasingly untenable. As the colonial era came to an end, native clergy gradually replaced foreign missionaries. With an indigenous leadership, many of these churches began to grow rapidly, not only evangelizing the population of their own nations, but also crossing national boundaries into such nations as Zaire that had never been English or American colonies. These growing Third World churches increasing took their places as independent provinces of the Anglican Communion. In 1982, for example, the Episcopal Church in Liberia, long a missionary diocese of the Episcopal Church in the USA, joined other West African nations in the previously established Church of the Province of West Africa. George Daniel Browne (1933–93), the first native-born Liberian to serve as a diocesan bishop, became the province's archbishop. In 1990 the Episcopal Church in the Philippines followed suit, becoming an independent province. In April of 1998 the Dioceses of Guatemala, El Salvador, Nicaragua, and Panamá became the *Iglesia Anglicana de la Región Central de América.*

The Anglican bishops who gathered each decade at the Lambeth Conference were aware of the shifting population within their communion. By 1998 African (224) and Asian (95) bishops slightly outnumbered the combined total from Europe, the United States, and Canada (316).[67] Issues of importance to Third World bishops became increasingly important on the bishops' agenda. "Structural violence"—oppression by existing governmental, social, and economic institutions—was a central concern in the 1988 Lambeth report on Christianity and the social order.[68] The bishops at the 1998 Conference discussed world debt, an issue of importance in the developing nations. The Third World bishops at the 1998 Conference also made it clear that they were not convinced by the pre-conference lobbying effort of Bishop John S. Spong to support the ordination and blessing of persons in same-sex relationships. Strong support by Third World bishops led to the adoption by a margin of 526 to 70 of a resolution that declared "homosexual practice as incompatible with Scripture" and indicated that the conference "cannot advise the legitimizing or blessing of same-sex unions, nor the ordination of those involved in same-gender unions."[69]

Three earlier Lambeth conferences had established bodies to provide additional opportunities for Anglicans to confer with one another. Lambeth 1948 created the Advisory Council on Missionary Strategy. Lambeth 1958 formed the Lambeth Consultative Body. Lambeth 1968 replaced both with the Anglican Consultative Council, which was composed of one to three representatives from each province in the Anglican Communion. Unlike the Lambeth Conferences, which always met in England with the Archbishop of Canterbury presiding, the Consulative Council varied its place of meeting and elected its own chair. The location of the first Council (Limuru, Kenya, in 1971) and its choice of chair (Nigerian high court judge Louis Mbanefo) bore witness to the increasingly international character of the Anglican Communion.

Those who attended the second gathering of the Council (Dublin, Ireland, 1973) established the ground rules for missionary activity in the postcolonial age. The primary responsibility for mission, they suggested, belonged to the indigenous church. Churches in the industrialized world should no longer set the agenda for Third World churches. The Council initiated a Partners in Missions consultation program through which provinces could decide jointly on directions to follow.

In the 1970s, a time in which the national church was facing budgetary problems, some Episcopalians used this reorientation of mission strategy as a rationale for decreased giving to mission. By the 1980s, however, such organizations as the Episcopal Church Missionary Community (formed in 1974), the U.S. branches of the South American Missionary Society (1976) and the Society for Promoting Christian Knowledge (1983), the Episcopal World Mission (1982), and Anglican Frontier Missions (1993) had helped to spark an interest in the now more cooperative overseas missionary work. In 1990 representatives of a number of these groups met to form the Episcopal Council for Global Missions. The council sponsored New Wineskins for Global Mission conferences (first conference, April 1994) and rallied opposition to a further cut in mission funding proposed by the Executive Board at the 1994 General Convention. Representatives from dioceses that were concerned with foreign missions created a parallel organization, the Global Episcopal Mission Network, in 1994.[70] The General Convention of 1997 restored missions as a subcategory in the list of canonical areas on which candidates for ordination were to be examined.[71]

As Archbishop of Canterbury Robert Runcie told the 1985 General Convention, the Anglican Communion became decreasingly English:

> We have developed into a worldwide family of Churches. Today there are 70 million members of what is arguably the second most widely distributed body of Christians. No longer are we identified by having some kind of English heritage. English is today the second language of the Communion. There are more black members than white. Our local diversities span the spectrum of the world's races, needs, and aspirations. We have only to think of Bishop Tutu's courageous witness in South Africa to be reminded that we are no longer a Church of the white middle classes allied only to the prosperous western world."[72]

Archbishop Runcie cited the example of South African archbishop Desmond Tutu, the leader of peaceful opposition to apartheid. The bishop was a speaker at the 1982 General Convention and the winner of the 1984 Nobel peace prize. After the downfall of racial apartheid in South Africa, he served as chair of the Truth and Reconciliation Commission (1995–98), which sought to uncover violations of human rights on all sides as a step toward greater reconciliation in his nation.

The awareness that the Anglican Communion itself was a diverse fellowship may have contributed to Episcopalians' greater willingness to enter ecumenical discussions with other

Fig. 56. Desmond Tutu in a 1989 meeting with
Presiding Bishop Edmond Browning

Christian denominations. In 1982 the participants in the
International Anglican-Roman Catholic Dialogue presented
agreed statements on the eucharist, the priesthood, and the
authority of the church for study by their respective denominations. In the same year the Episcopal Church began "interim
eucharistic sharing" with Christians of another tradition. The
relationship, initiated with what would become the Evangelical
Lutheran Church, was the first in which Episcopalians as a
denomination had engaged in joint celebrations of the eucharist.
In January 1983, Bishop John Allin and three Lutheran bishops
presided at a festival celebration at the National Cathedral that
inaugurated the sharing. In 1997 the General Convention overwhelmingly approved a proposed concordat that would have
brought Lutherans and Anglicans into closer cooperation. The
Lutheran General Synod of 1997, however, proved unable to
muster the two-thirds vote required by its polity for approval.
Lutheran proponents planned to resubmit a revised text to the
General Synod of 1999, which, if passed, might be considered
by the General Convention of 2000.[73]

Some groups had confidence that the proposals would eventually be accepted. In 1997 the members of the Conference of
Anglican Theologians (CAT) met jointly with theologians
from the Evangelical Lutheran Church. The following year the

group expanded its charter to become the Society of Anglican and Lutheran Theologians (SALT). That same year, 1998, was also the year in which Bexley Hall Divinity School entered an agreement with Trinity Lutheran Seminary in Columbus, Ohio, to cooperate in the training of Episcopal students at Trinity's campus.[74]

Episcopalians also participated in international ecumenical discussions with the Orthodox (beginning in 1966), Reformed (1978), and Methodist (1992) churches.[75] In the U.S. Episcopalians participated in the Consultation on Church Union (COCU), which began in 1962.

Presiding Bishop Frank Griswold

In 1997 the House of Bishops selected a new presiding bishop. Voting, which had been kept secret in previous elections, was made public. The bishops elected Frank Tracey Griswold III (b. 1937), Bishop of Chicago, on their third ballot.

Griswold had an elite background. A graduate of St. Paul's School in Concord, New Hampshire, he had attended the General Theological Seminary and had earned degrees from Harvard and Oxford. Yet, at the same time, he had a reputation in Chicago for having a common touch. He once spent two weeks living in an Episcopal community center in a troubled neighborhood, and he wore blue jeans to the office on a weekly basis. Griswold developed a collab-

Fig. 57. Presiding Bishop Frank Tracey Griswold

orative style of leadership in Chicago. His diocese had, for example, replaced its mandatory system of assessments with a voluntary system of parish giving to the diocese that he believed accorded with shared ministry.[76]

Outside of his diocese Griswold had demonstrated an interest in both ecumenism and liturgy. Prior to election as presiding bishop he served as the cochair of the U.S. Episcopal/Roman Catholic Commission; following it he became cochair of the Anglican/Roman Catholic International Commission.[77] He chaired the Standing Liturgical Commission and served on the General Convention's Prayer Book and Liturgy Committee.

A difficult task lay before Griswold as he assumed the position of presiding bishop. He inherited leadership of a church that was badly divided. There were indications early in his term, however, that he had the necessary gifts to turn the church away from the confrontational model of leadership of the early 1990s to a more conciliatory form of decision making.[78] At the time of his investiture in January 1998, he spoke of his desire for "communion, civility, conversation and... on all sides a change of heart."[79] Before 1998 was over those who attended national church meetings began to speak of a changed atmosphere. *Episcopal Life* characterized the spring 1998 meeting of the Executive Council, for example, as lacking "any feeling of crisis, which has absorbed the council's attention in the past."[80] Some who attended the pastoral retreat of the House of Bishops in the spring after Griswold's installation called it "a watershed" and cited "more conciliatory attitudes." The gathering was attended by the largest percentage of bishops since the initiation of nonlegislative meetings in 1991.[81]

One of the tasks that lay before the church was the evangelization of the members of what author Douglas Coupland had designated as the "X Generation," the generation of young people born in the 1960s and 70s.[82] The 1990 Gallup *Religion in America* poll indicated a declining adherence to the Episcopal, Lutheran, Methodist, and Presbyterian Churches among the young.[83] Griswold took a step in his first year in office to address one aspect of the problem—the lack of young clergy. He gave his support to an effort of four clergy—William

Danaher (b. 1965), Michael Kinman (b. 1968), Christine McSpadden (b. 1964), and Christopher Martin (b. 1968)—to organize a "Gathering for the NeXt Generation." One hundred thirty-four of approximately three hundred clergy under the age of thirty-five attended the gathering, which met at Virginia Seminary. The conference, which grew out of a series of informal meetings that William Danaher had hosted for young clergy in the New Haven area, provided a forum in which young clergy could voice their concerns. Those under thirty-five were a distinct minority in the church, for the average age of entering seminarians hovered around forty during the 1990s. Once ordained, they often felt that they were discounted or ignored because of their youth. The conference organizers recognized, however, that their contributions were absolutely vital in the Episcopal Church's effort to evangelize the young. William Danaher assisted in convening a series of local meetings for young clergy. Griswold began to meet with several diocesan bishops to plan a pilot project to attract young persons to the ordained ministry.[84]

As the second millennium came to a close, many Episcopalians were hopeful that the sustained conflict that had characterized the church of the 1980s and 1990s had come to an end.

NOTES

1. George Weinburg used the term "homophobia" in *Society and the Healthy Homosexual* (1972) to refer to a heterosexual fear of homosexuality. Patricia Beattie Jung used the term "heterosexism" in *Heterosexism: An Ethical Challenge to the Church* (1993) and other works to refer to an assumption of the exclusive correctness of heterosexual behavior.

2. Hunter expanded a 1990 magazine article into the book *Culture Wars: The Struggle to Define America* (1995). He identified those with an "orthodox" vision as defining *"freedom economically* (as an individual economic initiative) and *justice socially* (as righteous living)" and those with a "progressive" philosophy as defining *"freedom socially* (as individual rights) and *justice economically* (as equity)." See James Davison Hunter, *Culture Wars: The Struggle to Define America* (U.S.A.: Basic Books, 1995), 115.

3. Episcopal parochial reports included two membership figures: communicants and baptized members. Prior to 1986, parish clergy were asked to justify the number of communicants they reported by a series of computations. (The number of new confirmations, receptions, transfers, and restorations from the inactive list was added to the previous year's number, from which deaths, transfers, and those moved to the inactive list were subtracted.) In the pre-1986 forms, however, parish clergy simply stated the number of baptized people in the parish. The 1986 forms, which added the designation "became inactive or left without transfer" under the listing of baptized people, apparently caused clergy to scrutinize the baptized people figures more closely. As a result, the number of baptized people dropped from 2,972,607 (1985) to 2,504,507 (1986). The number of communicants in good standing, redesignated as the more restrictive category of "Confirmed Communicants in Good Standing," dipped from 1,881,250 to 1,772,271.

The 1986 parochial reports differed from earlier reports in a third way. Pentecost replaced Trinity as one of the four key Sundays on which attendance was reported.

4. "Report of the Committee on the State of the Church," in *The Blue Book: Reports of the Committees, Commissions, Boards, and Agencies of the General Convention of the Episcopal Church* (produced for the General Convention by Seabury Professional Services, 1982), 320.

5. Statistical summaries provided by Barbara Kelleher, administrative assistant to the Episcopal Church's statistical officer, Episcopal Church Center, 815 Second Avenue, New York, New York. Attendance figures are based on the totals for 1 Lent, Easter, 1 Advent, and Trinity (pre-1986) or Pentecost (post-1986). The average attendance for these four Sundays in 1980 was 1,051,818. In 1988, it had risen to 1,081,426.

The number of baptized members changed by less than 1.7 percent between 1980 (2,784,040) and 1985 (2,739,422).

6. *Religion in America, 1990* (Princeton, N.J.: The Princeton Religion Research Center, 1990), 32.

7. Margaret V. Uyeki, "Over Two Hundred New Churches in Five Years!" *Into the World* (New York: Education for Mission and Ministry Unit of the Episcopal Church Center, July/September 1984): 1.

8. Ronald L. Reed, "Good News in Financial Stewardship," in *Stewardship Report* (New York: Office of Stewardship of the Episcopal Church Center, Summer 1987), 7.

9. Eugene V. N. Goetchius and Charles P. Price, *The Gifts of God* (Wilton, Conn.: Morehouse-Barlow, 1984), 30.

10. Goetchius and Price, *Gifts of God*, 33–34.

11. *Guide for Congregational Self-Evaluation* (New York: Seabury Professional Services, n.d.), i.

12. "Report of the Committee on the State of the Church," 320.

13. *The Episcopalian* 150 (November 1985): 2.

14. Robert Libby, "Newest Episcopalians are spirited group," *Episcopal Life* 1 (June 1990): 6.

15. Edmond L. Browning, *No Outcasts: the Public Witness of Edmond L. Browning, XXIVth Presiding Bishop of the Episcopal Church*, ed. Brian J. Grieves (Cincinnati: Forward Movement, 1997), 15.

16. Browning, *No Outcasts*, 174–75.

17. Browning, *No Outcasts*, 145–46

18. In 1991 David Scott (b. 1936) and Allan Parrent (b. 1930) of Virginia Seminary's ethics department wrote a letter to President Bush that was critical of Browning's analysis of the Gulf War. In January 1994, the *United Voice* carried an article by Julia Duin questioning the reorganization of the Presiding Bishop's Fund for World

Relief. Duin noted that the shift in priorities made it possible for the fund to support projects, such as family planning, about which there was no consensus in the church.

19. *The Episcopalian* 150 (October 1985): 6.

20. Browning, *No Outcasts,* 24.

21. C. Kirk Hadaway and Penny Long Marler, "An Overview of Church Membership Data for the Episcopal Church: 1988–1991" (report commissioned for the Episcopal Church's Office of Evangelism, n.d.).

22. Hadaway and Marler, "An Overview."

23. John Shelby Spong, *Living in Sin? A Bishop Rethinks Human Sexuality* (San Francisco: Harper & Row, 1988), 154, 177–87, 211–12.

24. L. William Countryman, *Dirt, Greed, and Sex: Sexual Ethics in the New Testament and Their Implications for Today* (Philadelphia: Fortress, 1988), 237, 240–41, 244.

25. Carter Heyward, *Touching Our Strength: The Erotic as Power and the Love of God* (San Francisco: Harper & Row, 1989), 121.

26. Robert Williams, "Choosing integrity over Integrity," *Witness* 73 (June 1990): 16.

27. Robert Williams quoted in Kim Byham, "The Rise and Fall of Robert Williams," *The Witness* 73 (April 1990): 12.

28. Byham, "Rise and Fall," 12.

29. Williams quoted in Byham, "Rise and Fall," 12.

30. Browning, *No Outcasts,* 88–89.

31. Browning, *No Outcasts,* 89.

32. Diane Walker, "Same-sex Blessing Cancelled after Bishop Says 'No,'" *Episcopal Life* 6 (February 1995): 7.

33. Will Leckie and Barry Stopfel, *Courage to Love* (New York: Doubleday, 1997), 186–87, 203.

34. *Virginia Episcopalian* 99 (May 1991): 22. Committtee members David Scott of Virginia Seminary and Mrs. Scott T. Evans of the Diocese of North Carolina added a minority statement to the commission's report in which they strongly disagreeed with the committee proposals.

35. Edmond L. Browning, address to the joint session of the House of Deputies and House of Bishops (Philadelphia, 18 July 1997).

36. Robert W. Prichard, ed. *A Wholesome Example: Sexual Morality and the Episcopal Church* (Lexington, Kentucky: Bristol Books, 1993), 63.

37. Jeffrey Penn, "Mission Key to Renewal: Symposium," *Episcopal Life* 4 (September 1993): 1–2.

38. Nan Cobbey, "Structural Changes Cut Commissions but Little Else," *Episcopal Life* 8 (October 1997): 16.

39. *Episcopal Life* 4 (August 1993): 3.

40. Ed Stannard, "Panel Dismisses Complaint against Michigan Bishop," *Episcopal Life* 6 (January 1995): 7.; *Episcopal Life* 6 (July/August 1995): 5.

41. The Protestant Episcopal Church in the United States of America in the Court for the Trial of a Bishop, James M. Stanton, Bishop of Dallas, et. al. Presenters v. The Rt. Rev. Walter C. Righter, Respondent (May 15, 1996): 1.

42. Michael Barwell, "Two Bishops Sue over Use of Church's Name," *Episcopal Life* 9 (March 1998): 5.

43. *Report to the 72nd General Convention, Otherwise Known as the Blue Book* (Indianapolis, Indiana: the General Convention, 1997), 126.

44. Ed Stannard, "Cooke Resigns as Treasurer," *Episcopal Life* 6 (February 1995): 1; Edmond Lee Browning, television broadcast, June 24, 1995; Ed Stannard, "Auditor's Report Details How Cooke Took Funds," *Episcopal Life* 6 (July/August 1995): 1.

45. Pamela Darling, e-mail to author, 20 November 1998.

46. Thomas Bushnell, e-mail to author, 11 January 1999; Louie Crew, e-mail to author, 19 November 1998.

47. Wade C. Roof and William McKinney, *American Mainline Religion: Its Changing Shape and Future* (New Brunswick: Rutgers University Press, 1987), 142, 200.
Roof and McKinney based their figures on racial justice on a survey that asked about attitudes toward such questions as open housing and mixed socializing. The twenty-three groups included in the sample were identified as Episcopalians, United Church of Christ, Presbyterians, Methodists, Lutherans, Christians (Disciples of Christ), Northern Baptists, Reformed, the Southern Baptists, Churches of Christ, Evangelicals/Fundamentalists, Nazarenes, Pentecostals/Holiness, Assemblies of God, Churches of God, Adventists, Catholics, Jews,

Mormons, Jehovah's Witnesses, Christian Scientists, Unitarian-Universalists, and those with no religious preference. Episcopalians scored highest on the survey (i.e., were most open to integrated housing and socializing). Unitarians, Christian Scientists, and Jews were second, third, and fourth. On the other end of the scale, members of the Churches of God and Southern Baptists had the least progressive views.

The eighteen predominantly white denominations for which Roof and McKinney provided figures on black membership were the Episcopal Church, the United Church of Christ, the United Presbyterian Church, the Presbyterian Church in the U.S., the United Methodist Church, the Lutheran Church in America, the Lutheran Church—Missiouri Synod, the Christian Church (Disciples of Christ), the American Baptist Church, the Christian Reformed Church, the Reformed Church in America, the Southern Baptist Convention, the Churches of Christ, the Church of the Nazarene, the Church of God (Cleveland, Tenn.), the Christian and Missionary Alliance, the Seventh-Day Adventist, and the Roman Catholic Church. Of these denominations, only the American Baptist Church (27.1 percent), the Adventist (27.1 percent), and the Churches of Christ (8.1 percent) had higher percentages of black membership. The Southern Baptist Convention (0.6 percent), the Christian Reformed Church (0.6 percent), and the Christian and Missionary Alliance (0.6 percent) had the smallest percentage of black membership.

The majority of black American Christians are members of the seven predominantly black denominations: the African Methodist Episcopal Church, the African Methodist Episcopal Zion Church, the Christian Methodist Episcopal Church, the National Baptist Convention USA, the National Baptist Convention of America, the Progressive National Baptist Convention, and the Church of God in Christ.

48. Harold T. Lewis, *Yet with a Steady Beat: The African American Struggle for Recognition in the Episcopal Church* (Valley Forge: Trinity Press International, 1996), 166.

49. Voting for presiding bishop in the House of Bishops was still kept secret in 1985 and as a result no offical record of balloting was made public at that time. It was widely rumored in the church, however, that Bishop Walker of Washington ran second. The House of Bishops altered its rules for the 1997 election and made voting public. Bishop Herbert Thompson, Jr., of Southern Ohio ran first on the first ballot (89 votes to Frank Griswold's 86, with 39 votes divided among

three other candidates) and second on the two final ballots (106–96 and 110–96). See Jerry Hames, "Next Presiding Bishop Stresses Conversation," *Episcopal Life* 8 (September 1997): 6 and Doug LeBlanc, "The Bishop Belongs to All, PB-elect Frank Griswold Says," *United Voice*, General Convention edition (July 22, 1997).

50. Lewis, *Yet with a Steady Beat*, 168–69.

51. Paula D. Nesbitt, *Feminization of the Clergy in America: Occupational and Organization Perspectives* (New York: Oxford University Press, 1997), 63, 75.

52. Harris did not remain the only female bishop in the Anglican Communion for long, however. By the end of 1989, Anglicans in New Zealand had elected Penelope Ann Bansell Jamieson (b. 1942) as diocesan Bishop of Dunedin.

53. The ordination of Barbara Harris to the episcopate, which was attended by sixty-three bishops, was the event that apparently sparked the calling of the synod. The resolutions adopted at Fort Worth provided for a multi-step procedure for those congregations desiring a male episcopal visitor. The rector of the congregation would apply to the bishop designated to visit in his geographical area. The bishop would then seek permission of the diocesan bishop to visit. If permission were denied, the bishop would then consult with the presiding bishop in accordance with a procedure adopted by the 1988 General Convention. If the presiding bishop failed to mediate an agreement, the bishop would "nonetheless act in accordance with the missions given by consecration, obey God, and minister as requested." See "Resolutions of the Synod," resolutions adopted at the meeting of the Fort Worth Synod, June 1–3, 1989.

The strongest support for the synod came from the Midwest, from which three (William L. Stevens of Fond du Lac, Edward McBurney of Quincy, and William Wantland of Eau Claire) of the six bishops came. Members of the Catholic Fellowship of the Episcopal Church, formed in 1983 by those who affirmed "the appropriateness of the ordination of women and of the authorized *Book of Common Prayer*," attempted to make clear, however, that the Fort Worth group did not represent the opinions of all who were committed to "the catholic tradition in Anglicanism."

54. In 1993 a joint meeting of the Anglican primates and the Anglican Consultative Council had reaffirmed that there was a place in the Anglican Communion "for persons who do not accept ordination of women." See *Episcopal Life* 4 (March 1993): 15.

55. *Religion in America*, 35–37.

56. Ellis L. Larsen and James M. Shopshire, "A Profile of Contemporary Seminarians," *Theological Education* 24 (Spring 1988): 101.

57. *Episcopal Life* 4 (October 1993): 23.

58. Owanah Anderson, "NCIW and Seabury-Western Cooperate to Educate Clergy for Indian Country," *Episcopalian* 154 (May 1989): 6.

59. *Liturgical Texts for Evaluation* (New York: Church Hymnal Corporation, 1987), 60.

60. "Introduction," in *Commentary on Prayer Book Studies 30 Containing Supplemental Liturgical Texts* (New York: Church Hymnal Corporation, 1989), c-15.

61. Margo Maris, telephone interviews, 27 and 28 October 1998.

62. Maris, telephone interviews.

63. Rene Sanchez, "Diocese to Pay 8 Abused by Priest: Record Settlement Totals $23 Million," *Washington Post* (11 July 1998): A1 and 8.

64. Russell V. Palmore, Jr. (Chancellor of the Diocese of Virginia), presentation on sexual misconduct, 23 September 1993, Fredericksburg, Virginia. Not all the charge represented allegations of new behavior, however. Thirteen of the forty cases under review in 1992, for example, were for allegations concerning behavior from before 1982.

65. *Journal of the 71ˢᵗ General Convention of the Protestant Episcopal Church in the United States of America* (New York: Episcopal Church Center, 1994), 355, 603–04, 755–56, 845–52.

66. *Episcopal Life* carried news of trials and depositions with disturbing regularity during the 1990s. All the cases cited in the text were reported in the periodical or in press releases from the Episcopal News Service. The charismatic leader was Graham Pulkingham, who was suspended from the ministry in 1992 for sexual misconduct that had taken place in the 1970s (*Episcopal Life* 4 [May 1993]: 3). The seminary dean was Jack C. Knight (1941–98), a former head of Nashotah House Seminary. He was found guilty by a church court in 1994 of immoral conduct with two adult women (*Episcopal Life* 6 [February 1996]: 10). The bishops were Bishop David Johnson (1933–1995) of Massachusetts, Edward Chalfant (b.

1937) of Maine, and Steven Tsosie Plummer of Navajoland. Johnson took his own life in January of 1995. Shortly thereafter, church officials acknowledged that he had been involved in extra-marital relationships with adult females (*Virginia Episcopalian* 103 [March 1995]: 16). Chalfant resigned in May of the following year after acknowledging an extra-marital relationship with an adult female ("Maine Elects Pastoral-Care Expert as Bishop," *Episcopal Life* 8 [December 1997]: 20). In 1993 Bishop Steven Tsosie Plummer of Navajoland served a one-year leave of absence as a result of an acknowledged relationship with a juvenile male (Dick Snyder, "Navajo search for healing amidst turmoil," *Episcopal Life* 4 [September 1993]: 17; *Episcopal Life* 5 [August/September 1994]: 6).

Sandra Wilson (b. 1952) was an African American and William Lloyd Andries (b. 1936) was of Afro-Caribbean heritage. Both were priests. Wilson, the Director of the Union of Black Episcopalians, was temporarily inhibited from exercising her ministry in March of 1998 by the Bishop of Colorado following a formal complaint by three adult females (*Virginia Episcopalian* 107 [November 1998]: 19.). Andries of the Diocese of Long Island acknowledged a sexual relationship with a young Brazilian man, following the publication of a story in *Penthouse Magazine* alleging orgies had taken place in his church building. Andries left the ordained ministry, and an employee with responsibility for immigrant ministry lost his job at the Episcopal Church Center (Jerry Hames, "Investigation Continues in Long Island," *Episcopal Life* 8 [January 1997]: 6 and 9). A later diocesan investigation revealed that twenty-two of thirty-eight allegations in the *Penthouse* story were "untrue or unproven, and nine more were largely untrue." The magazine issued a guarded retraction ("Penthouse Issues Retraction," *Episcopal Life* 9 [July/August 1998]: 9). Bishop Plummer was a Navajo. J. Faulton Hodge, though later a priest, was sued in 1994 in civil court for sexual abuse of a minor male that had allegedly taken place when he was a lay worker. (Nan Cobbey, "Bishop's Son Accuses Priest of Sexual Abuse," *Episcopal Life* 5 [October 1994]: 5.)

67. Figures were based on the attendance at the opening of the Conference. Ed Stannard, "Lambeth Showcases Conservative Anglican World," *Episcopal Life* 9 (September 1998): 1.

68. "Christianity and the Social Order," in *The Working Papers for the Lambeth Conference 1988* (paper prepared at the Saint

Augustine's Seminary, held at Blackheath, London, England, 29 July–7 August 1987), 21–24.

69. Ed Stannard, "Sexuality Statement Made More Conservative," *Episcopal Life* 9 (September 1988): 4.

70. Nan Cobbey, "Evangelism Activists on a Mission," *Episcopal Life* 5 (June 1994): 1; Ed Stannard, "Budget Supports Missionaries, Variety of Ministries," *Episcopal Life* 5 (October 1994): 11; Margaret S. Larom, "Mission Network Stirred by Ways Love Multiplies," *Episcopal Life* 9 (July/August 1998): 16.

71. From 1919 to 1946 mission had been one of eight areas specified in canon law. From 1946 to 1970 it became a subcategory under church history. It was dropped altogether by the General Convention of 1970, but restored as a subcategory of Christian theology by the General Convention of 1997. See Robert W. Prichard, "The General Ordination Examination and the Changing Landscape of Theological Education," *Anglican and Episcopal History* 67 (September 1998): 299, 303, and 319.

72. *The Episcopalian* 150 (October 1985): 15.

73. J. Robert Wright of General Seminary and Walter Bouman of Trinity Lutheran Seminary in Columbus, Ohio, worked out a careful compromise over apostolic succession that seemed to be the major bone of contention in the concordat. According to the compromise, both sides would send three ecumenical observers to episcopal consecrations, while at the same time acknowledging the legitimacy of the other's forms of ministry. Over time the net effect of the participation of the Episcopal witnesses would be to share the apostolic succession with Lutherans. Some Lutherans feared that even this procedure would imply some negative judgment about existing Lutheran orders.

In 1998 the Lutheran-Episcopal Drafting Team offered a series of alterations to the concordat that it believed would make the document more attractive to Lutherans and more likely to pass on its second consideration in 1999. Among the proposed changes were an elimination of the requirement for three Lutheran and three Episcopal bishops at each installation or ordination of a bishop, though nothing in the proposed change would forbid the presence of such bishops. If adopted by the Lutherans in 1999, the revised concordat would be voted upon by Episcopalians in 2000.

74 . *Virginia Episcopalian* 107 (November 1998): 19.

75. *Ecumenical Bulletin* (January 1991): 1.

76. Marcy Darin, "Chicago's Become a More Open, Welcoming Diocese," *Episcopal Life* 9 (January 1998): 12.

77. "Griswold Named Co-Chair of International Roman Catholic Dialogue," *Episcopal Life* 9 (September 1998): 3.

78. Griswold, for example, refrained from weighing in aggressively on either side of the 1998 Lambeth debate on sexuality.

79. Ed Stannard, "Presiding Bishop-elect Sets Sights on a Church with 'a Change of Heart,'" *Episcopal Life* 9 (January 1998): 1 and 10.

80. Jerry Hames, "Council Sets Sail in New Triennium with Calm Seas," *Episcopal Life* 9 (April 1998): 11.

81. "Bishops Declare Improved Relations," *Episcopal Life* 9 (April 1998): 9.

82. Douglas Coupland, *Generation X: Tales for an Accelerated Culture* (New York: St. Martin's Press, 1991).

83. *Religion in America*, 34.

84. Tim Cherry, "Young Clergy Forge Bonds among Peers, Ask Church's Respect," *Episcopal Life* 9 (July/August 1998): 1 and 10; William Danaher, interview with author, 7 December 1998.

Acknowledgment of Sources for Illustrations

323

INDEX

Arminianism, 40n, 69n

Articles of Religion, 4, 12-13, 21, 24, 86, 115, 118, 137, 144, 156, 211

Asbury, Francis, 58, 90-93, 102n

Asian Americans, 180, 183

Aspinwall, William H., 152, 168-169n

Assembly of God, 267, 273n

Associated Parishes, 240-41

Association of Professional Women Church Workers, 237

Associations, 121

Atkins, Stanley, 265

Auchmuty, Samuel, 57

Authorized Services, 251-54

AWAKE, 291

Ayres, Anne, 160-61

Bahamas, 13, 34

Baldwin, Mary Briscoe, 130-31, 135n

Baptists, 14, 45, 51, 55, 61, 74, 80, 105, 116, 170n, 173, 188, 203, 205, 277, 282–83, 315–16n

Barbados, 33

Barrett, Ellen, 268

Barrett, George, 255, 257

Barth, Karl, 222

Bartlett, Allen, Jr., 292

Bass, Edward, 124

Bayne, Stephen, Jr., 231, 234, 259

Bedell, Gregory, 122

Bedell, Harriet, 217

Benediction of the Blessed Sacrament, 191-92

Bennett, Dennis and Rita, 266

Bennett, Joyce, 220

Berkeley, George, 29, 31

Berkeley-at-Yale Divinity School, 144, 184, 214, 221, 222, 237, 259-60

Bermuda, 2, 12-13, 15, 33

Bexley Hall, 116, 127, 222, 259, 309

Beyond Inclusion, 292

Biblical scholarship, 186, 222, 258

Bingham, Solomon, 130-31

Bishop Payne Divinity School, 181, 237, 244

Bishop Potter Memorial House, 159

Bishop Tuttle Training School, 217

Bishops—changing nineteenth-century patterns, 117-18

Bishops—colonial campaign for, 29, 61-2

Bishops—female, 257, 277, 298, 317n

Bishops—first in U.S., 85-93, 95-97

Bishops, House of—see General Convention

Bishops—missionary, 128, 144

Bishops—presiding, 97, 175, 198, 234, 245n

Bishops—suffragan, 182, 199, 214-15

Bittner, Merrill, 257

Black Americans, 16-17, 34, 38, 60-61, 70n, 74-76, 105, 111-14, 133n, 145-46, 179-82, 195, 214-16, 226n, 249, 254, 261-62, 273n, 294-97, 304, 315-16n, 319n

Black, Mary, 159

Black Awareness Coordinating Committee, 262

Black Economic Development Conference, 262

Blair, James, 27-28, 30, 32, 44-45

Blandy, Gray M., 235

Bliss, William Dwight Porter, 180, 188

Böhler, Peter, 50

Bonn Agreement, 201n

Book Annexed, 189

Book of Common Prayer, 4, 7-8, 11-13, 15, 21, 28, 36, 44, 52, 74-75, 85, 92, 96-97, 115, 190, 195, 204, 211, 216, 221, 241-42, 251-54, 265, 271-72n, 277, 300, 310

Book of Offices, 221, 240

Boone, William Jones, 131, 194

Booty, John, 270

Bosnia, 275

Boston, 27, 30, 34, 37, 44, 109, 144, 154-55, 160, 179, 182, 184, 196, 206

Bouman, Walter, 320n

Bowen, Nathaniel, 124

Bowie, Walter Russell, 212, 220, 233

Bowman, Locke E., 282
Boyle, Robert, 22, 28
Bozarth-Campbell, Alla, 257
Bracken, John, 109
Bradford, Samuel, 119
Bradner, Lester, 180
Brande, Vicente, 195
Bray, Thomas, 30, 32-34, 36-38, 50, 90
Brazil, 195, 201-2n, 239, 319
Breck, James Lloyd, 144-45, 168-69n, 192
Brent, Charles Henry, 191, 194, 197
Briggs, Charles A., 186
Broad Church, 173-196, 211-12
Brooks, Phillips, 184-85, 187
Brotherhood of Andrew and Philip, 179
Brotherhood of St. Andrew, 178-79
Brown, Dillard Houston, 295
Brown, Ida Mason Dorsey, 195
Brown, William Cabell, 195
Brown, William Montgomery, 188, 210-11
Browne, Edward Harold, 156
Browne, George Daniel, 295, 305
Brownell, Thomas, 124
Browning, Edmond, 269, 283-85, 288-94, 297, 308, 313-14n
Brunner, Emil, 222
Buchanan, Jane, 237
Burgess, George, 276, 313n
Burgess, John Melville, 215, 263, 295-96
Burnet, Gilbert, 23-24, 27-28, 33, 107
Burnham, Mary Douglass, 163
Bush, George, 276, 313n
Bushnell, Thomas, 294
Bussing, Elizabeth, 255-56
Butler, Joseph, 23, 62
Byham, Kim, 288

Cabral, Américo Vespucio, 195
California, 1, 130, 145, 153, 157, 160, 174, 186, 193, 241, 255, 257-58, 265, 292
Calvinism, 40n, 70n
Cambridge Camden Society, 148-49
Cambridge University, 2-4, 6, 23-24, 148

Cambrige Platonists, 24
Canada, 1, 26, 34, 75-76, 78, 86, 305
Cannon, Harriet Starr, 160
Carnegie, Andrew, 173
Case, Adelaide Teague, 237
Case of the Episcopal Churches . . . Considered, 84, 87, 114
Castro, Fidel, 264
Cathedral movement, 192-93
Cathedral of Our Merciful Saviour (Faribault, Minnesota), 192
Cathedral of Saints Peter and Paul (Chicago), 192
Cathedral of St. John the Divine (New York City), 193, 231, 241, 250, 261, 275
Catholic Fellowship of the Episcopal Church, 317n
Center for the Ministry of Teaching, 280
Center for Progressive Christianity, 292
Central America—see also individual countries, 153, 168-69n, 239, 284-85, 287, 289, 299, 305
Chalfont, Edward, 318-19n
Chambers, Albert, 265
Chandler, Thomas B., 62-63, 76, 117
Chaplains, military, 88, 147, 196-97
Charismatic movement, 264-67, 279-80, 282, 304, 318n
Charles I, 7-9, 11-13
Charles II, 13-15, 16, 22, 25
Charles, Otis, 292
Charleston, Steven, 300
Chase, Charlton, 124
Chase, Philander, 126-27, 129, 142
Chauncy, Charles, 62
Cheek, Alison, 257
Cheney, Charles E., 148, 167n
Cheyenne, 163
Chicago, 144, 148, 167n, 173-74, 178, 182, 192, 214, 234, 295, 299, 300, 302, 309
China, 131, 193-94, 196, 201n, 214, 220, 226n, 238
Chinnis, Pamela Pauly, 298
Christ Church, Philadelphia, 27, 30, 55-56, 58, 60, 70n, 84, 87, 91

Christian Nurture Series, 180, 321-32

Christian Social Union, 180

Christian Socialism, 180, 187

Christiani, Alfredo, 284

Christianity for the Third Millennium, 292

Choctaw, 300

Church Association for the Advancement of the Interest of Labor, 180

Church Congress (U.S.), 188-89, 206-7, 209, 211-12, 214, 223, 226n

Church Congress (England), 184

Church Divinity School of the Pacific, 174, 214, 231, 237-38, 240, 287

Church Hymnal Corporation—see also Church Publishing, 281, 301

Church Insurance Company, 303-04

Church parties, 7, 18n, 83, 118-123, 146-55, 184-85, 212-13

Church Periodical Club, 178

Church Publishing, 281

Church Training and Deaconess School, 160, 217

Church Union (England), 192

Church's Teaching Series, 231, 249, 281

Civil War (American), 112-14, 120, 137, 145-148, 158, 166n, 181

Civil War (English), 12-13, 75

Claggett, Thomas, 86-87, 97, 124

Clarendon Code, 13

Clarke, Lillian, 237

Claypool, John, 281

Clergy deployment, 255

Clinical Pastoral Education, 204-5, 233-34

Clinton, Bill, 276

Cobbs, Nicholas, 129-30

Cockburn, Catherine, 23

Cogley, John, 283

Coke, Thomas, 92-94, 102n

Colenso, John, 157

Coleridge, Clarence Nicholas, 295

Collier, Merrick William, 244

Colombia, 239, 264

Colorado, 162, 183, 265, 281

Columbia University—see also King's College, 81, 110, 231, 237

Commissaries, 27-31, 44, 61, 87, 116-17

Commissions on Ministry, 255

Committee of Bishops to Defend the Faith, 259

Communism, 210-11

Community of St. Mary, 160

Companions of the Holy Savior, 192

Compton, Henry, 25, 27, 32

Conference of Church Workers Among the Colored People, 179

Confirmation, 89-90, 252-53, 255, 270n

Congdon, Henry, 150

Congregationalists, 8, 13-15, 18n, 26, 34, 36-37, 40n, 43, 45, 51-52, 55, 61-62, 65, 68n,74, 88-89, 94, 105, 115, 120, 157, 163, 170n, 182, 249, 277, 302, 315-16n

Congress, Continental, 84

Congress, U.S., 113, 188, 196, 200n

Congress of Concerned Churchmen, 265

Congressional Board of Indian Commissioners, 185, 199n

Connecticut, 11, 14, 27, 36-39, 52, 56, 64, 77-79, 85, 87-88, 95-96, 101n, 118, 124-25, 126, 142, 144, 150, 156, 182, 214, 234, 266, 295, 300

Conscience clause, 267

Constance and her Companions, 160

Consultation on Church Union (COCU), 309

Cooke, Ellen, 293-94

Cooper, Myles, 53, 76

Corrigan, Daniel, 257

Costa Rica, 264

Council of Advice, Presiding Bishop's, 288

Countryman, William, 287

Coupland, Douglas, 310

Course of Ecclesiastical Studies, 115, 118, 122, 137

Cowley Fathers, 161

Craik, James, 152-54, 167n
Cranmer, Thomas, 3, 253
Crapsey, Algernon Sidney, 186
Crew, Louie, 268, 294
Crisis Theology, 221-23
Croes, John, 124
Cromwell, Oliver, 12, 15, 19n
Crummell, Alexander, 179
Cuba, 195, 201-2n, 215, 264, 299
Cudworth, Ralph, 24
Cueto, Maria, 264
Cuffe, Paul, 113
culture wars, 276-77, 312n
Cummings, Archibald, 30, 44, 54
Cummins, George David, 148, 167n
Cursillo Movement, 281
Cutler, Timothy, 27, 44, 52, 62-63

Dakota, 163, 183, 264
Danaher, William, 311
Daniel, Theodore Athelbert, 296
Daniels, Jonathan Myrick, 261
Darling, Pamela, 294
Darwin, Charles, 185
Dawley, Powel Mills, 231
Daughters of the King, 178
DeKoven, James, 153-56, 184
Deaconess Training School of the
    Pacific, 160, 217
Deaconesses, 158-160, 169-70n,
    178, 203-4, 214, 216-17, 236,
    255-56
Deaf—see Hearing Impaired
"Death of God" theology, 258
Dehon, Theodore, 124
Delany, Henry Beard, 182, 215, 276
Delaware, 30, 53, 56-57, 61, 63-64,
    70n, 79, 85, 90-92, 94, 101n,
    124, 142, 184
Deloria, Vine, Jr., 262-63
Demby, Edward Thomas, 182, 215,
    295
Dennis, Walter Decoster, 276
Denton, Robert C., 231
Depression, 205, 217-20, 222, 235-
    36, 276
Desegregation—see Segregation
Dewitt, Robert, 257
Disciples of Christ, 203, 205, 249
Disestablishment—see Establishment

Dix, Dom Gregory, 221
Dixon, Jane Holmes, 298
Doane, George Hobart, 140
Doane, George Washington, 140,
    144
Dom Pedro II, 195
Domestic and Foreign Missionary
    Society, 127-28, 130, 146, 175,
    177
Dominican Republic, 196, 264, 295
Donne, John, 6
Downs, Sturdie Wyman, 276
Dr. Bray's Associates, 37-38, 61,
    71n, 74
Drant, Emma B., 183
DuBose, William Porcher, 188-89
Duarte, Pedro, 195
Duché, Jacob, 55-6, 58, 84, 91
Dueling, 106-8
Duracin, Jean Zaché, 296
Dyer, Mrs. Randolph, 220

e-mail, 294
Eastburn, Manton, 144
Ecuador, 239
Ecumenism, 190-93, 213, 235
Education for Ministry (EFM), 281
Edward VI, 4
Edwards, Jonathan, 43
Edwards, O.C., 279
Ekklesia Society, 291
Elizabeth I, 1, 4-5, 8
Elliot, Stephen, 124, 145
El Salvador, 264, 284, 305
Ely, Richard T., 180
Emerging Church Network, 291
Emery, Julia Chester, 176-77
Emery, Margaret Theresa, 177
Emery, Susan Lavinia, 176-77
Empie, Adam, 118, 121
Emrich, Richard S., 244
Enlightenment, 21, 40n
Enmegahbowh, 162-63, 183
Enriching Our Worship, 302
Episcopal Charismatic Fellowship,
    282
Episcopal Children's Curriculum,
    282
Episcopal Church Missionary Com-
    munity, 306

Episcopal Churchwomen—see also Woman's Auxiliary to the Board of Missions, 238, 256, 298

Episcopal Council on Global Mission, 307

Episcopal Divinity School—see also Episcopal Theological School, 140, 145, 210, 260, 279, 287, 301

Episcopal Life, 291, 300, 310, 318-19n

Episcopal Pacifistic Fellowship—see Episcopal Peace Fellowship

Episcopal Peace Fellowship, 219-220, 260-61

Episcopal Renewal Ministries, 267

Episcopal Society for Cultural and Racial Unity, 261

Episcopal Synod of America, 299, 317n

Episcopal Teacher, 282

Episcopal Theological School, 140, 145, 186, 196, 210, 212, 231, 237-38, 240, 260-61

Episcopal Theological Seminary in Kentucky, 127

Episcopal Theological Seminary of the Southwest, 235, 237, 244, 258, 300

Episcopal party, 7, 18n, 83

Episcopal Women's Caucus, 256-57

Episcopal Women's History Project, 298

Episcopal World Mission, 306

Episcopalians United, 291, 294

Essays and Reviews, 185

Establishment of religion, 25-27, 79-82

Establishmentarian ideal, 198n

Evangelical and Catholic Mission, 265, 299

Evangelical and Reformed Church, 170n, 222, 233, 258

Evangelical catholics, 148, 150-55, 158, 168n, 185

Evangelical Episcopalians, 120-23, 126, 132n, 141-44, 147-48, 152, 155, 184

Evangelical Knowledge Society, 145

Evangelism, Decade of, 293

Evangelism, Standing Commission on, 293

Ewer, Ferdinand C., 153-54

Executive Council, 175, 238, 260

Faith and Order movement, 191, 235

Federal Council of Churches, 235

Fellowship of Reconciliation, 197

Ferguson, Samuel David, 295

Ferrando, Manuel, 195, 215, 273n

Finney, Charles Grandison, 151

First Promise, 291

Fleischer, Marie Moorefield, 257

Florida, 1, 129, 142-44, 163, 181, 195, 259, 267, 285

Ford, Hezekiah, 78

Fortune, Marie M., 302

Forty-two Articles—see Articles of Religion

Forward Movement, 300

Franklin, Benjamin, 53

Fraser, Thomas, 262

Free African Society, 111

Free church movement, 153, 178

Freedman's Commission—see Protestant Episcopal Freedman's Commission

Freeman, George, 129

Freud, Sigmund, 185

Frey, William, 290

Froude, Richard , 141

Froylan, Francisco Reus, 215, 272n

Fullam, Everett "Terry," 266

Fundamentalism 205-6, 208-9, 212-13, 221

Gallaudet College, 182

Gallaudet, Edward Minor, 183

Gallaudet, Thomas Hopkins, 182-83, 185

Gantt, Edward, Jr., 83, 88

Garden, Alexander, 30, 44

Gardiner, Theophilus Momolu Firah, 215, 295

Gardner, William E., 180

Garnier, Luc Anatole Jacques, 273n, 295

Garvey, Marcus, 216

Gaskell, Charles, 265

Gathering for the NeXt Generation, 311

Gavin, Frank, 212-13, 221

General Convention, (1785 and 86) 84-89, 124; (1789) 65, 94-98, 107, 114-115, 123-24; (1792) 94; (1795) 103n, 200n; (1798) 103n; (1799) 125, 200n; (1801) 115, 125, 200n; (1804) 115-16; (1808) 65, 107, 123-25, 200n; (1811) 124-25; (1814) 124; (1817) 98, 107, 124, 132n ; (1820) 121, 107-8, 124, 128; (1823) 97, 124, 128; (1826) 65, 119, 128; (1829) 128; (1832) 127-28, 200n; (1835) 128; (1844) 139-45; (1850) 200n; (1853) 151-52; (1862) 156; (1865) 146; (1871) 155; (1874) 192; (1880) 188, 200n; (1883) 179, 189-90, 200n; (1886) 173, 190, 200n; (1889) 159, 170n, 190, 200n, 243; (1892) 190, 200n, 243; (1895) 190, 200n; (1907) 190, 192;(1910) 191; (1913) 161, 174; (1916) 174-75, 181-82, 214; (1919) 175, 215-16; (1922) 190, 216; (1923 House of Bishops) 207-9; (1925) 175, 215-16; (1928) 211, 216; (1934) 177-78, 219; (1937) 213, 215; (1940) 230; (1943) 219, 234, 245n; (1946) 220, 233; (1949) 190, 220, 241; (1952) 236, 245n; (1953 House of Bishops) 242; (1955) 236; (1958) 237; (1961) 190, 254, 261; (1964) 234, 237, 251, 255; (1965 House of Bishops) 259; (1966 House of Bishops) 255, 259; (1967) 245n, 251, 255, 261-62, 272n; (1969) 255, 262; (1970) 251, 255-56, 297, 320n; (1973) 190, 251, 257, 263, 267-68, 271n; (1976) 253-54, 257, 265, 268; (1977 House of Bishops) 267-68; (1979) 254, 269, 290, 299, 300, 307; (1982) 190, 254, 278-80, 282, 301; (1985) 245n, 272n, 283, 307; (1988) 291, 293,301, 317n; (House of Bishops 1990) 288-89 (1991) 290, 302-03; (1994) 290, 303, 307; (1997) 290-91, 293-94, 299, 301-02, 307-08, 320n (2000) 308

General Convention Special Program, 262-64, 267, 277

General Council of the Confederate States, 145

General Theological Seminary, 116, 122-23, 143-44, 150, 165-66n, 209-210, 212, 221, 231, 237, 292, 320n

George I, 29

George III, 75

Georgia, 26, 30, 34, 43, 50, 54, 75, 78, 80, 97, 101n, 124, 129, 142-43, 145, 181, 225n, 267, 283

Gibbs, James, 35

Gibson, Edmund, 28, 38, 45

Gillespie, Joanna, 298

Girls' Friendly Society, 178

Global Episcopal Mission Network, 307

Glorious Revolution, 21, 25, 75, 81, 105

Glossolalia, 266, 273n, 279

Good, Deirdre J., 292

Gordon, William, 239

Godwyn, Morgan, 16

Goetchius, Eugene V.N., 279

Grace Cathedral (San Francisco), 193

Grafton, Charles C., 154

Grammer, Katharine Arnett, 237

Grant,Frederick Clifton, 222-23

Grant, Ulysses, 199n

Gray, Robert, 157

Great Awakening, xiv, 39, 43-65, 73, 114-15, 119-20, 141, 151

Greece, 130-31, 137-39

Green, William, 129

"Green Book"—see *Services for Trial Use*

Gregg, Alexander, 129

Griffiss, James E., 281

Griffith, David, 83-87

Griswold, Alexander, 122, 124-26, 142

Irish, Charles, 266
Isaac, Teleforo Alexander, 295
Ives, Levi Silliman, 121, 140, 158

James I, 2, 5, 7-9, 17
James II, 14-15, 21, 25, 81
James, Muriel, 238
Jamieson, Ann Bansell, 317
Japan, 193-95, 201n, 239, 284
Japanese immigrants, 183, 195, 233
Jarratt, Devereux, 56-58, 91, 93
Jarvis, Abraham, 90, 124
Jay, John, 113
Jay, John [II], 113
Jay, William, 113
Jenney, Robert, 30, 55
Jews, 80, 194, 316n
Johnson, David, 297, 318-19n
Johnson, Sally, 304
Johnson, Samuel, 37, 53-54, 62
Jones, Absalom, 111-14, 133n
Jones, Harold S., 263-64
Jones, Bayard Hale, 221
Jones, Paul, 197

Kamehameha IV, 195
Kansas, 129, 161
Keble, John, 141
Kehler, John Henry, 161-62
Keith, George, 33-36
Kelleran, Marian T., 237
Kemp, James, 110, 124-25
Kemper, Jackson, 128-30, 162
Kenrick, Francis Patrick, 139-40, 165n
Kentucky, 110, 129, 142-44, 148, 160, 183, 285
Kenya, 306
Kenyatta, Mohammed, 262
Kenyon College, 116, 127
Key, Francis Scott, 107, 111, 162
Kierkegaard, Søren, 222
King, Iris, 237
King, Martin Luther, Jr., 261
King's Chapel, Boston, 27, 30, 33, 86
King's College—see also Columbia, 37, 53-54, 75, 76, 80-81, 100-1n
Kinman, Michael, 311
Kinsolving, Charles, 262

Kinsolving, Lucien Lee, 195
Kip, William Ingraham, 130, 157
Knapp, Susan, 178
Knight, Jack C., 318n
Knudsen, Chilton, 298, 302
Koinonia Statement, 291
Krumm, John, 231, 269
Kuala Lumpur Statement, 291

La Iglesia de Jesús (The Church of Jesus), 195
Labor, 178-80
Ladd, William Palmer, 214, 221
Lambeth Conference, 155, 190, 216, 220, 239, 255, 293, 305-06
Lambeth Consultative Body, 306
Latitudinarian bishops, 21, 23-25, 40n
Laud, William, 8, 12, 15, 18n
Lawrence, Charles Radford, 297
Lawrence, William, 186, 207, 209-10
Lay, Henry, 166n
Leaming, Jeremiah, 87
Lee, Alfred, 124, 184
Lee, Henry, 129
Lee, Robert E., 147, 226n
Leo XIII, 192, 201n
Lewis, Harold T., 297
Li Tim Oi, Florence, 220
Liberal Catholicism, 212-13
Liberal Evangelical Congress, 212-13
Liberia, 114, 130-31, 179, 201n, 215, 295, 305
Lichtenburger, Arthur, 234
Lift Every Voice and Sing, 254, 301
Littlejohn, Abram, 159
Liturgical Revival, 221, 239-42, 251-54
Liturgical Texts for Evaluation, 302
Liturgy of the Lord's Supper, 251-52
Living the Good News, 281-82
Livingston, William, 63
Locke, John, 22-23, 45-46
London Company, 2, 6
Longley, Charles, 156-57
Louisiana, 125-26, 129, 142-43, 145, 148, 160, 226n, 285
Louttit, Henry, 259

Loveland, Clara O., 237
Lowrie, Walter, 222
Luther, Martin, 4
Lutheran-Episcopal Concordat, 308
Lutherans, 58, 80, 116, 156-57, 169-70n, 188, 222, 227n, 230, 249, 266, 278, 308-10, 315-16n, 320
Luwum, Janani, 284
Lyell, Charles, 185

McBurney, Edward, 295n
McClenanchan, William, 55-56, 63, 71n
McCoskry, Samuel, 129-30
McGarvey, William, 192
McGee, Eleanor Lee, 257
McGill, Ernest, 181
MacGuire, George Alexander, 215-16
Machado, Antôntio, 195
McIlvaine, Charles P., 126, 142, 155, 167n
McLeod, Mary Adelia R., 298
MacQuery, Thomas Howard, 186
McSpadden, Christine, 311
Madison, James, 78, 86, 94, 97, 109, 124
Magaw, Samuel, 56, 91-92, 102n
Maine, 33, 109, 122-24, 129, 142-43, 191, 216, 319n
Maris, Margo, 302-03
Martin, Christopher, 311
Martin, Richard Beamon, 295
Mayson, Henry Irving, 276
Mbanefo, Louis, 306
Malcolm X University, 262
Malines Conferences, 192
Manning, William T., 207-08
Manteo, 5
Marriage, 108, 268-69, 276, 281, 286, 289-90, 292
Marriage Encounter, 281
Mary I, 4
Mary II, 21, 23, 25, 28
Maryland, 10-12, 15, 25-26, 28-30, 32-34, 38-39, 43, 52-54, 56, 65, 75, 77-78, 80-85, 86-88, 91, 93-94, 97, 101-102n, 110, 121, 124-25, 142, 155, 158-61, 167n, 175, 182

Massachusetts, 2, 11, 14, 16, 27, 30, 33, 36-39, 44, 55, 62, 77-79, 85, 87, 96, 97, 101n, 109, 122, 124-25, 142-45, 179, 182, 186, 196, 207, 211, 215, 260, 263, 295-98, 304, 318n
Maurice, Frederick Denison, 153-55
Mayhew, Jonathan, 62
Mazakute, Paul, 163
Meade, William, 113, 121-25, 134n
Meem, John G., 195
membership in the Episcopal Church, 34, 38-39, 60-61, 74, 157, 173-74, 181, 183-84, 277-78, 285-86, 294, 304, 312-13n, 316n
Memorial Papers, 152
Mercersberg Seminary, 151
Meredith, Mrs., 110
Methodists, 47, 50-51, 57-59, 65, 74, 90-95, 102n, 105, 147, 170n, 179, 188, 203, 249, 266, 278, 282, 309-10, 315-16n
Mexico, 195, 201-02n, 226n
Meyers, C. Kilmer, 257
Michigan, 128-30, 142-43, 225n, 243, 286, 288, 292, 295
Micks, Marianne H., 238
Millennium[3], 292
Miller, Charles, 86
Miller, Dickenson Sargeant, 209-10
Miller, Randolph Crump, 231-32
Mills, Cedric Earl, 276
Minard, Catherine, 159
Minnesota, 130, 162-63, 183, 192, 302-04
Missionary Society for the West, 145
Mississippi, 128-29, 142, 285
Missouri, 129-30, 142-43, 160, 220, 225n, 233, 265, 286
Modernism, 186, 204-13, 221-22, 233
Modern Churchman's Union, 212, 225n
Modest, Leon, 261-62
Mollegen, Albert T., 223, 230
Monastic orders, 3, 160-61, 170n, 203-04

Montana, 162, 173, 259
Moore, Benjamin, 107, 110, 117, 124, 132n
Moore, Elizabeth Channing, 122
Moore, Paul, Jr., 268-69
Moore, Richard Channing, 118, 121-22, 124
Morality, 28, 32, 106-109, 132-33n, 152, 268-70, 276, 286-93
Moravians, 50, 80
Morgan, J.P., 173, 193
Morris, James W., 195
Morris, Robert, 84
Mortalium Animos, 192
Morton, Sarah, 109
Mosheim, John Lawrence, 156
Moss, Susan, 302
Muhlenberg, William Augustus, 150-53, 160, 179, 185
Murakami, Paul, 183
Murray, John Gardner, 175
Murray, Pauli, 256
Music, 51, 65, 153, 220, 254

Nashotah House, 144, 155, 192, 221, 281, 318n
Nation-Wide Campaign, 175
National Association for the Advancement of Colored People (NAACP), 179
National Coalition for the Ordination of Women to the Priesthood and Episcopacy, 257
National Consultation of Episcopalians on Same-Sex Unions, 292
National Council (Episcopal Church), 175, 177, 214, 238, 261
National Council of Churches, 235
Native Americans, 5, 34, 74-78, 125, 128, 144, 162-63, 183, 199n, 243, 262, 264, 300, 304, 319n
Navajo, 183, 300, 319n
Navajoland Area Mission, 300
Neale, John Mason, 148
Nebraska, 129, 162
Neill, Hugh, 56, 61, 71n
Nevin, John Williamson, 151
Nemiken, Raisa, 264

Neo-orthodoxy, 222, 230-34, 257-58
New birth, 47-51
New Hampshire, 11, 30, 78, 101n, 114, 122-25, 142, 309
New Jersey, 14, 26, 27, 29, 34, 39, 52-53, 57, 63-64, 79, 80, 85, 93-94, 101n, 116-17, 124, 142, 160, 286, 293
New Mexico, 162, 173, 225n, 262, 283, 288
New Wineskins for Global Mission conferences, 307
New York, 14, 25-27, 29-30, 37-38, 43-44, 52-53, 57-58, 63-64, 70n, 75, 77, 79, 80-81, 85-86, 88, 91-92, 94, 101n, 110-11, 113, 117-18, 120-26, 128, 142, 147, 149-51, 153, 156, 159-60, 174-76, 178, 182, 184, 193, 207, 210, 212, 215, 217, 219, 222, 231, 234, 237, 241, 250, 256, 258, 260, 266, 268-69, 278, 281, 284-85, 292, 295, 298
New York City, 25, 27, 30, 38, 43-44, 53, 57-58, 70n, 76-77, 82, 87, 91-92, 94, 111-12, 120, 131, 147, 150, 153, 155, 174-76, 178, 182, 184, 193, 210, 212, 217, 219, 222-23, 231, 234, 237, 241, 250, 258, 266, 281, 284, 292, 298
New York Ecclesiological Society, 150
New York Training School for Deaconesses, 159, 178
Newfoundland, 1, 34
Newman, John Henry, 141, 166n
Newton, Isaac, 22
Newton, R. Heber, 186
Nicaragua, 295, 305
Niebuhr, H. Richard, 234
Niebuhr, Reinhold, 222, 233-34
Nigeria, 306
Nippon Seikokai (the Holy Catholic Church in Japan), 195
Nonjurors, 23, 75, 88-90, 103n, 105
North Carolina, 1-3, 5, 14, 25, 28, 30, 33-34, 44, 57, 75, 80, 97-98, 101, 118, 121, 124, 142, 147, 158, 181-82, 214-15, 217, 225n, 262, 285, 290, 295, 314n

for the Preservation of the *Book of Common Prayer*

Vietnam—see War in Vietman
Vincent, Boyd, 215
Vinton, Alexander, 185
Virgin Birth, 186
Virgin Islands, 295-96
Virginia, 1-2, 4-6, 8-12, 15-17, 26-28, 30, 32-4, 39, 43-44, 54, 56, 58, 61, 64-65, 73, 75, 77-79, 80-81, 83-86, 94, 97, 101n, 109-110, 114, 118, 121, 124-25, 142-43, 145, 148, 161, 181, 183, 225-26n, 234, 237, 243-44, 318
Virginia Company, 6-7, 9
Virginia Theological Seminary, 116, 123, 169n, 223, 230-31, 237-38, 243-44, 246n, 256, 264, 279, 282, 311, 313-14n
Voices Found, 301
Voorhees College, 181

Wager, Anne, 38
Wainwright, Jonathan Mayhew, 63
Walker, Oris George, Jr., 296
Walker, John, 243, 264, 284, 295-96, 316n
Wantland, William, 264, 293, 317n
War in Vietnam, 260-61
War of 1812, 113, 118
Warburton, William, 26
Washburn, Edward A., 184
Washington, 173
Washington, D.C., 107, 121, 126, 160, 179, 182-83, 193, 230-31, 257, 263, 278-79, 281, 284, 298, 316n
Washington, George, 77, 108
Washington, Martha, 110
Washington National Cathedral (Washington, D.C.), 193, 250, 278-79
Wayland, Francis, 152
Waynick, Catherine M., 298
web pages, 294
Webb, Thomas, 58, 90
Webber, Robert E., 283
Weems, Mason Locke, 83, 88, 102n, 108, 110
Weil, Louis, 280
Welles, Edward, 257
Welles, Noah, 62

Welsh, Herbert, 199n
Welsh, William, 159, 185
Wesley, Charles, 47-48, 50-51, 65, 91
Wesley, John, 47-48, 50-51, 56-59, 62, 65, 70n, 91-93, 95
Wesley, Samuel, 50
Wesley, Susanna, 50
West, Edward, 240-41
West Indies, 34, 214-15
West Virginia, 183, 195
Western Theological Seminary—see also Seabury-Western, 174, 214
Whatcoat, Richard, 92, 102n
Whigs, 29, 63, 81, 105
Whipple, Henry Benjamin, 130, 162, 183, 185
Whitaker, Alexander, 17
White, John, 5
White, Stan, 283
White, William, 79, 83-87, 92, 93-97, 102n, 106, 110-12, 114-15, 117, 122, 124, 129, 156, 175, 182
Whitefield, George, xiv, 43-57, 59, 61, 68-69n, 73
Whitehouse, Henry John, 167n
Whittingham, William R., 155, 159, 167n
Wilberforce, Robert Isaac, 155
Wildes, George, 184
Wilkerson, David, 266
William III, 21, 23, 25
William and Mary, the College of, 28, 30, 78, 81, 86, 109
Williams, Arthur Benjamin, Jr., 296
Williams, Channing Moore, 193
Williams, Eleazar, 125
Williams, John, 144, 156
Williams, Peter, Jr., 112-13
Williams, Robert, 287-88
Williamsburg, 38, 44
Wilmer, Richard H., 159, 166n
Wilmer, William, 109, 121-23
Wilson, Bird, 166n
Wilson, Sandra, 319n
Wilson, Woodrow, 197
Windham House, 217, 237, 256
Wisconsin, 126, 129-30, 144, 153, 156, 183, 192, 286

Wolf, Geralyn, 298
Woman's Auxiliary to the Board of Missions, 176-78, 237-38, 256
Women's History Project, 298
Women's Ordination Now, 257
Wonder, Love, and Praise, 301
Wood, Mary Elizabeth, 196
Wood, R. Stuart, 292
Wood, Sally, 109
World Council of Churches, 191, 235
World War I, 156, 203, 222
World War II, 205, 219-20, 229-30, 233, 235, 238-39, 242, 305
world wide web, 294

Wren, Christopher, 22
Wright, Harold Louis, 276
Wright, J. Robert, 320n
Wyoming, 162, 173, 183

X generation, 310-11

Yale University—see also Berkeley-at-Yale, 36-37, 53-54, 60, 214, 232, 234, 260

"Zebra Book"—see *Authorized Services*
Zielinski, Frances, 256